500 F GARDEN PLANTS

FOR CANADIAN GARDENERS

RAINCOAST BOOKS
Vancouver

First published in 2000 in Canada by Raincoast Books
9050 Shaughnessy Street,
Vancouver, BC V6P 6E5
http://www.raincoast.com

500 Popular Garden Plants for Canadian Gardeners
ISBN 1 55192 325 4

First published in 1997 by Random House Australia Pty Ltd
http://www.randomhouse.com.au

Sydney New York Toronto
London Auckland Johannesburg
and agencies throughout the world

Adapted from 500 Popular Garden Plants for
Australian Gardeners.
First published in 1997

Cataloguing-in-publication Data available from the Publisher

Page Layout: Joy Eckermann

Printed by Sing Cheong Printing Co. Ltd, Hong Kong
Film separation by Pica Colour Separation, Singapore

CONTENTS

INTRODUCTION

At some time, nearly every gardener has stood before a withered piece of vegetation and wailed 'everything I plant dies!' But these deaths are usually due to poor choice rather than gardening incompetence. *500 Popular Garden Plants* will help plant lovers choose the right plants and turn plant killers into green-thumb gardeners.

American plant nurseries carry a huge variety of plants from a wide range of climates and soil types. While these nurseries are paradise to serious plant collectors, the busy gardener frequently returns home with a potentially expensive failure.

Transplant shock is another reason for instant death among new plants. Most plants found in nurseries begin their lives in a protected environment where the professionals at the nursery attend to their needs and whims on a daily basis. Suddenly these plants are sent to live in a very different set of conditions on the retail-nursery bench and then, just as suddenly, they are expected to adjust to yet another lifestyle in the home garden. No wonder some die!

The 500 plants listed in this book are the well-loved 'toughies' which, if given the right climate, position and treatment, will survive these changes with style.

This book is written specifically for American gardeners and features plants which thrive in American gardens.

The entries give general descriptions, essential cultural advice and, where appropriate, potential size, flowering time or light requirements. The entries are accompanied by color photographs. A climatic zone map helps to give the gardener an idea of the climate range in which perennial plants can grow in their garden.

Designed as an easy-to-follow guide for the inexperienced, this user friendly book will turn any 'failed' gardener into the proud owner of an easy-care, flourishing garden.

Hardiness Zone Map

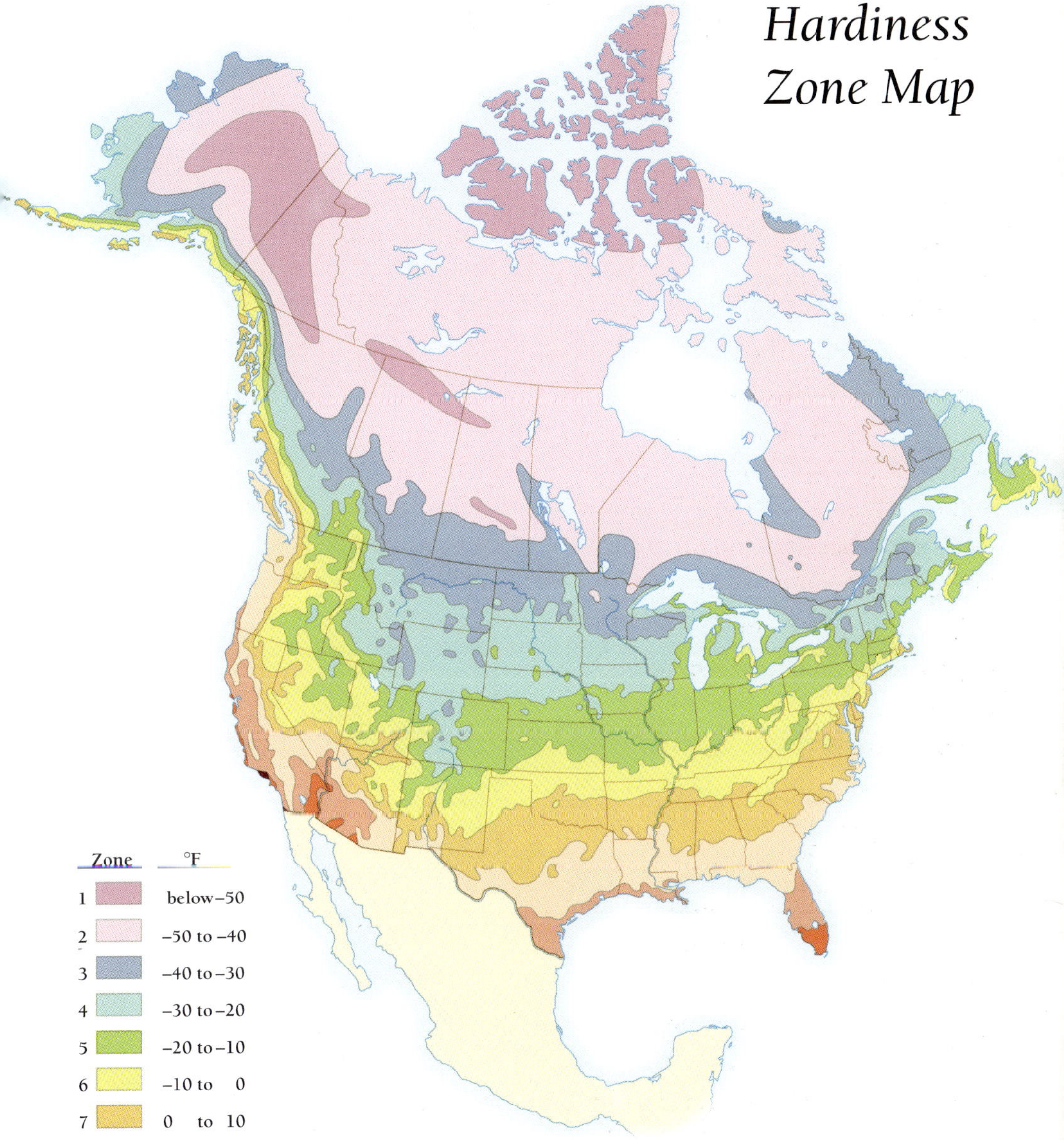

Zone	°F
1	below –50
2	–50 to –40
3	–40 to –30
4	–30 to –20
5	–20 to –10
6	–10 to 0
7	0 to 10
8	10 to 20
9	20 to 30
10	30 to 40
11	above 40

Hardiness zones are based on the average annual minimum temperature for each zone.

YOUR GARDEN

A beautiful garden grows out of the interaction between the site, the climate, the soil and the needs and desires of its owner. There is no 'right' way to make a garden—there is only the way that works best for you. Most of us make our garden on the land around the house, and it augments our living space. Thinking about how you want to live in your garden is a good starting point for planning and creating this area, which will change in color and shape with the seasons.

A terracotta pot and yellow irises are featured in this herb and perennial garden.

PLANNING THE GARDEN

Plan for the climate

When gardeners think of climate, it is usually in terms of how it affects the choice of plants, but it influences the basic layout of a garden also. Barbecues and swimming pools flourish where summers are sunny and pleasant; in a hot climate shade is a necessity; and in any climate you will almost certainly face winds, hot or cold, which you will want to break.

If you can arrange a balance of sun and shade, you have the option of sitting in either, and you gain a greater choice of plants that you can grow. But shade doesn't stay in one place. The sun moves daily from east to west, but it also shifts with the seasons, being higher in the sky in summer than in winter. The pool of shade cast by a tree, for example, is larger in winter than in summer—and a corner behind the shed may get sun in summer but not during the winter.

It is a general rule that the south side of the house is the sunny one, and the north is in the shade of the house itself. Most of us like the morning sun, but on a hot summer day the last thing we want is the hot afternoon sun streaming in the windows. If you can arrange trees on your south side to shade the house on summer afternoons, it will make life more comfortable. The west side can do with summer shade too, but here you will probably welcome the winter sun.

Deciduous trees, which drop their leaves as the summer cools into autumn and clothe themselves again in spring, will fill the bill here, and so might grapes or wisteria trained on pergolas. Beneath them is the ideal place for a terrace for sitting out and entertaining.

Arrange suitable shade and you can make yourself comfortable on most aspects.

When you are planning for sun and shade, think of your comfort inside the house as well as in the garden. Regardless of whether you have curtains, once the sun is in through a window, its heat is in too. Shading the outside of the glass is the only way to keep it out. Architects use cornices, eaves and verandas to achieve this. Gardeners use plants: trees, shrubs and climbers which can be allowed to climb the walls and hang trails of greenery over the windows or trained over pergolas to form green roofs. Plants give cooler shade than structures do, because their constant transpiration of water makes them natural air-conditioners.

Wind

Gardens need to be screened from the cold winds in winter and the hot ones of summer. Not only for your own comfort, but because wind dries out the garden as effectively as it does the washing on the line. Trees and shrubs are more effective than structures for the purpose. If the wind hits a wall it just rebounds and comes down with renewed force, but foliage filters the wind and provides you with shelter for a distance downwind about eight times the height of the planting. In a hot climate, you can use greenery as an air-conditioner simply by turning a sprinkler on it, converting a hot dry breeze into a gentle cool one.

Not all wind is undesirable. In most areas there are evening summer breezes that you won't want to block, and you'll be thinking of less dense plantings on that aspect. It isn't possible to give rules for all this, as wind patterns vary so much from place to place.

It can be a worry when the prevailing wind (or the hot summer sun) comes from the same direction as a wonderful view. Perhaps the best way to deal with it is to use fairly open-growing trees which will break the wind or sun a bit but not block the view too much, or to group the plants so that they frame segments of the view. If the problem is essentially a summer one, you might use deciduous trees, which will at least give you back the view in winter.

A garden blend of fuchsias, geraniums, lobelias, roses and begonias.

The pink flowers of this daisy bush bloom through spring and summer.

Monet's garden at Giverny inspires gardeners everywhere.

Lobelias and pelargoniums are an eye-catching combination.

Privacy

How much privacy you need in the garden is a matter of temperament; some people like more seclusion than others. A new garden is apt to be dominated by fences and the neighbors' houses, but before you rush to surround yourself with dense growth, take a careful look. Ignore the fence for a moment—you can mask it with creepers and shrubs—and concentrate on the neighbors' houses. If you arrange some trees or tall shrubs to mask these from your view, leaving the skyline open elsewhere, will that be sufficient?

It can be difficult to visualize how this is going to look; try taking snapshots and sketching some foliage on them to see how much cover you'll need. (This can be a good way of visualizing any changes you propose to the garden.)

Front gardens

Almost always, the house is set on the land so that you have front and back yards. As it is usually more private, the back yard is frequently where most people enjoy their family activities. Even where local zoning ordinances allow a front fence, the front garden is still basically a threshold to your property, a link between the street and the front door. It may be possible to screen a section to make a front patio (using hedges where fences aren't permitted), but there is still the need to have access to the house. You do need to have a clear path from the entrance to the front door, and to ensure it is well lit at night.

The front yard is the scene of the visitor's first and last impressions. It is also neighborly to have a garden that looks pleasing from the street and you will want to show off the architecture of the house, and perhaps your gardening skills, to advantage.

Duranta repens grows behind the pond while *Acanthus mollis* provides dramatic texture.

On the other hand, however, you may not want to spend a high proportion of your gardening time on an area you don't use much yourself and you may opt for a low-maintenance design. It's up to you, but a word to the wise: in these days of high crime, it isn't a good idea to shroud the front of your house too much in greenery or with high fences. Burglars appreciate privacy too!

City gardens

People are discovering that they can make delightful gardens in small back yards.

A confined space does call for some editing of the wish list—you just can't include all the activities or all the plants you might want. The answer is to develop the garden as a living room; think of it as a courtyard and pave most of it. The walls and fences can be clad with climbing plants or with trained espalier shrubs. If space allows, you might be able to contrive a pocket-handkerchief-sized lawn; but city conditions are against it. Surrounding buildings often block the sun, and few lawn grasses like shade. Chances are you'll wear the grass out underfoot anyway; and you need to consider where you are going to store the lawn mower.

The big problem is apt to be privacy. Even with the high fences that most city zoning laws allow, the dominant feature of your view is likely to be the neighbors' walls and windows. Pergolas might screen them from your view; trees are effective too, though they will probably eventually confine your choice of plants to shade lovers.

Also you need to choose carefully to be sure that the trees don't have structure-damaging roots.

One splendid tree spreading its leafy, and perhaps flowery, canopy over the whole garden can set the style far more effectively than several smaller ones.

Side gardens

If the areas beside the house are large enough to use as living spaces, you can usually extend a screen (built or planted) from the facade of the house to the side fence and thus incorporate the area into the back yard. Depending on aspect, this can be a nice place for a secluded patio, for the vegetable garden or for the compost heap; and trees planted there can be useful in framing the house. Often, however, it is simply a narrow strip, just wide enough to separate the house from the neighbors. Here there is little to do but treat it as a passageway, putting down a path and training plants on the fence and the house. Make the plants interesting enough to be worth visiting. Watering a long narrow area is difficult and tedious. Even if you decide to use hand-held hoses and movable sprinklers elsewhere in the garden, consider an in-ground system here.

PLANT SELECTION

Choosing plants for the design

Half the art of successful planting design is learning to see plants as a whole. Don't just focus on the flowers, however gorgeous. Does the plant have attractive foliage, and is it attractive for a long time? Does it have an attractive habit, graceful and open, or neat, rounded and compact, boldly upright, cascading or whatever? What sort of texture does it suggest to the eye: fine, medium, coarse or bold, matte or glossy? Does it offer features other than flowers or fancy leaves—interesting bark or fruit perhaps, or fragrance? Is it easy to grow in your soil and climate, or will it need constant attention?

The other half is learning to think of plants in terms of the role you want them to play in your garden design. This is particularly useful if you don't know everything there is to know about plants. It's much easier to talk to someone from a nursery or search through a book to get some ideas.

Simplicity is another key factor. It is much easier to arrange just a few species

Salvia viridis is a dramatic contrast to drifts of orange and yellow marigolds.

effectively than to try to weave an intricate tapestry of many.

The most common mistake in planting is to crowd your plants. Space the young plants in accordance with their mature spread or you'll end up with a tangle. Where we have given the width of a plant take note; where it isn't given, assume that it will spread to a width about two-thirds to three-quarters of its height, unless it is noted as 'spreading' or 'upright', in which case you can assume a greater or lesser figure.

Tulips can be contrasted with colorful blue bulbs.

Native or exotic?

Gardeners have always used their native plants. The cypresses, umbrella pines and box of the great formal Italian gardens are all Italian natives and the camellias and chrysanthemums of Japanese gardens are native to Japan, though after centuries of cultivation they can scarcely be described as wildflowers.

On the other hand, gardeners have always taken delight in importing choice plants from foreign lands: there are carvings on ancient Egyptian and Assyrian temples praising the rulers who had the benevolence to introduce trees and flowers that had never grown in those countries before.

Native plants can create a feeling that the garden belongs to a particular land which is hard to achieve with exotics (using the term in the strict scientific sense of 'coming from a foreign place or environment'). However, many countries have diverse climates and ecosystems and plants that are native to some regions will be foreign in the different soils and climates of others.

Local plants do have the practical advantage that they are born to your own environment, and the chances are that they will flourish with little attention. Regardless of where you live, there will be native plants of great beauty to choose from. Most gardeners ignore the debate and grow what they like, no matter where it comes from, mixing native and exotic plants as their fancy suggests.

Climate

We have discussed the influence of climate on the design of the garden, but mainly from the point of view of your comfort. But your climate also determines, more than anything else, the selection of plants you can grow. The earth has many types of climate, from tropical to arctic, and nature has evolved plants to grow in all of them. Take those plants from the wild and bring them into a garden, and they will be happiest and easiest to grow where the climate matches that of their homeland. If it is markedly different, the plant will either not grow at all or it will lose its character. And it is not only the familiar phenomenon of a tropical plant freezing to death when struck by frost; the reverse is true too. Cold-climate plants need their winters to flourish. For example, we always say that cherries need a cold climate to grow, but this is

Cinerarias are the mainstay of a colorful winter garden.

not strictly true. A cherry tree once grew in the Botanic Gardens in Singapore. But it never flowered or even lost its leaves; in the tropical climate of Singapore, it had become a non-flowering evergreen.

Nevertheless, it is frost that provides the sharpest division. Though it is true that plants that can stand frost vary in the amount they can survive, plants from warm climates with no frosts have never evolved defensive mechanisms to allow themselves to cope with being frozen. Take them to a frosty climate, and they die from having their cell walls ruptured by the freezing and expansion of their sap. In the USA, 'hardiness zones' have been worked out for the entire country, based on the minimum temperatures expected and how long they occur. American gardeners have developed the habit of saying that a plant is hardy to zone 7 (or 3 or whatever) or 'suitable for zones 5 to 9'. We have included these ratings in our plant entries.

The plant entries also describe the growing conditions each plant requires, and any particular characteristics, such as whether it is hardy or frost-tender. We have noted if a plant is drought-tolerant; summer humidity is important here, not just rainfall.

Buying plants

These days, gardening is big business. Every suburb has its garden center; florists do a flourishing trade in potted plants; even supermarkets sell plants. It has never been easier to buy what you need to furnish the garden. If you can't find just what you are looking for, you can often find it advertised in the gardening press by one of the many mail-order nurseries.

Supermarkets and chain stores tend to buy nationally from one or more of the big wholesale growers. But the fact they are selling a particular plant doesn't guarantee its suitability for your climate—you need to rely on your own research here. Also, conditions in an artificially lit, air-conditioned store aren't always ideal for plants (except indoor plants). Try to buy as soon as possible after the plants arrive. Ignore any plants that look as though they are suffering stress. Bulbs and perennials in packets can often be a good buy here, but check them carefully—some-times stock gets left on the shelves long after the planting season has finished and the seeds are dead.

At garden centers and nurseries, you can expect the staff to be able to give good advice about the plants they sell. Often they will also be aware of what does well in their area. You should still look carefully at the quality and condition of the plants. Are they healthy, vigorous-looking and free from disease? Naturally, there won't be weeds in the pots. Be prepared to pay a fair price; bargains are often plants left over from last season.

Bare-rooted stock, like roses, fruit trees and perennials in season, should be plump and healthy, with plenty of roots. Reject any that look shriveled and dried out, or which seem to be trying to grow prematurely. Bulbs should be firm; if you find any that feel squashy or mildewy, examine the others carefully.

Compost

No garden should be without its compost heap. Compost is the most readily available source of organic matter, and it is free but for the labor in making it. All you need to do is gather together all the fallen leaves, grass clippings, cabbage stalks and other once-living debris of the garden, throw them on a heap, and come back a little while later to find compost. That little while may be several months or even a year, but eventually you'll find, under a skin of leaves and twigs that haven't completely rotted, a pile of the black, moist crumbly stuff that works such magic on any soil.

Compost enthusiasts may throw up their hands in horror. 'Compost making is a scientific process!' they'll say. 'A heap like that takes too long to rot, half the nitrogen will have evaporated as ammonia, and the compost won't be as rich as manure, as it would have been had it been made properly.' True; but compost isn't all that rich in N:P:K—that is not the point. It is intended mainly to keep the soil supplied with humus, its direct value as fertilizer being secondary. Let us, however, look at the standard recipe for compost making, with the understanding that apart from piling up the heap just about all the manipulations directed are optional.

First, you gather together roughly a cubic meter of compostable stuff. This can be almost anything of organic origin, though the bulk will be plant matter. (Don't put meat in the heap.) Ideally, you want a mix of coarse and fine material, so that the heap will be neither

A tumbler type of composter is quick to turn waste into enriched compost.

too open to rot properly nor so well-packed that air can't get into it. Coarse ingredients include cabbage and tomato stalks from the vegetable garden, straw, weeds complete with roots and a bit of dirt, twiggy prunings (no thorns) and the like; fine includes lawn clippings, shredded paper and small fallen leaves. Cooked vegetables are apt to go soggy and putrefy, and left-overs from the salad bowl are dubious—the oil tends to set like lacquer and preserve them. Perfectionists will keep the coarse and fine material separate, so that they can put them on in layers, like a layer cake.

You need to keep the heap compact. The best way to do this is to put it in a compost bin. Better still, have two, side by side. Bins can be made of wood, bricks, or chicken wire stretched between four stakes, as you please and as your handyperson skills allow. (You can buy compost bin kits made from treated pine.) There is no need for a concrete floor; placing the bin on the ground allows worms to enter the heap and assist with the rotting.

Into the bin, you throw about 8 in (20 cm) of material, and on that you sprinkle a nitrogen-rich 'starter' to encourage the bacteria and fungi that will do the rotting to begin their work. You can buy compost starters that claim to contain cultures of the bacteria and fungi. No doubt they do, but it is a rare garden (a roof top in the city, perhaps) that doesn't already contain plenty of them blowing in the air. To the mix, add left-over artificial fertilizer, manure (rotted or otherwise), ash and the like. They will all help enrich the compost.

Keep piling in layers of material and starter, and when the bin is full, water it. Then you should cover it with a tarpaulin to keep the rain off; you don't want it to get too wet or it may putrefy. (If it does, it is too compact and too wet. Take the tarpaulin off, and pierce the heap several times with a sharp stake to let some air in.)

Almost at once, there will be frantic activity from the bacteria. The heap will start to get very hot in the middle, and there will be a smell of ammonia. No doubt this represents nitrogen being lost, but most of it will stay in the heap. When the ammonia smell passes (in a couple of weeks to a month) the heap is ready to be turned inside out, so that the bits on the outside get the benefit of the heat and activity of the middle. This is what the second bin is for—simply pitchfork everything into it, and the compost should be well turned. Then you can start on making a new heap in the first bin. Once again, you will be able to smell ammonia; but this time when it fades there is no need to turn it as this would disturb the worms, which will now come in and refine the compost. When most of them leave, the compost is ready to be shoveled out into the garden. It will be black, crumbly and sweet-smelling, and free from weeds

Slow-release fertilizer pellets ensure on-going nutrition to plants.

and diseases, which will have been killed by fermentation.

Even so, it isn't wise to count on this last quality—it is better to dispose of diseased material. It should not be added to compost heaps.

The compost will keep for a while, but it is meant to be put in the garden to improve the soil. The lazy gardener can make compost without even going to the trouble to make a heap. Just spread your compostable material straight on your beds as mulch, sprinkle it with a bit of blood and bone to ensure it doesn't take nitrogen from the soil as it starts to rot, and let it rot down in place. This has the fancy name of 'sheet composting'. There are neater mulches, more suitable for putting in the front garden where the neighbors might see them, but it is fine for the vegetable garden.

The makers of horticultural gadgetry have jumped on the compost bandwagon. In small gardens, the plastic compost bins are very useful; they take up less room than a full-sized bin and don't look quite so untidy. Some even come on a stand which enables you to turn them over and over, which the makers claim will accelerate the rotting process and give you compost in a couple of weeks. They don't hold much and are really only useful for the impatient or those who have a small garden. Shredders, alias chippers, are useful gadgets—they chop up prunings and other garden waste into small pieces. This allows you to compost bigger, woodier material, and the neat, same-sized pieces are also great for sheet composting.

Planting

The actual planting of a plant takes only a few minutes, but how you do it is as important as anything else you ever do to it. Plant with care, and you get it off to a good start; do it carelessly and badly and you can cripple it for life.

There are four rules for successful planting:

Rule 1. Never put a ten dollar plant in a one dollar hole. If you haven't been able to dig the whole bed, dig as much as you can. Make your hole wider than the plant's roots so that it has plenty of nice, soft soil in which to spread its roots.

Rule 2. Disturb the roots as little as possible. If the plant is growing in a container, it has to be removed. Tip the pot upside down, holding the plant in the fingers of one hand, and give the rim a sharp tap to release the pot from the root ball. It can then just be lifted off. If the pot is too big to do this, lie it on its side and tap; the plant should slide out sideways. Advanced trees and shrubs are often grown in large plastic bags. These are best cut away with scissors, and then you can lift the plant (cradling the roots, not grabbing the stem and expecting it to take the weight of the soil) off the bottom.

If the plant is at all potbound and the roots are showing signs of going around in circles, gently release them and tease them out, or they will continue to circle forever and not break out into the surrounding ground. This might sound like breaking the rule, but not so if you do it gently and quickly, so that the roots don't get a chance to dry out. (If you're reluctant to do this, cut the circling roots by slashing the root ball in two or three places with a sharp knife; new, outward-going roots will grow where you cut.)

Seedlings growing in small containers are tipped out the same way as other plants are removed from pots. The easiest way to separate them is to cut their roots apart with a sharp knife. Try to pull them apart, and you'll invariably lose soil and maybe bits of root as well.

Trees and shrubs are also sold as 'balled and burlapped'. A 'balled and burlapped' tree is grown in the field, and when dug to be sold, has its root area wrapped in burlap and tied with string. These are easy to handle. Simply carry them by the root ball and undo the string when the tree is safely in its hole. Leave the burlap in place; it will soon rot and the roots will grow through its remains.

Fruit trees and roses are often sold bare-rooted, that is, without soil. These need care to ensure they don't dry out. Plan on planting them as soon as you get them home. Drying out is the worst disturbance you can inflict on any roots. Once they are unwrapped, keep them in a bucket of water. If need be, disentangle the roots, and trim any broken ones with sharp pruners. (Planting is simple enough: make your hole, spread the roots out over a small mound in the bottom, fill up with crumbly soil and water heavily to settle the soil around the roots.)

Rule 3. Set the plant at the same depth as it was originally. This is easy enough with container grown plants, and balled and burlapped and bare-rooted trees usually show a mark on the stem where the soil was in the nursery. Add or take away soil to adjust the hole's depth. With most plants, a little too deep or shallow won't matter, but do try not to set the roots too deep or there is a real danger of smothering them.

Grafted plants are normally set with the graft union just at soil level, though citrus and lilac are two major exceptions to this. Citrus are prone to collar rot, which is almost certain to occur if the graft is buried. Lilac, on the other hand, must have the graft set well below the surface. This is because it is normally grafted on the closely related privet, which is really too vigorous for it. Burying the graft enables the lilac to make its own roots and eventually smother the privet, which otherwise would push the lilac off after a few years.

Annuals can go in a shade deeper than they were in the container, and most perennials are set with 2–3 in (5–8 cm) of soil above the crown. As a general rule, bulbs are set so they have as much soil over their noses as they are tall, though most can be a bit shallower or deeper. Many have the remarkable ability to pull themselves down to where they feel comfortable.

Rule 4. Water the plant in well. First of course you need to fill the hole in around the roots with well-crumbled soil, and many people like to enrich this with compost to help the plant make the transition from the enriched soil of its container to the garden soil. Water in well with the hose or water poured from a bucket.

Naturally, you will water and mulch the new plant for as long as it needs it.

A few don'ts. With the exception of annuals, don't plant any plant while it is actively growing if you can avoid it. Even minimal disturbance to the roots will affect their ability to support the activity above, though if you must choose between planting and the risk of the plant drying out in its pot, plant. Don't plant out of the correct season for the plant unless you really have to, but especially not when the weather is hot and dry. *Warm* weather planting from containers is fine, and most plants will establish faster than they would in late fall or winter; but you do need to take extra care—its new home is probably less sheltered than the nursery was. Give it some shade for a few days (a

Time-saving watering systems are relatively easy to install.

newspaper teepee is just the thing for seedlings; a few leafy twigs or some shade cloth for a shrub) and water regularly at least until autumn.

WATERING AND CONSERVING WATER

The water we put on our gardens accounts for a high percentage of our total water usage, and an alarming percentage of that water is wasted.

The golden rule is to water only when the plants actually need it and to water thoroughly so that the water actually penetrates to where the roots are. Frequent light sprinklings only encourage roots to stay near the surface, where they suffer as soon as the soil dries out again. Deep watering sends the roots deep where the soil dries out at a much slower rate.

How often you water depends on the weather and even more on your soil. Sandy soils absorb moisture more quickly than clay soils do, but they don't absorb as much, so excess runs away more easily and what has been held is used up faster. Clay soils are the opposite; they absorb water slowly (especially when they are quite dry) but they hold onto it for longer. Watering heavy soils takes patience—you can't apply the water as fast as you can on sand. Loam, as in so much else, is the best balance, absorbing the water fairly quickly and holding onto it well. On any soil, you shouldn't apply water faster than the soil can absorb it.

Similarly, you shouldn't waste water by evaporation. This will happen if you water in the heat of the day, especially if a dry wind is blowing, and the loss will be worse if you deliver the water in a fine spray. Much of it will evaporate even before it hits the ground!

Water in the early morning or evening, when the air is cooler and stiller, or in the middle of the night, when the air is coolest and water pressure highest.

Plants send signals that they are suffering water stress long before they actually wilt, and the observant gardener should watch for these signals and learn to recognize them.

Pruning

It may seem paradoxical, but the reason we cut bits of plants is to encourage them to grow.

The guiding rule is always to prune to a place where growth will come. Most trees and shrubs grow by first extending their branches, and then making side shoots from growth buds in the axils (the 'armpits') of the leaves. To encourage these buds (the lateral buds) to grow, you shorten the branch, cutting to just above a leaf. To encourage the main branch (or the trunk of a young tree) to grow taller, you shorten any side shoots to divert the plant's energy into the end shoot, the terminal bud. If you want to remove the branch altogether, you cut it right back to a junction with another, diverting the energy to that branch. However you cut, don't leave stubs. If you are cutting to above a leaf, cut just above it; if back to another branch, cut close. Stubs and stumps won't grow, they'll only rot, and the rot may spread into the living wood. Cut at the right place, and the wound will heal over.

To encourage side shoots, shorten leading shoots; to encourage leading shoots, shorten side shoots. The real art of pruning is in deciding which to do. Many shrubs, though not all, bear most of their flowers and fruit on side shoots, and shortening the leaders encourages not only a bushier plant, it leads to more flowers. On the other hand, you might want to encourage the leading shoots. For example, if you wanted to encourage a young tree to grow tall quickly, you would shorten the side branches.

When do you remove a branch altogether? It might be dead, when it is no use to the plant; it might be senile, and the plant is already replacing it with strong new growth, as when you remove a branch of a mock-orange, or a rambling rose that has already flowered; it might be weak and feeble, its energy better diverted to other branches; it might be spoiling the desired shape of the plant, when you might want to shorten it simply for symmetry; or it

Using a sharp pruning saw, make a cut at the base of the branch, close to the trunk. Then, saw cleanly from above.

This clean cut, close to the trunk junction, will heal over in less than a season.

might be crowding out other, better placed or stronger branches.

The last scenario is the key to pruning trees. Usually, trees can grow perfectly well without pruning, though the prudent gardener removes dead branches before they fall on someone; but often a tree is too big or too densely shady for its position. All too often, it gets cut back (lopped) to make it smaller. This is usually a disaster. Lopping may indeed make the tree smaller, but at the cost of ruining its shape. Also, it usually responds by making great bunches of new shoots so that it is shadier than before. Controlled, regular lopping, called pollarding, has its place in city streets, where a lollipop-shaped tree looks appropriate: in a garden, you are almost always better to thin out the crown of the tree, removing superfluous branches to let in the light.

With shrubs, thinning is also often the wisest course as it reveals the lines of the branches and allows the light into the plant to encourage strong new growth. Every species, however, is different, and you need to study how the plant grows. If, like a mock-orange, a hydrangea, a poinsettia, a raspberry or a rose, it grows by renewing itself, annually making new shoots to take the place of those that have spent their energy in flowers, then the basic job is thinning out the old wood to make way for the new, and these are the plants that call for the most attention from the pruning shears. (You can usually recognize them by their thicketing, multi-stemmed habit, with unbranched young stems and twiggy older ones.) If it grows more like a miniature tree, for example, camellias, bottlebrushes, hibiscus or crepe myrtles, then it will need less pruning; usually the judicious removal of weak or overcrowded branches is all you need to do when you prune.

Plants will not languish if you don't prune. Even roses, normally pruned each winter or early spring, can remain unpruned for a while, and you only have to see a neglected rosebush covered with roses to wonder whether we don't prune too much. When a description says 'prune in winter', interpret this to mean that winter is the time to prune if you think the plant will benefit from it. Many trees and shrubs can flourish without ever needing pruners or saws.

Fruit trees are a special case. Here the aim is to keep the tree small enough to make spraying and harvesting of the fruit easy, as well as to encourage the plant to put its energy into maximum numbers of fruit. You can leave fruit trees unpruned (this is the rule with

Rosa 'Claridge' shown as a standard can be kept in shape by regular pruning.

Planting many of the same type of rose allows uniform pruning to help maintain the formal appearance.

citrus, avocados, and most subtropical fruit) if you don't mind getting out the ladder to tend them.

The next question is when to prune. First, never prune anything during the period when it is actively growing and the sap is running; you risk making it bleed to death. There are a few exceptions; for example, you can pinch back the tips of such things as lavender, rosemary and the bushier natives to encourage the growth to be bushy, and you can pinch the long shoots of wisteria to keep the plant from getting out of bounds; but if you find yourself cutting into strong wood at this time, you will regret it.

Unless you are hoping that fruit or berries will follow, prune after flowering and before growth begins. This means that spring bloomers, almost all of which bloom on the growth they made last year, are pruned in late spring or summer; they include such plants as forsythia, weigelas, flowering quinces and wild roses. Prune them in winter, and you are cutting away the wood that will shortly be flowering. (You can do your pruning while the plants are in bloom, taking the cut off branches inside for flower arrangements.) Summer bloomers usually flower on growth made in spring, and in their case 'after flowering' means during winter.

Unless you expect spring flowers from them, most trees can be thinned in winter; but the after-flowering rule applies here also, so you can do the job in late summer or early autumn after growth has slowed down. This can be the better time if the aim is to let in sunshine; you can see the effect more easily if you prune a deciduous tree which still has its leaves.

The next rule is to use the right tools; you'll do far more harm by tearing your plant apart with the wrong tool than from ignorance. If the branch is too big for hand pruners, you will need long-handled loppers or a pruning saw; if you find yourself wishing for a chainsaw, call in a professional. Tree surgery is dangerous work, and chainsaws lethal in the hands of the inexperienced. Keep your tools sharp so they cut cleanly. Ragged cuts heal poorly and infections can get in. If you aren't used to using a whetstone, send your tools to be sharpened professionally.

ORGANIC GARDENING

It is easier to define organic gardening in terms of what it is not. Basically, it is gardening without the (often dubious) benefits of modern chemicals. Organic gardeners don't use weedkillers; they pull weeds out by hand. They don't spray bugs and fungi with chemicals, or at least not with the newer ones developed by the petrochemical industry. They prefer to squash caterpillars or, when spraying can't be avoided, to use old-fashioned chemicals like Bordeaux mixture or home-made sprays like garlic water. (Infuse a few garlic cloves in 2 cupfuls or so of boiling water, as though you were making tea; when it reeks of garlic, it is ready to use.) Or use dishsoap or Safer's soap for minor insect problems. Organic gardeners don't use chemical fertilizers, they rely on compost and on manure.

The basic philosophy of organic gardening—returning what we can to the soil and avoiding chemicals that might damage the environment—is simply common sense. A fertile soil is one which contains a flourishing population of micro-organisms, and they cannot endure long without the constant replenishment of humus that comes from compost or manure. Chemical fertilizers don't help them, and they leach from the soil to pollute waterways and other soils. Sprays, no matter how non-toxic their manufacturers hope them to be, should always be regarded as poisonous and dangerous to the environment until proved otherwise.

Any gardener who really cares about the soil and their garden will make compost; will give preference to organic fertilizers like manure and blood and bone rather than chemicals like superphosphate and sulphate of ammonia; and will use chemical sprays only when absolutely necessary, after less drastic controls of pests and diseases have failed. Most gardeners practice this philosophy. The days when people used to spray their gardens from fence to fence every season are long over.

Whether the result of strict organic gardening practices is indeed more flavorful, more nutritious vegetables and healthier flowers is hard to say. Some scientific research suggests that the nourishment contained in an orange is the same whether it was 'organically' or 'chemically' grown. But it will be as free as it might be of chemical residues and the soil that grew it will, or should, be still healthy and fertile; and that is worth aspiring to.

GARDENING IN CONTAINERS

There are many reasons to grow plants in containers.

First, you can give a potted plant individual care, with a soil mix designed to suit it, watering or not just as it needs it, and a position in sun or shade as it needs. Some plants with specialized needs such as epiphytic orchids and some cacti are usually grown as pot plants for this reason. Young plants, whether grown from seeds or cuttings, are usually grown in pots while they are too delicate to take their chances in the competition of the open garden. They will suffer less shock when they are transplanted than they would if they were lifted from the open ground; and most nurseries grow most of their plants in pots for this very reason.

Then, you might want to grow your

plant on a paved terrace, on a veranda, even on a balcony or roof. Here, pots can make the difference between having plants or not having them. Or you might be renting your house on a short lease, and want to be able to take your plants with you when you go—plant them in the ground and you are making a present of them to your landlord.

Put a plant in a handsome container, and you give it importance. You might want to use a potted plant or a group of them to create a focal point—next to the front door, at the head of a set of steps, or around a swimming pool. You might want to take advantage of how portable container plants are to arrange a changing display, retiring one plant as its flowers fade and bringing in another that is just coming into bloom. This way you can have interest all year.

Most plants can be grown in pots. You can grow full-sized trees in containers, but few gardeners will want to deal with something so cumbersome. A half-barrel is about as big as most of us can cope with—and even that will need two people to move it—but it is quite big enough to grow a shrub. Bearing in mind that a container plant like this draws the eye, choose one that looks good for much of the growing season, or in milder climates, the entire year. Think of long-flowering, handsome evergreens

Potted plants can create a focal point in the garden.

such as oleanders, hibiscus, camellias, azaleas, hydrangeas, even citrus. There are also many others.

Smaller pots offer their own possibilities—annuals, spring bulbs (which often flower a week or two earlier in the warmth of a pot than they do in the open ground); ferns; even vegetables and climbing plants. (Try training a moonflower or a pink mandevilla up a tripod of tall stakes to make a marvellous column of bloom.)

A cluster of small or medium-sized pots has more impact than just one, and you can mix and match your plants just as the mood takes you—one of the joys of container gardening.

Window boxes are a European idea. Geraniums and petunias are the traditional window-box plants, but you can plant any sort of low or trailing things you fancy. Ferns and fuchsias would be nice in a shaded spot; and what about some herbs conveniently outside the kitchen window? The important things are to make the box itself generous in size—8 in (20 cm) is not too wide or deep—and to fix it securely in place.

The containers themselves offer great choice. Plastic pots have been much improved in recent years, and there are more to choose from than just the old black ones, useful as they are as temporary homes for plants that are going to be planted out. The material doesn't age well, however, and though its lightness is usually an asset, it won't be if you are planning a tall plant which might be blown over in a high wind.

Terracotta is the material with several thousand years of tradition behind it, and even in the plainest models its warm color is flattering to almost any plant displayed in it. It has an advantage over plastic in that it is porous; it is harder to overwater a plant in terracotta. Salts

The blue-green foliage of *Picea pungens* is shown to great effect in this pot.

from fertilizer tend to make a white bloom on the surface, which isn't pretty. It does wash off easily, but also it can be minimized by painting the inside of the pot with olive oil before you plant—a trick practiced by the ancient Romans.

Glazed earthenware and porcelain pots have been fashionable for years. They offer good accommodation for plants, with three caveats: they are sometimes rather fragile; the fancier ones are apt to distract from the plants they are supposed to be showing off; and some of the large Chinese ones have no drainage holes. This is because they aren't flower pots at all; they are goldfish bowls. You can drill holes in them, but it's a risky business. Better to make mini-water gardens in them.

Wood is traditional for containers too, whether in the form of cut-down barrels (harder to come by than they used to be) or in more elaborate designs like the

A garden urn creates interest and variety in your garden vista.

caisses de Versailles originally designed for the gardens of Louis XIV. Wood has the great ability to keep the roots of any plant growing in it cool, no matter how hot the summer. Choose wooden containers as much for their durability as their looks. Teak, western red cedar and oak are the timbers of choice; treated pine is a reasonably economical alternative. All will last longer if they are oiled or painted. Wood is the material of choice for window boxes.

Reinforced concrete is the material of the most daring modern architecture, but did you know it was first developed around 1800 to make flower pots? Their walls have to be thick, so there is no point in trying to make them small; most concrete pots are tub-sized and heavy. The weight is a disadvantage; few concrete tubs are truly portable. So is the ease with which the material can take molded decoration, usually with unhappy results. The most attractive concrete pots are simple in design, and these days are often colored and finished to resemble stone. You can paint them, though moisture from inside usually flakes the paint off in a couple of years and they then look shabby.

Splendidly carved urns and vases of stone and marble are sometimes available, though they are fabulously expensive. Should you be fortunate enough to have one, you have a work of art which could be the focal point of the entire garden.

Whatever the material, make sure your container has adequate drainage holes; nothing will kill your plants faster than wet feet. For the same reason, it isn't wise to stand an outdoor pot in a saucer, which will stay full in wet weather. Do this only for real water lovers such as arum lilies, willows or Louisiana irises. Over the holes it is customary to place a few pieces of broken pot to keep the soil from washing out. (Unless you are in the habit of breaking pots, these crocks are hard to come by; try pieces of brass, wire mesh or hardware cloth, which will also keep out worms, which rapidly wear out their welcome in the confines of a pot.) Cover them with a layer of gravel for drainage; and then add your potting soil and plant, ensuring you have a couple of inches between the finished level of the soil and the rim for water.

A time-honored potting mix, suitable for most plants, can be made from equal parts of good garden soil, sharp sand, and peat moss or the coarser material from the compost heap, with a handful of complete fertilizer added to each

Once you purchase an elegant pot, you have the basis for a creative display that can change every year. Pastel petunias one year can be replaced with different colored plants the following year.

wheel barrowful. Unless you are planning to have a lot of potted plants, you'll probably find it easier to buy one of the ready-made potting mixes which every garden center carries these days. Premium grade is worth the extra money, and you can buy special mixes for acid-loving plants such as azaleas. Water-retaining granules which you add to the potting mix are also available. They aren't cheap, but they do reduce the need for frequent watering. A point to watch: always use fresh potting mix; it can be tempting to reuse soil that has held annuals or bulbs, but don't. It will have lost structure and nutrients and the new plants will suffer accordingly.

Planting is just the same as when planting in the open ground—follow the four rules. Make sure your plant is accurately centered in the container, or it will annoy you every time you look at it. Looking after container plants is simple. Water them when they need it (in summer, this can mean every day) and fertilize them regularly, as the constant watering leaches nutrients from the soil rather quickly. Here, slow-release fertilizers are well worth their high cost.

Annuals are simply discarded at the end of their season, but other plants will eventually need repotting when they exhaust their soil. If they can go into a larger container, fine; if not, you may have to prune the roots. This is easy—simply tip the plant out of its container, shave half an inch or so off the sides of the root ball with a sharp knife, replant, then water well.

ANNUALS & PERENNIALS

Annuals and perennials bear some of the brightest and most beautiful of all flowers. Annuals are short-lived, but the plants are generous with their blooms. They grow quickly and give you something to admire while your slower growing, permanent plants are developing. With the current fashion for cottage gardens, perennials are enjoying a revival. Coming up unfailingly year after year, they can be displayed in borders, or you can tuck a few among and in front of shrubs, or beside a path. You can also blend them with annuals and shrubs for a kaleidoscope of color.

Achillea filipendulina 'Gold Plate'

Agapanthus praecox subsp. *orientalis*

ACHILLEA

Yarrow, milfoil

There are about 200 species of *Achillea*, most native to Europe, Asia and North America. Their large, flat heads of masses of tiny daisy flowers are borne in shades of white, yellow, pink and red.

Cultivation

They are hardy perennials, easily grown and tolerant of poor soils, but doing best in sunny, well-drained sites in temperate climates. They multiply rapidly and are easily propagated by division in late winter or from softwood cuttings in early summer. Flowering stems may be cut when spent or left to die down naturally in winter, when the clumps should be hard pruned to stimulate strong spring growth. Fertilize in spring.
Flowering time Spring–summer. *Zone 6.*

Achillea filipendulina 'Gold Plate'

A strong-growing, erect cultivar reaching 4 ft (1.2 m) or more with a spread of 24 in (60 cm). It has aromatic, bright green foliage, and bears flat heads of golden-yellow flowers, 4–6 in (10–15 cm) wide. It is a valuable border plant.

AGAPANTHUS

African lily, agapanthus

Native to southern Africa, these strong perennials have strap-like foliage and showy flowers. The flowers are blue or white, in many flowered umbels, and are borne on a long erect stem.

Cultivation

The plants enjoy full sun, and will grow in any soil as long as it is well watered. They naturalize readily, soon forming large clumps. Propagate by division in late winter, or from fresh seed in late summer or autumn. Remove spent flower stems at summer's end, and dead leaves at the end of winter. Frost-hardy to half-hardy.
Flowering time Summer. *Zone 7.*

Agapanthus praecox subsp. *orientalis*

A half-hardy species, this is probably the best known agapanthus. It has large dense umbels of blue flowers carried on strong stems over broad dark green leaves in summer. It grows to 30 in (75 cm) high and 24 in (60 cm) wide, and is ideal for pot culture. Prefers full sun and moist soil.

AGERATUM HOUSTONIANUM

Floss flower

Native to tropical Mexico, this annual has dull hairy heart-shaped leaves and showy blue, lavender, mauve-pink or white fluffy flowerheads. The tall cultivars form clumps of 12 in (30 cm) high and wide and are useful for bedding and cut flowers. The dwarf varieties form clumps of 6 in (15 cm) high and wide and are excellent for edging and containers.

Cultivation

Any well-drained soil is suitable, preferably compost-enriched. They are half-hardy and prefer a sunny position with protection from cold wind. Keep moist, especially during spring and summer. Young plants benefit from tip pruning and spent flowers should be removed. Propagate from seed sown in spring.

Flowering time Summer-autumn. *Zone 8.*

AJUGA REPTANS

Carpet bugleweed, blue bugle

This excellent perennial ground cover forms a showy carpet in sun or part shade. Its bright blue flower spikes appear above metallic green crinkled leaves. There are various cultivars with different colored leaves: 'Burgundy Lace' has cream and maroon variegated leaves; 'Atropurpurea', dark purplish bronze; 'Multicolor', white, pink and purple. They grow 4–12 in (10–30 cm) high and spread rapidly from runners.

Cultivation

Fully hardy, they grow in most conditions but prefer shade and cool moist soil. Those with variegated foliage do better in sun. Propagate by division in spring. Remove spent flowerheads and watch for fungus disease.

Flowering time Spring. *Zone 6.*

Alcea rosea

Ageratum houstonianum

Ajuga reptans

ALCEA ROSEA

syn. *Althaea rosea*

Hollyhock

A native of the eastern Mediterranean and central Asia, this stately biennial has tall spikes of flowers which can reach 6 ft (1.8 m). Flowers come in a range of colors including pink and cream.

Cultivation

They are fully hardy but need shelter from wind, benefiting from staking in exposed positions. They prefer sun, a rich, heavy well-drained soil and frequent watering in dry weather. Propagate from seed in late summer or spring. Rust disease can be a problem.
Flowering time Summer. *Zone 6.*

Amaranthus tricolor 'Flaming Fountain'

Alchemilla mollis

ALCHEMILLA MOLLIS

Lady's mantle

This old-fashioned, low-growing perennial is ideal for ground cover, the front of borders or for rock gardens. It is clump-forming, growing to a height and spread of 15 in (40 cm). It has decorative, wavy-edged leaves which hold dew or raindrops. It bears masses of small sprays of greenish yellow flowers, similar to *Gypsophila*.

Cultivation

They are fully hardy, preferring partial shade, moist, well-drained soil and a humid atmosphere. Propagate from seed or by division in spring or autumn. Cut back to 1½ in (35 mm) when they finish flowering.
Flowering time Summer. *Zone 7.*

AMARANTHUS TRICOLOR

Native to tropical Africa and Asia, this quick-growing annual has given rise to many cultivated strains, some used as leaf vegetables (Chinese spinach), others as bedding plants with brilliantly colored leaves. They are bushy annuals, reaching about 3 ft (1 m) high and 18 in (45 cm) wide. Tiny red flowers appear in summer. 'Flaming Fountain' has leaves that are deep green at the base, then bronze tinted higher up, and then entirely blood red at the top. 'Joseph's Coat', has brilliant bronze, gold, orange and red variegated 8 in (20 cm) long leaves which retain their coloring into late autumn.

Cultivation

A sunny, dry position with protection from strong winds is essential, and they enjoy a fertile, well-drained soil, mulched during hot weather. They are marginally frost hardy and in cool climates are usually brought on under glass before planting out in late spring.

Prune when young to thicken growth. Prepare soil for planting with plenty of manure, and water seedlings regularly. Protect from snails, caterpillars and aphids. Propagate from seed.
Flowering time Summer. *Zone 8–11.*

ANCHUSA

Summer forget-me-not, alkanet

Natives of Europe, north and south Africa and western Asia, this genus consists of about 50 species of annuals, biennials and perennials. All species are suitable for herbaceous borders and are easily grown in beds and containers.

Cultivation

Fully to frost-hardy, they grow best in a sunny position in deep, rich, well-drained soil. In very hot areas planting in semi-shade helps maintain the flower color. Feed sparingly and water generously. The plants require plenty of room as they can make large root systems. Cut flower stalks back after blooming to promote new growth. Propagate perennials by division in winter, annuals and biennials from seed in autumn or spring.
Flowering time Early summer. *Zone 7.*

Anchusa azurea

syn. *A. italica*

This fully hardy perennial grows to 3–4 ft (1–1.2 m) high. It has coarse, hairy leaves and an erect habit with tiers of brilliant blue flowers borne in spring to summer. Cultivars include the rich blue 'Morning Glory', light blue 'Opal' and deep blue 'Loddon Royalist'.

ANEMONE × HYBRIDA

Windflower

Japanese anemones bring a touch of spring to the temperate autumn garden. They are members of a large genus, the different species of which flourish in different habitats. They were introduced to European gardens from Japan, though they are actually native to China. Varieties are available with either single or double flowers in white and pink.

Anchusa azurea 'Loddon Royalist'

Anemone × hybrida

Cultivation

If the soil is rich and the position lightly shaded, these plants can look magnificent, growing 5 ft (1.5 m) tall and displaying hundreds of flowers.
Flowering time Autumn. *Zone 6.*

ANTIRRHINUM MAJUS

Snapdragon

Native to the Mediterranean region, this perennial is valued for its showy flowers. There are many cultivars (usually grown as annuals), ranging from tall—30 in (75 cm); to medium—19 in (50 cm); to dwarf—10 in (25 cm). They have a spread of 12–19 in (30–50 cm). They form dense bushes of many upright stems carrying spikes of frilly, two-lipped, sometimes

Aquilegia vulgaris

Antirrhinum majus

double, flowers, in a range of colors including orange, yellow, red, purple, pink and white.

Cultivation

They prefer a fertile, well-drained soil in full sun with some protection from wind. Plants should be dead-headed to prolong flowering and early buds can be pinched out to increase branching. Half-hardy. Propagate this plant from seed in spring or early autumn.
Flowering time Spring–autumn. *Zone 8.*

AQUILEGIA

Columbine

These graceful, clump-forming perennials, native to Europe, North America and much of Asia, are grown for their interesting form and varied color range. They are also useful cut flowers, and the dwarf and alpine species make good rock garden plants. Foliage is fern-like and the flowers are mainly bell-shaped and spurred. The common name, 'columbine', comes from the Latin for dove, as the flowers were thought to resemble a cluster of doves. *A.* McKana hybrids feature an extensive range of pastel shades and bicolors. They are fully hardy and their flowers are large and noted for their delicate long spurs behind the petals.

Cultivation

Fully to frost-hardy, they prefer a well-drained light soil, enriched with animal manure. Plant in an open, sunny site, protected from strong winds and with some shade in hot areas. They look their best in bold clumps with a foreground planting of other annuals. Keep moist and give plenty of liquid fertilizer during growth. In cold climates columbines are perennials and need to be cut to the ground in late winter, but growing them as biannuals usually gives best results. Propagate from seed in autumn and spring. The plants are short-lived, but self-seed readily.
Flowering time Spring–summer. *Zone 6.*

Aquilegia vulgaris

Granny's bonnets

This is the true columbine, one of the parents of the modern hybrids. It is a variable species, growing to 3 ft (1 m) high with a spread of 19 in (50 cm). *A. vulgaris* bears funnel-shaped, short spurred flowers in colors of pink, crimson, white and purple, on long stems from the center of a loose rosette of gray-green foliage that resembles maidenhair fern. Fully hardy, it flowers from spring to early summer.

ARMERIA MARITIMA

Sea pink, thrift

A tufted evergreen perennial with a mound-like mass of narrow, dark green leaves, and dense flowerheads of small white to pink flowers. The plant grows to 4 in (10 cm) high and spreads to 8 in (20 cm), making it good for edging. Sandy soil and good drainage are essential and they thrive in dry, sunny situations, particularly near the coast. The species is native to the mountains and rocky coasts of the Mediterranean and Asia Minor and resents wet conditions or heavy soils.

Cultivation

Fully hardy. Propagate from seed in autumn, or semi-ripe cuttings in summer.

Flowering time Spring–summer. *Zone 6.*

Armeria maritima

ARTEMISIA

Wormwood

A large genus of plants and herbs, mostly native to arid regions in the northern hemisphere. They have insignificant flowers but are an attractive addition to a flower border where their feathery foliage provides interest throughout the year. There are both shrubby and herbaceous, annual, biennial and perennial.

Cultivation

Mostly fully to half-hardy, they prefer an open, sunny situation with light, well-drained soil. Prune back lightly in spring to stimulate growth. Propagate from softwood or semi-ripe cuttings in summer or by division in spring. Transplant during winter.

Flowering time Summer. *Zone 6.*

Artemisia arborescens

Artemisia arborescens

Evergreen perennial with silvery white foliage, reaching a height of 4 ft (1.2 m) and spread of 30 in (75 cm). Small bright yellow flowers are borne in summer and early autumn. Half-hardy. Trim well in spring. This is a good plant for the back of a border.

ARTHROPODIUM CIRRHATUM

Rengarenga lily

Native to New Zealand, this plant belongs to a genus of evergreen, tufted perennials, grown for their starry white flowers on 3 ft (1 m) tall wiry stems. It has a basal tuft of sword-shaped leaves and fleshy roots, which the Maori of New Zealand used in medicines.

Cultivation

Grow this half-hardy species in fertile soil against a sunny, sheltered wall. Propagate by division in spring or by seed in spring or autumn.
Flowering time Late spring. *Zone 9.*

ASTER

Michaelmas or Easter daisy, aster

Native to the northern hemisphere, this large genus of perennials and deciduous or evergreen sub-shrubs contains over 250 species. Easily grown, they vary in height from miniatures suitable for rock gardens to 6 ft (1.8 m) tall giants suitable for the back of a herbaceous border. Leaves are sometimes dark colored, sometimes hairy. Showy, daisy-like flowerheads come in a wide range of colors, including blue, violet, purple, pink, red or white, all with a central disc of yellow or black.

Aster novi-belgii 'Ernest Ballard'

Arthropodium cirrhatum

Cultivation

Grow in sun or partial shade in hot areas in a well-drained soil, preferably enriched with leaf mold. Keep moist at all times and feed complete plant food in spring and summer. Shelter from strong winds and stake the taller species. Cut the long stems down to ground level and tidy the clumps when flowers have faded. Propagate by division in spring or late autumn or from softwood cuttings in spring. Replace plants about every three years; the most vigorous types are best lifted annually, and two or three strong side shoots planted again.
Flowering time Late summer. *Zone 6.*

Aster novi belgii 'Ernest Ballard'

Aster novi-belgii has given rise to many garden forms in colors ranging from palest mauve to violet and deep pink. 'Ernest Ballard' is named after one of the leading breeders of asters. It flowers in autumn and grows about 3 ft (1 m) tall.

ASTILBE

Goat's beard

Native to the Orient, these easily grown fully hardy perennials are ideal used as a trouble-free ground cover in damp spots. They grow best on the edge of ponds and in damp hollows, but are also suitable for borders and rock gardens. Foliage is attractive and fern-like, and in young plants often a coppery red. Flowers appear in tall, fluffy plume-like panicles, in white, cream, many shades of pink, red and purple.

Cultivation

Plant in rich, deep soil with plenty of water, in partial shade and do not allow to dry out. Propagate by division of

established clumps from late winter to spring, or from seed or division in autumn. Yearly winter side-dressing or rich compost maintains vigor. Cut down to ground level in late autumn and lift and divide every three years. Astilbes make good cut flowers.
Flowering time Summer. *Zone 6.*

Astilbe × _arendsii_ 'Bressingham Beauty'
This leafy, clump forming perennial bears small, star-shaped, rich pink flowers on strong stems in summer. Its broad leaves are divided into oblong to oval, toothed leaflets.

BEGONIA
Begonia
This large genus of perennial plants are grown for their colorful flowers and ornamental foliage. Most of the 1,000-odd species can be grown outdoors only in areas with temperate to subtropical climates. Tuberous rooted or fibrous, they range in habit from dwarf to tall and scandent. Some are hardy and others are very sensitive to frost.

Cultivation
All require a light, rich well-drained soil that is slightly acidic. They need shelter from wind and strong sunlight. There are various groups of begonias, each with different cultivation requirements.
Flowering time Winter–spring. *Zone 9.*

Begonia Semperflorens group
Bedding begonia, wax begonia
Bushy, evergreen perennial cultivars within this classification are often grown as bedding annuals. They are also useful for borders, especially in shaded gardens. Freely branching plants, with soft succulent stems, they have rounded glossy green, bronze or variegated 2 in (5 cm) long leaves. Flowers are showy, single or double in colors of bright rose-pink, light pink, white or red. They grow best in partial sun or shade and a well-drained soil. Propagate in spring from seed or stem cuttings and pinch out growing tips to encourage bushy growth. Frost-tender, these begonias can be dug up and potted for indoor winter use in frosty areas.

Begonia Semperflorens hybrids

Astilbe × *arendsii* 'Bressingham Beauty'

Bellis perennis

Bergenia cordifolia

BELLIS PERENNIS

English daisy, double daisy

The common daisy of English lawns has given rise to a variety of garden strains with fully double flowerheads of red, crimson, pink or white, all with a gold center. They grow to a height and spread of 6–8 in (15–20 cm) and make ideal front border, edging or rock garden plants.

Cultivation

They grow in sun or semi-shade and prefer well-drained, rich, moist soil. Check for rust disease. They are usually grown as annuals or biennials from seed that is sown in summer. Remove the spent flowerheads regularly to prolong flowering.

Flowering time Spring. *Zone 6.*

BERGENIA CORDIFOLIA

Heartleaf, saxifraga

Native to Siberia, this tough perennial has large, roundish, crinkle-edged, heart-shaped leaves and produces racemes of rosy red flowers on 12–15 in (30–40 cm) stems in spring. It is long-flowering and useful for cutting. Cultivars include 'Red' with deep carmine flowers and 'Purpurea', magenta pink, with purple-tinted leaves in winter. It grows to a height of 18 in (45 cm) and spread of 24 in (60 cm).

Cultivation

Fully hardy, it makes an excellent border plant or trouble-free ground cover among deciduous trees and shrubs. It thrives in sun or shade and requires a fairly good soil with plenty of humus. Propagate by division from autumn through spring, after flowering. Water well in hot weather and remove spent flowerheads to prolong flowering.

Flowering time Winter–spring. *Zone 6.*

BRASSICA OLERACEA, ACEPHALA GROUP

The Acephala Group (the kales and ornamental kales) are flat-leafed or curly-leafed cabbages that do not form a head, popular in northern Europe because of their tolerance to cold. Some forms can grow thick, knobby stems up to 6 ft (1.8 m) or more tall. Ornamental kales, used for bedding and also sold in pots by florists, have leaves usually lobed or dissected, and strikingly veined with purple, pink, yellow or white. The Osaka Series is a modern strain of mixed colors, the leaves undivided but with frilled edges.

Brassica oleracea, Acephala Group

Cultivation

Most brassicas love a lime-rich, moist, well-drained soil. Seedlings should be raised in seedbeds and then carefully planted out 6 to 8 weeks later in a sheltered, sunny spot in soil that has been used previously for a different crop. *Flowering time* Spring. *Zone 6–11.*

CALENDULA OFFICINALIS

Pot marigold, English marigold

Originally native to southern Europe and long valued for its medicinal qualities, this species is known in gardens only by its many cultivars and seedling strains, popular winter- and spring-flowering annuals that remain in bloom for a long time. There are tall and dwarf forms, all of bushy habit, the tall growing to a height and spread of 24 in (60 cm) and the dwarf to 12 in (30 cm). All forms have lance-shaped, strongly scented, pale green leaves and single or double flowerheads.

Calendula officinalis

Cultivation

Calendulas are mostly fairly frost-hardy plants and are readily grown in well-drained soil of any quality in sun or part-shade. Flowering will be prolonged with regular deadheading. Propagate from seed, and watch for aphids and powdery mildew.

Flowering time Early summer–autumn (grown as an annual). *Zone 6–10.*

CALLISTEPHUS CHINENSIS

China aster

An erect, bushy annual with a short flowering season. It is a fairly fast-growing plant. There are various cultivars available, ranging from tall, up to 24 in (60 cm) with a spread of 18 in (45 cm) to very dwarf, up to 8 in (20 cm) with a spread of 12 in (30 cm). Leaves are oval, toothed and mid-green and the flowers come in a wide range of colors including white, blue, pink and red.

Callistephus chinensis

Campanula medium

Cultivation

This species needs sun, protection from wind and extremes of heat and a light sandy, fertile, well-drained soil with added lime. Water plants well and mulch in hot weather to keep the root system cool. It is a fairly fast-growing plant. *C. chinensis* is half-hardy. Stake tall cultivars and remove spent flowers regularly. Propagate from seed in mid-spring as the plant is prone to damping off and wilt. Choose resistant varieties.
Flowering time Summer–autumn. *Zone 8.*

CAMPANULA

Bellflower

Native to the temperate parts of the northern hemisphere, this large genus includes about 250 species of annuals, biennials and perennials. They are very useful specimens for rock gardens, borders, wild gardens and hanging baskets. Many of the species are classed as rock and alpine plants. The leaves vary in shape and size. The flowers are mostly bell-shaped and blue, with some white varieties available.

Cultivation

All do best in a moderately enriched, moist, well-drained soil. They grow in sun or shade, but flower color remains brightest in shady situations. Protect from drying winds and stake the taller varieties, which make good cut flowers. Remove spent flower stems. Feed regularly, particularly during the growing season. Propagate from seed or by division in spring or autumn, or by softwood or basal cuttings in spring or summer. They are fully to half-hardy. Transplant during winter. Watch for slugs.
Flowering time Spring–summer. *Zone 6–7.*

Campanula medium
Canterbury bells
A biennial species, this is a slow-growing, erect clump-forming plant. It produces spires of bell-shaped single or double, white, pink or blue flowers, towering 3 ft (1 m) over a rosette of lance-shaped fresh green leaves that spreads to 12 in (30 cm). Dwarf cultivars grow to 24 in (60 cm). Flowers in spring and early summer. Grow as border plants in semi-shade.

Campanula persicifolia
This is perhaps the best known species with nodding, bell-shaped blue or white flowers borne above narrow, lance-shaped bright green leaves in summer. Pinch individual spent flowers off upright stems as soon as they fade. Fully hardy, it is a spreading rosette-forming perennial reaching a height of 3 ft (1 m) and spread of 12 in (30 cm).

Campanula portenschlagiana
Native to the mountains of southern Europe, this is a low-growing evergreen plant, well suited to rock gardens. Grows to a height of 6 in (15 cm) with an indefinite spread. It has dense, small, ivy-shaped leaves, and a profusion of open, bell-shaped, violet flowers are borne in late spring and early summer. Plant in cool, part-shaded positions with good drainage. Fully hardy.

CATHARANTHUS ROSEUS
syn. *Lochnera rosea, Vinca rosea*
Pink periwinkle
In its original form this shrubby perennial is a rather slender plant about 24 in (60 cm) high, with white to rose pink flowers shading to a darker red eye in the center. Garden forms are generally lower and more compact with larger flowers in a wider range of colors, blooming almost throughout the year in warm climates but mainly in spring and summer in cooler climates. Some mixed color series have flowers ranging from purple through pink to white, while others have mainly pale colors (or white) with prominent red eyes. All parts of the plant contain poisonous alkaloids from which drugs of value in the treatment of leukemia have been refined.

Campanula persicifolia

Campanula portenschlagiana

Centaurea cyanus

Celosia argentea, Plumosa Group

Cultivation

In cooler areas *Catharanthus* can be grown in a sunny greenhouse or as summer bedding plants. In warm climates they are moderately tolerant of deep shade, the fiercest sun, and a dry atmosphere. Grow in free-draining soil, which should be kept moist in the growing period. Tip prune to keep bushy, but not so heavily as to inhibit flowering. Propagate from seed or from cuttings in summer.

Flowering time Spring, summer. *Zone 9–12.*

CELOSIA ARGENTEA, PLUMOSA GROUP

syn. *Celosia cristata*, *C. pyramidalis*

Probably native to tropical Asia, this erect, summer-flowering annual can reach 3 ft (1 m) or more in height. The leaves are mid-green; the silvery white flowers appear in summer in dense, erect, pointed spikes with a silvery sheen. The species is best known in the guise of two strikingly different cultivar groups—the Plumosa Group, with erect, plume-like heads of tiny deformed flowers in a range of hot colors, and the Cristata Group (cockscombs), with bizarre wavy crests of fused flower stalks also in many colors. The Plumosa Group are favored for cut flowers and sale in pots for indoor decoration. Some dwarf strains are no more than 6 in (15 cm) tall, while the old-fashioned bedding strains are about 24 in (60 cm). Most strains are sold as mixed colors.

Cultivation

In cool climates celosias are treated as indoor plants, or planted out for summer bedding after raising seedlings indoors in spring. They are better adapted to hot climates, withstanding the fiercest summer heat. They require full sun, rich, well-drained soil and constant moisture. Propagate from seed in spring.

Flowering time Summer (grown as an annual). *Zone 10–12.*

CENTAUREA

Knapweed

Mostly native to Europe, Asia and Africa, this large genus of annuals and perennials are grown for their graceful flowerheads which have thistle-like centers surrounded by finely rayed petals in shades of bright red, deep purple, blue and golden yellow. Some species are inclined to sprawl and need trimming back or staking.

Cultivation

Fully hardy, they need sun and well-drained soil. They are particularly useful in dryish conditions on alkaline soil. Propagate by division or seed in autumn, late winter or spring. Transplant during winter or spring.
Flowering time Spring–summer. *Zone 6.*

Centaurea cyanus
Cornflower

One of the best known annuals, this fast-growing upright plant reaches a height of 3 ft (1 m). It is a hardy species with lance-shaped gray-green leaves and a spring or early summer display of double daisy-like flowerheads in shades of pale and deep pink, cerise, crimson, white, purple and blue. Tall and dwarf cultivars are available. Best displayed in large clumps and will flower for months if deadheads are removed regularly. Once known as bluebottle, the wild form was used to make ink.

CERATOSTIGMA PLUMBAGINOIDES

syn. *Plumbago larpentae*
Chinese plumbago, perennial leadwort, dwarf plumbago

Native to western China, this bushy perennial grows to 18 in (45 cm) high with rather erect, crowded stems arising from much-branched rhizomes. It has oval, mid-green leaves that turn a rich orange and red in autumn. The flowers are plumbago-like, with small clusters of single cornflower blue blooms appearing on reddish, branched stems in late summer and autumn.

Cultivation

Ceratostigma species will grow in any moist, well-drained soil in sun or part-shade. Propagate from seed or semi-ripe cuttings, or by division. In cold climates they will reshoot from the roots even though the top growth may die back to ground level.
Flowering time Summer, autumn. *Zone 6–9.*

Ceratostigma plumbaginoides

CHEIRANTHUS

Wallflower

These perennial flowering plants are now grouped under the name *Erysimum*. They are well known as winter and spring bedding subjects. Short-lived species are best grown as biennials. The older types are scented while the newer cultivars have little fragrance.

Cultivation

Fully to half-hardy, they do best in fertile soil in an open sunny position. Propagate from seed in spring or greenwood or softwood cuttings in summer. Cut plants back occasionally so only a few leaves remain on each stem.
Flowering time Winter-spring. *Zone 6.*

Cheiranthus cheiri
English wallflower

A bushy perennial grown as an annual or biennial. Cultivars vary in height from tall, up to 24 in (60 cm), to dwarf, with a height and spread of 8 in (20 cm). Fragrant 4-petaled flowers appear in spring in colors ranging from pastels to deep browns, bronze, orange, bright yellow, dark red and scarlet. They are fully hardy and self-seeding. They must not be allowed to dry out in summer and should be cut back after blooming and again in autumn. They grow best in cooler areas.

CHRYSANTHEMUM

Chrysanthemum

Native to temperate zones, this large genus is valued for its ease of culture, rapid growth and showy flowers. It includes annuals, perennials and sub-shrubs, most of which are evergreen. All have daisy-like flowers, each flowerhead in fact made up of a large number of individual florets. Color range includes yellow, orange, brown, white, pink, red and purple. The leaves are usually deeply cut or divided, often feathery, and oval to lance-shaped.

Cheiranthus cheiri

Cultivation

Fully to half-hardy, chrysanthemums grow best in an open, sunny site in a rich, friable, well-drained soil. Stake tall plants and pinch out growing tips of young plants to encourage lateral branching. Suckers should not be allowed to develop until the plants have flowered. Propagate annuals by seed sown in spring; perennials by dividing basal growth or by striking cuttings taken from plant material that is in active growth in spring; and sub-shrubs by softwood cuttings in spring or hardwood cuttings in winter.

Flowering time Spring–autumn. *Zone 7.*

Chrysanthemum carinatum

syn. *Chrysanthemum tricolor*

Painted daisy

This spectacular annual species is from Morocco and grows to 24 in (60 cm),

Chrysanthemum carinatum

Chrysanthemum frutescens

Cleome hassleriana

spreading to 12 in (30 cm) with banded, multi-colored flowers in spring and early summer. Hardy to half-hardy. 'Monarch Court Jesters' comes in red with yellow centers or white with red centers, and the Tricolor Series has many color combinations. Excellent as bedding plants and cut flowers.

Chrysanthemum frutescens

Now called *Argyranthemum frutescens*, this is a soft-wooded shrub from the Canary Islands. It is rather tender, but in mild-winter climates it is one of the most valuable small shrubs, bearing daisy flowers in white, pink or pale yellow nearly all through the year. It suits any soil as long as drainage is good and the plant gets plenty of sunshine.

Chrysanthemum × superbum
Shasta daisy

Now classified as *Leucanthemum × superbum*, this lovely, herbaceous perennial flowers from late spring to autumn if flower stems are promptly cut to the ground. Its white flowers can be as much as 6 in (15 cm) wide. Single and double-flowered varieties are also available.

CLEOME HASSLERIANA

syn. *Cleome spinosa*

Spider flower

Mainly native to tropical America, this fast-growing, bushy annual is valued for its unusual spidery flowers. An erect plant, it grows to 4 ft (1.2 m) tall with a spread of 18 in (45 cm). It has hairy spiny stems and large, palmate leaves topped in summer with heads of airy, pink or white flowers with long protruding stamens. Flowers will last until winter. A good background bedding plant and useful in new gardens for their rapid growth.

Cultivation

Half-hardy, they require sun and fertile, well-drained soil. Shelter from strong winds and water regularly. Taller growth can be encouraged by removing side branches and dead flowers should be removed. Propagate by seed in spring or early summer. Watch for aphids.

Flowering time Summer–autumn. *Zone 10.*

CONSOLIDA

Larkspur

The name larkspur comes from the nectar at the back of the flowers, hidden in the open blooms but clearly visible on

Chrysanthemum × superbum

Coreopsis grandiflora

Consolida ambigua

the unopened buds. This genus is not difficult to grow and will succeed in any temperate or even mildly subtropical climate.

Cultivation

They like sun and rich soil and being sown in autumn to flower late the following spring.

Flowering time Spring–summer. *Zone 9.*

Consolida ambigua

These dainty versions of their cousins the delphiniums are superb cut flowers. They come in shades of blue, purple, pink, crimson or white. Sow in autumn for late spring bloom. The plants grow about 3 ft (1 m) tall and a light stake is often advisable as they can become top heavy. They love rich soil and sunshine.

COREOPSIS

This genus of annuals and perennials has daisy-like flowers in shades of gold or yellow, some bicolors. The perennials make excellent herbaceous border plants, and look striking with shasta daisies and blue delphiniums.

Cultivation

Fully to frost-hardy, they prefer full sun and a fertile well-drained soil but also grow well in coastal regions and on poor, stony soil. Propagate perennials by division of old clumps in winter or spring, or by spring cuttings. The annuals also prefer full sun and a fertile, well-drained soil; they will not tolerate a heavy clay soil. Taller varieties may need staking. Propagate from seed in spring or autumn and deadhead them regularly.

Flowering time Mainly summer. *Zone 6.*

Coreopsis grandiflora

This hardy perennial is often seen growing wild along roadsides. The golden yellow, single, daisy-like flowers carried during summer are held on strongly upright stems reaching to 3 ft (1 m) in height. An easy-care plant, *C. grandiflora* responds especially well to ample moisture provided during the growing season.

Coreopsis tinctoria

Tickseed

A fast-growing showy annual that produces clusters of bright yellow,

Coreopsis tinctoria

daisy-like flowerheads with red centers throughout summer and autumn. It grows to a height of 2–3 ft (60–90 cm) and spread of 8 in (20 cm) and is fully hardy. Provide support for the plant with branched twigs or fine bamboo stakes. *Coreopsis tinctoria* makes a very good cut flower.

COSMOS

Mexican aster

Native to Mexico and Central America, this small genus of annuals and perennials has been grown in gardens for over a century. Some annual species are particularly tall, ideal for the back of borders and excellent for late summer and autumn cutting.

Cultivation

They require a sunny situation with protection from strong winds and will grow in any well-drained soil as long as it is not over-rich. Mulch with compost or animal manure and water well in hot, dry weather. Fully to half-hardy. Propagate annuals by seed in spring and autumn, half-hardy species by basal cuttings in spring. Remove dead-heads regularly, and in humid weather watch for insect pests and molds.
Flowering time Late spring–autumn.
Zone 7.

Delphinium, Pacific Hybrid

Cosmos bipinnatus

Cosmos bipinnatus

An upright, bushy annual, growing to about 6 ft (1.8 m) in height with a spread of 19 in (50 cm). Though too tall for bedding, it is a fine border plant with large rose-pink, white or maroon flowerheads held against delicate feathery foliage. Half-hardy, it flowers in late summer and autumn.

DELPHINIUM, PACIFIC HYBRIDS

This group of short-lived perennials is usually grown as biennials. They were bred in California with the main parent being the perennial *Delphinium elatum*. They are stately plants to 5 ft (1.5 m) or more in height with star-like single, semi-double or double flowers of mostly blue, purple or white, clustered on erect rigid spikes. Some of the named cultivars are: 'Astolat', a perennial with lavender-mauve flowers with dark eyes; 'Black Knight', with deep rich purple flowers with black eyes; 'Galahad' has pure white flowers. 'Guinevere' bears pale purple flowers with a pinkish tinge and white eyes; 'King Arthur' has purple flowers with white eyes; and 'Summer Skies' has pale sky-blue flowers.

Dianthus × allwoodii

Cultivation

Very frost hardy, most like a cool to cold winter. They prefer full sun with shelter from strong winds, and well-drained, fertile soil with plenty of organic matter. Apply a liquid fertilizer at 2 to 3 week intervals. To maintain type, propagate from cuttings or by division though some species have been bred to come true from seed.

Flowering time Spring. *Zone 3–9.*

DIANTHUS

Pink

A very large genus including the carnation, maiden pink, cottage pink, sweet William and many other cultivated annuals, biennials and evergreen perennials. Most species are popular as massed border plants and for cutting. Perennial species include some small-flowered plants, excellent for rock gardens and chinks in stone walls and between paving stones.

Cultivation

Fully to half-hardy, *Dianthus* likes a sunny position, preferably protected from strong wind, and well-drained, slightly alkaline, soil. Regular watering and twice-monthly feeding produces

Dianthus caryophyllus cultivar

Dianthus barbatus

good flowers. The taller varieties will require staking. Prune stems back after flowering to encourage new growth. Propagate perennials by layering or cuttings in summer; annuals and biennials by seed in autumn or early spring. Watch for aphids, caterpillars and thrips. Some species are susceptible to rust and virus infections.
Flowering time Spring–summer. *Zone 10.*

Dianthus barbatus
Sweet William

A short-lived perennial, usually treated as a biennial, it self-sows readily and is useful for bedding and cut flowers. It is slow growing, to a height of 19 in (50 cm) and spread of 6 in (15 cm). In late spring and early summer, it bears many small, fragrant flowers in bright reds, pinks and bicolors, on a flat-topped crown.

Dianthus caryophyllus cultivars
Carnation

Fairly fast-growing evergreen perennials of short duration, carnations have a tufted erect habit and showy, perfumed, semi-double or double flowers. The range of colors includes pink, yellow, white and red. Striped flowers are called fancies; those edged in a contrasting color, picotees.

Dianthus × *allwoodii*
Perpetual flowering pink

These densely leafed, tuft-forming perennials of hybrid origin have gray-green foliage and an abundance of erect flowering stems each carrying solitary or up to four fragrant, single to fully double flowers in shades of white, pink or crimson, often with dark centers and with plain or fringed petals. They grow 12–19 in (30–50 cm) high with a spread of 8–10 in (20–25 cm) and are frost-hardy.

DICENTRA

Herbaceous perennials native to the colder regions of northern Asia and North America, they are grown for their attractive sprays of pendent, heart-shaped pink, red or white flowers, which are carried on arching stems above lacy gray-green leaves. They grow to a height of from 3 in (8 cm) to 16 ft (5 m).

Cultivation

Plant in a rich, well-drained soil of coarse texture. Propagate by late winter divisions, from spring basal cuttings or seed in autumn.
Flowering time Spring–summer. *Zone 6.*

Dicentra formosa
Western bleeding heart

This spreading plant grows to 18 in (45 cm) high and has a spread of 12 in (30 cm). Dainty pink and red flowers appear throughout spring and summer. The form 'Alba' has white flowers.

Dicentra spectabilis
Bleeding heart

This popular garden perennial grows 24–36 in (60–90 cm) tall with a spread

Dicentra formosa 'Alba'

Dicentra spectabilis

Digitalis purpurea

of 18–24 in (45–60 cm). Pink and white heart-shaped flowers on long arching stems appear in late spring and summer. After flowering, the foliage usually dies down to the ground. 'Alba' is a pure white form with green-yellow markings and pale green leaves that will grow true from seed.

DIGITALIS

Foxglove

Natives of Europe, northern Africa and western Asia, these biennials and perennials, some of which are evergreen, are grown for the strong accent value of their tall flower spikes in the summer border. They are very effective planted in groups in a shrub border under taller trees to provide shade and protection from wind. They come in many colors including magenta, purple, white, cream, yellow, pink, apricot and lavender.

Cultivation

Fully to frost-hardy, they grow in most conditions, doing best in cool, humid climates in semi-shade and moist, well-drained soil. Cut flowering stems down to the ground after the spring flowering to encourage development of secondary spikes. Propagate from seed in autumn; they self-seed readily.
Flowering time Spring–summer. *Zone 6.*

Digitalis purpurea

The common foxglove, this short-lived perennial is grown as a biennial. Ideal for providing a backdrop in a border or for naturalizing in open woodlands because of its upright habit, it reaches a height of 3–5 ft (1–1.5 m) and spread of 24 in (60 cm). Tall spikes of tubular flowers in shades of purple, white, pink, rosy magenta and pale yellow appear between late spring and early autumn above a rosette of rough, oval, deep green leaves. *D. purpurea* is fully hardy. All parts of the plant, but especially the leaves, are poisonous.

ECHINACEA PURPUREA

syn. *Rudbeckia purpurea*

Purple coneflower

Native to North America, this showy perennial has large daisy-like, rosy purple flowers with high, orange-brown

Echinacea purpurea

central cones. The 4 in (10 cm) wide flowers are borne singly on strong stems. Leaves are lance-shaped and dark green. Of upright habit, it grows to 4 ft (1.2 m) and spreads 19 in (50 cm).

Cultivation

Fully hardy, it prefers a sunny spot and a rich, moist but well-drained soil. Deadhead regularly. In cold climates the entire plant can be cut back in autumn. Propagate by division or root cuttings from winter to early spring.
Flowering time Summer–early autumn. *Zone 6.*

ECHINOPS RITRO

This perennial suits the herbaceous border, and its globe-like, spiky flowers can be cut and dried for winter decoration. It has large, deeply cut, prickly leaves with downy undersides and silvery white stems. In summer, when in bloom, it has round, thistle-like, purplish blue flowerheads. It grows to 30 in (75 cm).

Eschscholzia californica

Echinops ritro

Cultivation

This frost hardy and heat tolerant plant requires nothing more than a sunny aspect with a well-drained soil of any quality. Like most herbaceous perennials, cut them to the ground in autumn or early winter. Propagate by division or from seed.
Flowering time Summer. *Zone 3–10.*

ESCHSCHOLZIA CALIFORNICA

Californian poppy

The official floral emblem of California, this is one of the brightest garden annuals, suitable for rock gardens, the front of borders, and gaps in paving. The cup-shaped flowers open out from gray-green feathery foliage into vivid shades of orange, bronze, yellow, cream, scarlet, mauve and rose. Of a slender, erect habit, they grow to 12 in (30 cm) high with a spread of 6 in (15 cm).

Cultivation

Fully hardy, they grow well in poor, very well-drained soil and should be deadheaded regularly to prolong flowering. As their flowers close in dull weather, they should be planted in a sunny situation. Propagate from seed sown in spring. They do not transplant easily so sow where the plants are to remain. Watch for snails.

Flowering time Spring–autumn. *Zone 8.*

GAILLARDIA × GRANDIFLORA

These hybrids of *Gaillardia aristata* and *G. pulchella* are the most commonly grown of the blanket flowers. The plants form mounds up to 3 ft (1 m) high and wide and have narrow, slightly lobed hairy leaves. The flowerheads, 3–4 in (8–10 cm) in diameter, come in bright colors: red, yellow, orange and burgundy. They are propagated by division or from cuttings to provide named cultivars. 'Burgunder' ('Burgundy') has deep maroon-colored flowers; 'Dazzler' has bright orange-yellow flowers with maroon centers; 'Kobold' ('Goblin') has compact growth to 12 in (30 cm) high and rich red flowers with yellow tips.

Cultivation

These hardy plants tolerate extreme heat, cold, dryness, strong winds and poor soils. Plant in full sun in well-drained soil and stake if necessary. In cool climates the stems of perennials should be cut back in late summer in order to recover before frosts. Propagate from seed in spring or early summer.

Flowering time Summer–autumn. *Zone 3–10.*

GAURA LINDHEIMERI

Native to North America, this bushy, long-flowering perennial is useful for backgrounds and mixed flower borders. It has loosely branched stems covered with tiny hairs, and produces beautiful, pink-suffused, small white flowers which give a misty pink effect. Leaves are lance-shaped and mid-green. Grows

Gaillardia × grandiflora 'Kobold'

Gaura lindheimeri

to 4 ft (1.2 m) in height with a spread of 3 ft (1 m), and is fully hardy.

Cultivation

It is easily grown, thriving in hot dry climates and preferring full sun and a light, sandy, well-drained soil. Propagate from seed in spring or autumn or from cuttings in summer.
Flowering time Spring–autumn. *Zone 6.*

GAZANIA

These low-growing perennials, some grown as annuals, are valued for their ease of culture and large, brightly colored flowers. They are useful for bedding, rock gardens, pots and tubs, and for binding soil on sloping land. Leaves are either entire or deeply lobed, long and narrow, and dark green on top, silver-gray and woolly beneath. The large daisy flowers are in a range of colors from cream to yellow, gold, pink, red, buff, brown and intermediate shades, usually marked with bands or spots of contrasting color at the base of the petals.

Cultivation

Grow in full sun in sandy, fairly dry, soil. Give an annual mulch of compost and water during dry periods. They are half-hardy and salt resistant so are useful in coastal areas. Propagate by division or from cuttings in autumn or from seed in late winter to early spring. Remove spent flowers and dead leaves, and tidy up at the end of the growing season.
Flowering time Late spring–summer.
Zone 9.

***Gazania*, Sunshine hybrids**

This is another carpeting perennial that is better grown as an annual in cooler climates. It grows to a height and spread of 8 in (20 cm). There is a large range of colors, many of them with dark centers.

GERANIUM

Cranesbill, geranium

There are over 400 species of perennial geraniums found all over the world in cool, alpine and temperate regions. They are useful for rock gardens, informal ground covers and plants for the front of the border. They make small, showy clumps with pink to blue or purple flowers.

Cultivation

Fully to half-hardy, most prefer a sunny situation and damp, well-drained soil. Propagate from semi-ripe cuttings in summer; seed in spring or by division in autumn. Tidy up regularly to encourage bushy growth. Transplant in winter.
Flowering time Spring–summer. *Zone 6.*

***Geranium* 'Johnson's Blue'**

Fully hardy, this rhizomatous perennial has cup-shaped lavender-blue flowers

Gazania, Sunshine hybrids

Geranium 'Johnson's Blue'

Geum chiloense 'Mrs. Bradshaw'

throughout summer. Leaves are deeply divided. It has a spreading habit, and grows to a height of 12 in (30 cm) and spread of 24 in (60 cm). Propagate by division or cuttings.

GERBERA JAMESONII

Barberton daisy, Transvaal daisy

Native to South Africa, this is one of the most decorative of all daisies and is an excellent cut flower. From a basal rosette of deeply lobed, lance-shaped leaves, white, pink, yellow, orange or red flowerheads, up to 2–4 in (5–10 cm) wide, are borne singly on long stems in spring and summer. Modern florists' gerberas derive from crosses between *Gerbera jamesonii* and the tropical African *G. viridifolia*. Some have flowerheads as much as 12 in (30 cm) across, in a wide range of colors, as well as double, for example 'Brigadoon Red', and quilled forms.

Cultivation

They need full sun to part-shade in hot areas and fertile, composted, well-drained soil. Water well during summer. Gerberas make good greenhouse plants, where they require good light and regular feeding during the growing season. Propagate from seed in autumn or early spring, from cuttings in summer or by division from late winter to early spring.

Flowering time Spring, summer. *Zone 8–11.*

GEUM CHILOENSE

syn. *Geum coccineum* of gardens, *G. quellyon*

Scarlet avens

This Chilean native reaches a height of 24 in (60 cm) with a spread of 12 in (30 cm). It forms a basal rosette of deep green, pinnate leaves to 12 in (30 cm) long. The vivid scarlet, cup-shaped flowers appear in terminal panicles in summer. 'Lady Stratheden' (syn. 'Goldball') has semi-double, golden-yellow flowers. 'Mrs. Bradshaw' bears rounded semi-double scarlet flowers.

Cultivation

Frost hardy, they prefer a sunny, open position and moist, well-drained soil. Propagate from seed in autumn or by division in autumn or spring.

Flowering time Summer. *Zone 5–9.*

GYPSOPHILA

Baby's breath

Native to Europe, Asia and North Africa, these annuals and perennials, some of which are semi-evergreen, are grown for their masses of small, dainty, white or pink flowers which make an excellent foil for bolder flowers. *G. paniculata* is a favorite cut flower as the tiny flowers last a long time in water.

Cultivation

Plant in full sun with shelter from strong winds. Fully hardy, they will tolerate most soils but do best in deep, well-drained soil that contains some organic matter in the form of compost or peat. They will grow well on limestone soils. Cut back after flowering to encourage a second flush of flowers. Propagate from cuttings of small lateral shoots in summer or from seed in spring or autumn. Transplant when dormant during winter.

Flowering time Summer. *Zone 6.*

Gypsophila paniculata

HELIANTHUS

Sunflower

Native to the Americas, these tall, showy-flowered annuals and perennials are grown for their large daisy-like, golden-yellow blooms. The plants have coarsely hairy, sticky-feeling leaves, and tall, rough stems which bear mostly yellow flowers with brown or yellow discs. Fully hardy, they prefer full sun and protection from wind, otherwise staking may be necessary.

Cultivation

Soil should be well-drained. Fertilize in spring to promote large blooms and water deeply in dry conditions. They may become invasive and should be cut down to the base after flowering. Propagate from seed or by division in autumn or early spring.

Flowering time Summer–autumn. *Zone 6.*

Helianthus annuus

Helianthus annuus

An upright annual, fast growing to a height of 6 ft (1.8 m) or more. Large daisy-like, 12 in (30 cm) wide, yellow flowerheads with brown centers are borne in summer. They are coarse, leggy plants with heavily veined, mid-green leaves.

HELICHRYSUM

Everlasting, strawflower, paper daisy, immortelle

This large genus of mainly annuals and short-lived perennials is notable for its papery, daisy flowers, commonly called everlastings. The most spectacular species occur naturally in Australia.

Cultivation

They are fully hardy to frost-tender and require a warm, sunny situation and a moderately fertile sandy or gravelly soil with free drainage. The plant adapts to most soils except heavy clay. Water regularly and shelter from strong winds. To use as dried decoration, cut flowers when just open, tie in bundles loosely wrapped in a paper sheath and hang upside-down in a well-ventilated place. Propagate perennials by division, seed or suckers in spring and annuals from seed in spring.

Flowering time Summer–autumn. *Zone 8.*

Helichrysum bracteatum

Strawflower, everlasting daisy

Native to Australia, this annual or short-lived perennial has an upright, branching habit and grows to a height and spread of 30 in (75 cm). It has tough, hollow stems, rough narrow leaves and from summer to early autumn bears clusters of daisy-like blooms. Flowers are multi-colored. Half-hardy. 'Dargan Hill Monarch' is the name of the golden-flowered cultivar commonly grown which often lives for two or three years, while the many-colored garden hybrids raised in Europe (red, pink, white, yellow) are definitely annuals.

Helichrysum bracteatum

HELLEBORUS

Lenten rose

Native to southern Europe and western Asia, these perennials, some of which are evergreen, are useful plants for cooler climates. They bear open, cup-shaped flowers in shades of green and purple and are effective planted in drifts or massed in the shade of deciduous trees.

Cultivation

Fully to half-hardy, they grow best in semi-shade and a moisture-retentive, well-drained soil that is enriched with organic matter. Never let the plants dry out in summer. Cut off old leaves of deciduous species in early spring just as buds start to appear. Top-dress with compost or manure after flowering. Propagate from seed or by division in autumn or early spring. The plants have poisonous properties.

Flowering time Winter and spring. *Zone 7–8.*

Helleborus orientalis

Helleborus orientalis

The most easily grown of the genus, this species is evergreen and clump-forming, growing to a height and spread of 18 in (45 cm). The large nodding flowers come in a variety of colors from white, green, pink and rose to purple, sometimes with dark spots. Fully hardy, it flowers in winter or early spring.

HEMEROCALLIS

Day lilies

Long-lived perennials, originating from China, Japan and east Asian countries, these have been intensively hybridized, resulting in a vast flower shape and color range mainly within the yellow-orange-pink tones. Mostly herbaceous, the dense pale green foliage emerges in early spring followed by flowers which, although lasting only a day, are freely produced for many months.

Cultivation

Given a full sun position, good soil and ample moisture these are easy-care plants but will respond to fertilizing and watering as they grow. At the end of winter cover the dormant plants with a mulch of rich compost then feed regularly to extend the flowering time. Propagate by division every three years.
Flowering time Spring–summer. *Zone 8.*

***Hemerocallis* 'Stella d'Oro'**

A hybrid with a seemingly constant blooming habit throughout the warmer months. It is a low to medium growing, about 12–24 in (30–60 cm) high, clump forming plant with strap-like leaves remaining neat throughout the season if care is taken to remove snails.

HEUCHERA

Alum root, coral bells

These evergreen perennials from North America are good as ground cover or as rock garden or edging plants. They form clumps of scalloped leaves, often tinted bronze or purple, from which arise very slender stems bearing masses of dainty white, crimson or pink bell flowers.

Cultivation

Fully to frost-hardy, they grow well in either full sun or semi-shade, and like a well-drained, coarse, moisture-retentive soil. Propagate species from seed in autumn or by division in spring or autumn; cultivars by division in autumn or early spring. Divide established clumps every 3 or 4 years.
Flowering time Spring. *Zone 8.*

***Heuchera* 'Palace Purple'**

This species is grown for its striking, purple, heart-shaped foliage and sprays

Hemerocallis 'Stella d'Oro'

Heuchera 'Palace Purple'

Hosta fortunei var. albopicta

Hosta sieboldiana

of white flowers in summer. It is clump forming, growing to a height and spread of 19 in (50 cm) and is fully hardy.

HOSTA

Plantain lily

Natives of Japan and China, these easily grown, fully hardy perennials are valued for their decorative foliage. They all produce wide, handsome leaves, some being marbled or marked with white, others a bluish green. All-yellow foliage is also available. They do well in large pots or planters, are excellent for ground cover, and add an exotic touch planted on the margins of lily ponds or in bog gardens. Tall stems of nodding white, pink or mauve bell flowers appear in warmer weather.

Cultivation

They prefer shade, and rich, moist, neutral, well-drained soil. Feed regularly during the growing season. Propagate by division in early spring, and guard against snails and slugs.
Flowering time Summer–autumn. *Zone 6.*

Hosta fortunei

This group of clump-forming hybrid perennials has oval to heart-shaped leaves in different colors. 'Aurea Marginata' has mid-green leaves with creamy yellow edges and tolerates full sun; var. *albopicta*, pale green with a creamy yellow center. All bear racemes of trumpet-shaped violet flowers in summer. They grow to a height of 30 in–3 ft (75 cm–1 m).

Hosta sieboldiana

A robust, clump-forming plant growing to a height of 3 ft (1 m) and spread of 5 ft (1.5 m). It has large, puckered, heart-shaped bluish gray leaves and bears racemes of trumpet-shaped white flowers in early summer. There are many beautiful variegated cultivars.

IBERIS

Candytuft

These annuals and perennials are mainly from southern Europe, western Asia and the Mediterranean area. They are highly regarded as decorative plants and are excellent for rock gardens, bedding and bordering. Showy flowers are borne in either flattish heads in colors of white, red and purple, or in erect racemes of pure white flowers. They are widely used in floral arrangements.

Cultivation

Fully to half-hardy, they require a warm, sunny position and a well-drained, light soil, preferably with added lime or dolomite. Water regularly. Propagate

Impatiens walleriana

from seed in autumn—they may self-sow but are unlikely to become invasive—or semi-ripe cuttings in summer.
Flowering time Spring–summer. *Zone 8.*

Iberis amara
Candytuft, hyacinth-flowered candytuft
Native to the United Kingdom and Europe, this fast-growing, fully hardy annual has lance-shaped, mid-green leaves and produces showy, flattish heads of numerous, fragrant, small, pure white flowers in early spring and summer. Of an erect, bushy habit, it reaches a height of 12 in (30 cm) and spread of 6 in (15 cm).

Iberis sempervirens
A low, spreading, evergreen perennial, this species is ideal for rock gardens. It has narrow, dark green leaves and dense, rounded heads of white flowers in spring. It is fully hardy, and grows to a height of 6–12 in (15–30 cm) and spread of 19–24 in (50–60 cm). The cultivar 'Snowflake' is attractive. Trim lightly after flowering.

IMPATIENS WALLERIANA

syn. *I sultanii*
Busy Lizzie
Native to tropical East Africa, this succulent, evergreen perennial is grown

Iberis amara

Iberis sempervirens

as an annual in cool climates. It has soft, fleshy stems with reddish stripes, oval, fresh leaves and flattish spurred flowers. There are many cultivars.

Cultivation
Half-hardy, this is a popular indoor plant and useful for bedding in partial shade. Water well.
Flowering time Spring–autumn. *Zone 8.*

KNIPHOFIA

Red-hot poker, torch lily, tritoma
Native to southern Africa, these stately perennials, some of which are evergreen,

make a brilliant display in the garden for a long time. They are upright, tufted plants with long, grass-like foliage and tall bare stems carrying showy, brightly colored, tubular flowers.

Cultivation

Fully to half-hardy, they require an open position in full sun and a well-drained soil with plenty of water in summer. They tolerate wind well and are often seen growing close to the coast. From spring on, fertilize monthly to increase size and quality of blooms. Remove dead flower stems and leaves in late autumn. They are excellent cut flowers. Propagate species from seed or by division in spring; cultivars by division in spring. Attractive to bellbirds and other birds that feed on nectar.

Flowering time Winter–summer. *Zone 8.*

Lamium maculatum 'Beacon Silver'

Kniphofia 'Maid of Orleans'

***Kniphofia* 'Maid of Orleans'**

This summer-flowering cultivar has dense racemes of yellow buds that open into creamy white flowers. It is frost-hardy and grows to a height of 4 ft (1.2 m).

Kniphofia uvaria* var. *nobilis

A tall, clump-forming perennial with strappy, blue-green leaves and robust straight flower spikes topped with deep orange blooms. Flowers in late summer and looks well when grouped with *Agapanthus* species. Grows to a height of 4 ft (1.2 m) with a spread of 19 in (50 cm). It is extremely hardy but responds to being divided every three years.

LAMIUM MACULATUM

Dead nettle

A semi-evergreen perennial, native to Europe and the Middle East, this plant is a popular flowering ground cover. It has mauve-tinged, deeply toothed leaves with central silvery stripes and clusters of pinkish flowers in spring and summer. Mat-forming, it grows to a height of 10 in (25 cm) with a spread of 3 ft (1 m). There are several cultivars, such as 'Beacon Silver'.

Cultivation

Fully hardy, the plants prefer full or partial shade and a moist, well-drained

Kniphofia uvaria var. *nobilis*

soil. Propagate by division of the root mass in autumn or early spring.
Flowering time Spring. *Zone 8.*

LIATRIS SPICATA

syn. *L. callilepis*

Gay feather, blazing star

This low-growing perennial from America is a desirable cut flower and a good butterfly and bee-attracting plant. The flowers are lilac-purple and are produced in crowded, fluffy spikes. They open from the top downwards, the opposite of most flowering spikes. The species has thickened, corm-like rootstocks and basal tufts of grassy foliage. Clump-forming, it grows to a height of 24 in (60 cm).

Cultivation

The plants require a sunny situation and well-drained light soil of reasonable quality. They are fully hardy but do not like high humidity. Propagate by division in early spring or from seed in spring or autumn. Transplant when dormant during winter.
Flowering time Late summer. *Zone 8.*

LIMONIUM

Statice, sea lavender

These sub-shrubs and perennials, sometimes grown as annuals, are popular for their papery, many colored flowers. Flowers should be cut just as they open and hung upside-down to dry in a cool, airy place. They are good mixed border plants and are easily grown in full sun and well-drained, sandy soil. Their tolerance to seaspray and low rainfall make them a good choice for seaside and low maintenance vacation house gardens.

Cultivation

Plants benefit from light fertilizing in spring while flowerheads are developing. Propagate by division in spring, from seed in early spring or autumn, or from root cuttings in late winter. Transplant during winter or early spring.
Flowering time Spring–summer. *Zone 8.*

Limonium latifolium

A fully hardy, tall-stemmed perennial bearing clusters of lavender-blue or bluish white flowers for a long period

Limonium latifolium

Liatris spicata

Linaria purpurea 'Canon J. Went'

over summer. Clump-forming, it grows to a height of 12 in (30 cm) and spread of 18 in (45 cm), with large leaves.

Limonium sinuatum

This statice is a bushy, upright perennial, almost always grown as an annual. It produces dense rosettes of oblong, deeply-waved, dark green leaves and bears masses of tiny blue, pink or white papery flowers on winged stems. Flowers in summer and early autumn. It is fairly slow-growing to a height of 19 in (50 cm) and spread of 12 in (30 cm).

LINARIA PURPUREA

Purple toadflax

This perennial from Europe is naturalized in some areas and grows to 3 ft (1 m). It bears violet-tinged purple flowers in summer. 'Canon J. Went' is a tall example of the species with tiny pale pink flowers.

Cultivation

It requires rich, well-drained, preferably sandy soil, moderate water and full sun. Seed sown directly in autumn or very early spring will germinate in 2 weeks.

Limonium sinuatum

Seedlings need to be thinned to a 6 in (15 cm) spacing and weeded to ensure no over-shadowing of these fine plants. Cutting back after the first flush will produce more flowers.

Flowering time Summer. *Zone 6–10.*

LOBELIA

This large genus of annuals and perennials is widely distributed in temperate regions, particularly America and Africa. Growth habits vary from low bedding plants to tall herbaceous perennials. They are all grown for their ornamental flowers and neat foliage and make excellent edging, flower box, hanging basket and rock garden specimens. Some are suitable in wild gardens or by the waterside.

Cultivation

They are best grown in a well-drained, moist, light loam enriched with animal manure or compost. Most grow in sun or semi-shade but resent wet conditions in winter. Prune after the first flush of flowers to encourage repeat flowering, and fertilize weekly with a liquid manure during the season. Fully hardy to frost-tender. Propagate annuals from seed in spring, perennial species from seed or by division in spring or autumn and perennial cultivars by division only. Transplant from late autumn until early spring.

Flowering time Spring–summer. *Zone 8.*

Lunaria annua

Lobularia maritima

***Lobelia erinus* 'Cambridge Blue'**

Edging lobelia

This low-growing compact annual from South Africa has a tufted, sometimes semi-trailing, habit with dense oval to lance-shaped leaves. It bears small, 2-lipped blue flowers continuously through spring, summer and early autumn. It grows to a height of 4–8 in (10–20 cm) and spread of 8–12 in (10–15 cm), and is half-hardy. Water sparingly and feed regularly.

LOBULARIA MARITIMA

syn. *Alyssum maritimum*

Sweet alyssum, sweet Alice

Native to southern Europe and western Asia, this fast-growing, spreading annual is a widely popular edging, rock garden or window box plant. It produces masses of tiny, honey-scented, 4-petalled white flowers. Lilac, pink and violet shades are also available. It has a low, rounded compact habit with lance-shaped grayish green leaves and grows to a height of 3–6 in (8–15 cm), and a spread of 8–12 in (20–30 cm).

Cultivation

Fully hardy, it grows best in a dryish position in full sun and likes a fertile, well-drained soil. Good for coastal and beach situations. Shear back after flowering to encourage continuous flowering. Propagate from seed in spring. *Flowering time* Winter–early autumn. *Zone 6.*

Lobelia erinus 'Cambridge Blue'

LUNARIA ANNUA

syn. *L. biennis*

Honesty

A fast-growing biennial, native to southern Europe and the Mediterranean coast, it has attractive flowers and curious fruits. It has pointed oval, serrated, bright green leaves, and bears heads of scented, 4-petaled rosy magenta, white or violet-purple flowers. These are followed by circular seed pods with a silvery, translucent membrane, which are used in dried floral arrangements. Erect in habit, it grows to a height of 30 in (75 cm).

Cultivation

Fully hardy, it will grow in either sun or shade, but prefers partial shade and

moderately fertile well-drained soil. Propagate from seed in spring or autumn. It self-sows readily.
Flowering time Spring–early summer. *Zone 7.*

LUPINUS

Lupin

A large genus of annuals and perennials mainly native to North America and southern Europe, grown for their ease of culture, rapid growth and large spikes of showy pea flowers in a range of colors including blue, purple, pink, white, yellow, orange and red. They are useful grouped with bearded irises in bedding schemes and are good naturalized.

Lychnis coronaria 'Alba'

Lupinus Russell hybrids

Cultivation

Grow in cool climates in an open, sunny position and a well-drained alkaline soil. They enjoy high humidity and should be mulched in dry areas. Spent flowers should be cut away to prolong plant life and to prevent self-seeding. Fully frost-hardy. Propagate species from seed in fall and selected forms from cuttings in spring. Watch for slugs and snails.
Flowering time Spring–summer. *Zone 6.*

Lupinus Russell hybrids

This fine strain of strong-growing perennial lupins bears long spikes of large brilliant, strongly colored flowers (in shades of cream, pink, orange, blue or violet), some of which are bicolored, in late spring and summer. They produce a magnificent clump of handsome, deeply divided, mid-green leaves, growing to a height of 3 ft (1 m) with a spread of half that. There are also dwarf strains. Cut back flowering stems to ground level in late autumn and divide and replant clumps between autumn and early spring every two or three years.

LYCHNIS

Native to the temperate regions of the northern hemisphere, these annuals, biennials and perennials are grown for their attractive flowers, borne in cymes in white through to reds and magenta.

Cultivation

They are fully hardy, and like cool, elevated places, preferably on sunny sites with an easterly or southerly slope to minimize soil temperatures. They grow in any well-drained soil and an annual feeding in late winter to early spring is beneficial. Remove spent stems after flowering and deadhead often. Propagate by division or from seed in autumn or early spring. They self-seed readily.
Flowering time Summer. *Zone 6.*

Lychnis coronaria
Rose campion

A clump-forming perennial, sometimes grown as a biennial, this plant grows to a height of 24 in (60 cm) and a spread of 18 in (45 cm). It forms a dense clump of silvery white, woolly leaves. Bright scarlet flowers bloom in summer. Fully hardy, it thrives in most areas and self-sows readily. 'Alba' is a white-flowered cultivar.

MATTHIOLA
Stock

This genus of annuals, biennials and perennials is native to the Mediterranean region. They have soft gray-green foliage and densely clustered, scented flowers in shades of white, lilac and purple, deep reds and pinks, and yellow. Tall and dwarf, single and double varieties have been developed.

Cultivation

Fully hardy to frost-tender. Grow in a sheltered position in sun or semi-shade, and in a fertile, well-drained soil that has been freshly turned with manure and lime. Sow seed of annuals in late summer to early autumn; perennials under glass in spring.
Flowering time Spring–summer. *Zone 7.*

Matthiola incana
Stock

This upright biennial or short-lived perennial from southern Europe is best grown as an annual. It has a bushy habit and grows up to 24 in (60 cm) in height with a spread of 12 in (30 cm). These stocks are fully hardy with lance-shaped, gray-green leaves, and fragrant, spikes of mauve flowers borne in spring.

MIMULUS × *HYBRIDUS* HYBRIDS

These hybrids between *Mimulus guttatus* and *M. luteus* blend parental characters. The funnel-shaped, open-mouthed flowers can be up to 2 in (5 cm) wide and come in red, yellow, cream and white, or mixed variations of these, plus red mottling, spotting or freckling. Although reasonably hardy, they rapidly deteriorate in hot sunlight and become straggly after a few months, and so are treated as annuals. 'Ruiter's Hybrid' bears orange trumpet-shaped flowers with wavy petal margins.

Cultivation

Grow these plants in full sun or part-shade in wet or moist soil. Propagate from seed in autumn or early spring.
Flowering time Spring, summer (mostly grown as an annual). *Zone 6–10.*

Matthiola incana

Mimulus × *hybridus* 'Ruiter's Hybrid'

Myosotidium hortensia

Monarda didyma

MONARDA DIDYMA

Bergamot, Oswego tea

A native of North America, this perennial species of bergamot has long been grown for the oil extracted from its young leaves. Today, with their great variety of colorful forms, they are highly regarded cottage or herbaceous garden plants. A well-behaved clump-forming plant with small, soft gray-green leaves and flowerheads, in white and pink tones, held aloft, it grows about 30 in (75 cm) high.

Cultivation

Like most perennials, it will repay the gardener with strong healthy foliage growth and good flower quality if the

Myosotis 'Blue Ball'

soil is well prepared and mulched at the time of planting. It grows well in full sun. Propagate by dividing the dormant clumps in late winter.

MYOSOTIDIUM HORTENSIA

Chatham Islands forget-me-not

Native to the Chatham Islands off the coast of New Zealand, this evergreen, clump-forming perennial is the giant of the forget-me-not family, growing to a height and spread of around 24 in (60 cm). It has a basal mound of large, glossy, rich-green, pleated leaves, and bears large clusters of bright blue flowers on tall flower stems.

Cultivation

Half-hardy, it requires semi-shade and a humus-rich moist soil. It can withstand salt winds and benefits from a mulch. Propagate by division in spring or from seed in summer or autumn. They will naturalize freely.
Flowering time Spring–summer. *Zone 8.*

MYOSOTIS

Forget-me-not

This genus of annuals and perennials includes 34 New Zealand natives among its 50 or so species, but those most commonly cultivated come from the temperate regions of Europe, Asia and the Americas. They are grown for their dainty blue (sometimes pink or white) flowers that complement plants of stronger color. Most species are useful in rock gardens, border displays or as ground cover under trees and shrubs.

Cultivation

Fully hardy, they prefer either a semi-shaded woodland setting or a sunny spot with the protection of other larger plants. Soil should be fertile and well-drained. Before flowering, they respond well to feeding. Discard plants after flowering. Propagate from seed in autumn. Once established, the plants will self-seed freely.
Flowering time Spring–summer. *Zone 6.*

***Myosotis* 'Blue Ball'**

This fully hardy, delightful perennial is usually grown as an annual. It has a bushy, compact habit, growing to a height of 8 in (20 cm) with a spread of 6 in (15 cm), and bears tiny blue flowers in spring and early summer. It is good for edging.

Nemophila insignis

Nemesia strumosa

NEMESIA STRUMOSA

Indigenous to southern Africa, this colorful, fast-growing annual is a popular bedding plant, and also useful for planting between summer-flowering bulbs, in rock gardens and window boxes. They are bushy plants with lance-shaped, pale green toothed leaves, growing to a height of 8–12 in (20–30 cm) and spread of 10 in (25 cm). Many trumpet-shaped flowers in colors of yellow, white, red or orange are borne on short terminal racemes.

Cultivation

The plants prefer a well-dug, moderately fertile, mildly acid or neutral, well-drained soil, and a wind-sheltered, sunny position. They cannot tolerate very hot, humid climates. Prune spent flowers to prolong flowering and pinch out growing shoots of young plants to encourage a bushy habit. Propagate from seed in early autumn.
Flowering time Spring. *Zone 9.*

NEMOPHILA INSIGNIS

syn. *N. menziesii*

Baby blue-eyes

A charming Californian wildflower, this fast-growing, spreading annual is a useful ground cover under shrubs, in rock gardens and borders, and is effective overplanted in a bed with spring bulbs. It bears small, bowl-shaped, sapphire-blue flowers with a well-defined concentric ring of white in the center. It has dainty, serrated foliage, and grows to a height of 20 cm and spread of 15 cm.

Cultivation

It is best planted in a cool, partly shaded site in fertile, well-drained soil that does not dry out in summer. These plants dislike heat and transplanting. Propagate from seed sown outdoors in early autumn. Watch for aphids.
Flowering time Spring. *Zone 8.*

Nepeta × faassenii

Nicotiana alata

NEPETA × FAASSENII

Catmint

This bushy, clump-forming perennial is useful for separating strong colors in the shrub or flower border, and very effective in rock gardens, or as a border plant. It forms spreading mounds of grayish green leaves that are aromatic when crushed.

Cultivation

Fully hardy, it prefers cool conditions and a sunny situation but will grow in semi-shade. Any fertile, well-drained soil will suit. Propagate by division in early spring or from softwood cuttings in spring and summer.
Flowering time Summer. *Zone 8.*

NICOTIANA

Flowering tobacco

These annuals and perennials are mainly of South American origin and are an ornamental species of tobacco. The older species are grown for the fragrance of their warm-weather flowers which usually open at night; the newer strains have flowers that remain open all day but have limited perfume.

Cultivation

They are half-hardy to frost-tender, requiring full sun or light shade and a fertile, moist, but well-drained soil. Propagate from seed in early spring.
Flowering time Late spring–early autumn. *Zone 8.*

Nicotiana alata

syn. *N. affinis*

A short-lived perennial, often grown as an annual, this half-hardy plant bears clusters of attractive, tubular flowers in lime green, white, red or various shades of pink. Rosette-forming, it has oval, mid-green leaves and grows to a height of 3 ft (1 m). It flowers through summer and early autumn.

PAPAVER

Poppy

With their characteristic cupped petals, and nodding buds turning skywards upon opening, poppies are popular bedding flowers.

Cultivation

They are fully hardy and prefer little or no shade and moist, well-drained soil. Sow seed in spring or autumn; many species self-seed readily.
Flowering time Spring–summer. *Zone 6.*

Papaver nudicaule

Iceland poppy

This tuft-forming perennial is in fact almost always grown as an annual. It bears large scented flowers, colored white, yellow, orange and pink in winter and spring. The plant has pale green leaves, long hairy stems, and grows to a height of 12–24 in (30–60 cm) with a 4 in (10 cm) spread. Give this native of North America and Asia Minor full sun. Sow in late summer to early autumn. The species is good for bedding and cutting.

Papaver orientale

Oriental poppy

This frost-hardy perennial bears spectacular single or double flowers in early summer. Originally from Asia, cultivars offering different colors abound, but a common feature is the dark basal blotch on each petal. Foliage of hairy, lance-like, bluish green leaves can become straggly. As this plant will grow to a height and spread of 18 in (45 cm), it may need support.

Papaver rhoeas

Corn poppy, field poppy

The cupped flowers on this fast-growing annual from Asia Minor are small, delicate, scarlet and single, although cultivated varieties (Shirley poppies) offer hues including reds, pinks, whites and bicolors. Double-flowered strains are also available. It will grow 24 in (60 cm) high with a 12 in (30 cm) spread. Flowering time is early summer, and the leaves are light green and lobed. Give them all full sun.

Papaver nudicaule

Papaver orientale

Papaver rhoeas

Pelargonium graveolens

Pelargonium zonale

PELARGONIUM

Geranium

These frost-tender perennials are often grown as annuals for summer bedding in colder climates. In warmer climates with long hours of daylight, they flower almost all the time, although they do not do well in extreme heat and humidity.

Cultivation

Plant in pots or beds. The site should be sunny with light, well-drained, neutral soil. If in pots, fertilize regularly and cull dead-heads. Avoid over watering. Use softwood cuttings for propagation in spring through autumn. The species in this genus are mainly from South Africa. Including hybrids and cultivated varieties, the genus is divided into three large groups: zonal, ivy-leaved and regal or show geraniums.

Flowering time Spring–summer. *Zone 9–10.*

Pelargonium graveolens

Rose geranium

The deeply lobed, furry leaves of this species give off an aroma of roses when crushed. It is a shrubby plant, growing 12–24 in (30–60 cm) tall and wide. The smallish flowers are rose pink with a purple spot on the upper petals. The common 'rose geranium' of gardens is not the same as the original South African *Pelargonium graveolens* and is probably of hybrid origin.

Pelargonium zonale

Zonal geranium

This South African species is rarely seen in gardens; however its hybrids, the zonal geraniums, are among the most popular of all the summer flowers. Bushy aromatic perennials, they can be grown either from seed or cuttings. Zonal geraniums are frost tender and they can be grown as annuals in cold climate areas.

PENSTEMON

This large genus includes shrubs, sub-shrubs, annuals and perennials, all of which do best in fertile, well-drained soil and full sun. Most of the species are native to North America, but hybrids are grown all over the world for their showy flower spikes in blues, reds, white and bicolors. Tall varieties suit sheltered borders; dwarf strains are bright in bedding schemes. The genus comprises mainly evergreens and semi-evergreens.

Cultivation

Propagate from seed in spring or autumn, by division in spring, or from cuttings of non-flowering shoots in late summer (the only method for cultivars). Cut plants back hard after flowering. *Flowering time* Spring–summer. *Zone 8.*

Penstemon* × *gloxinioides

Beard tongue

These hybrids between *P. hartwegii* and *P. cobaea* are the most widely grown penstemons in gardens. They include the two-toned, strong-growing 'Huntington Pink'; the tall, dark 'Midnight' and not-so-tall but also dark 'Prairie Dusk'; and one that flowers profusely called 'Apple Blossom'. All grow about 30 in (75 cm) tall and are fine plants for the middle of a border.

PEROVSKIA ATRIPLICIFOLIA

Russian sage

This tall, tough species produces soft, gray-green foliage that beautifully complements the haze of pale lavender-blue flowers that appear on panicles in late summer and autumn. The plants are upright to 5 ft (1.5 m), with a spread of 3 ft (1 m) or more. They are long lived.

Cultivation

They are very easily grown in any well-drained, rather dry soil in a sunny position. It is often best to contain their growth by planting them beside a path, wall or border edge. They are very frost hardy and may be propagated from seed or cuttings of non-flowering stems. *Flowering time* Summer, autumn. *Zone 5–9.*

Petrovskia atriplicifolia

Penstemon × gloxinioides

PETUNIA

Petunia

Mostly grown as annuals, these perennials like well-drained, fertile soil and a sunny location. They thrive where summers are hot, but need shelter from the wind. Hues of white, purple, red, blue, pink and a mix are available. Fairly fast-growing, the branching plant has dark green elliptical leaves. Flowers of some of the larger grandiflora hybrids are damaged by rain but others, such as the multiflora hybrids, are much more resilient.

Cultivation

Sow seed early in spring. Pinching back hard encourages branching. Fertilize the plants every month only until the onset of hot weather. Cucumber mosaic and tomato spotted wilt can attack species of petunia and they need to be dead-headed at frequent intervals.
Flowering time Late spring–autumn.
Zone 10.

Petunia* × *hybrida

The subject of extensive hybridization, these plants are being bred with specific habits to be used as flowers for massed summer displays, or cascading types just right for hanging baskets or containers, and miniatures with smaller flowers for patio tub culture. The color range also is being ever expanded to include cream and glistening sheen to the blooms.

Phlox paniculata

Phlox subulata

PHLOX

These evergreen and semi-evergreen annuals and perennials, mostly native to North America, are grown for their profuse, fragrant flowers. The name phlox means 'flame', an appropriate epithet for these brightly colored, showy flowers, popular in bedding and border displays.

Cultivation

Grow in fertile soil that drains well but remains moist. Choose a sunny or partially shaded location.
Flowering time Spring–summer. *Zone 8.*

Phlox paniculata

Summer phlox, perennial

This tall perennial can grow to more than 3 ft (1 m), although height varies a little among the many named varieties. In summer it bears long-lasting, terminal

Petunia × *hybrida* cultivar

flowerheads comprising many small, 5-lobed flowers. Colors range through violet, red, salmon and white according to variety. Eelworm is this species' enemy. Watch out also for spider-mites and mildew. Propagate from root cuttings in winter or by division early in spring. Mulch in winter. It is fully hardy.

Phlox subulata

Moss phlox, creeping phlox

The flowers that bloom through spring in terminal masses on this prostrate alpine perennial are mauve, pink, white and shaped like stars, the petals being notched and open. The fully hardy, evergreen species is suited to growing in rock gardens where it will get sun. Its fine-leaved foliage will grow carpet-like to 4 in (10 cm) high with a spread twice that. Start in spring or summer using cuttings from non-flowering shoots. Trim back after flowering.

PLATYCODON GRANDIFLORUS

Balloon flower, Chinese bell flower

This perennial originates from Japan and China. In summer, balloon-like buds open out into 5-petaled flowers like bells, colored blue, purple, pink or white. 'Fuji Blue' grows up to 30 in (75 cm) and has single purplish blue flowers up to 24 in (60 cm) across.

Platycodon grandiflorus 'Fuji Blue'

Cultivation

Plant the fully hardy species in full sun in well-drained sandy soil. Use rooted basal cuttings of non-flowering shoots to propagate in summer, sow seed in spring or autumn, or divide in spring. *Flowering time* Summer. *Zone 8.*

PORTULACA GRANDIFLORA

Moss rose, sun plant

This annual, native to South America, grows slowly, attaining a height of up to 8 in (20 cm) and a spread of 6 in (15 cm). Its small, lance-shaped, fleshy leaves are bright green and its branching stems are prostrate. Its large open flowers, which may be single or double, bloom in red, pink, yellow or white.

Cultivation

Plant this half-hardy plant as ground cover, or in a rock garden or border, in

Portulaca grandiflora

Primula malacoides

Primula vulgaris hybrid

Primula obconica

well-drained soil in a sunny location. The flowers close in dull conditions and overnight. Sow seed in spring.
Flowering time Summer–early autumn. *Zone 9.*

PRIMULA

Primula, primrose

Fragrant, colorful flowers on stems above a rosette of basal leaves is characteristic of this genus, mostly from the temperate regions of the northern hemisphere. The flowers can be flat, trumpet-shaped or bell-shaped.

Cultivation

Primulas like fertile, well-drained soil, partial shade and ample water. Propagate from seed in spring, early summer or autumn, or by division or from root cuttings. Remove dead-heads and old foliage after blooming.
Flowering time Winter–spring. *Zone 7.*

Primula malacoides

Fairy primrose

Small, open flowers bloom in spiral masses on this frost-tender perennial, mostly grown as an annual. It is a native of China. The single or double flowers range in color from white to pink to magenta. Its oval-shaped, light green leaves have a hairy texture, as does its erect stem. The species reaches a height and spread of 8 in (20 cm) or more.

Primula obconica

Poison primrose

Dense flower clusters grow in an umbellate arrangement on hairy, erect stems on this perennial. A native of China, it grows to 12 in (30 cm) high and as much or more in spread. Flowering time is winter through spring. The yellow-eyed, flattish flowers range in color from white through pink to purple. The light green leaves are elliptical, serrated and form a basal rosette. This is popular as a container or bedding plant.

Primula vulgaris

English primrose, common primrose

This is a very familiar wildflower in Europe and it likes its cultivated conditions to mirror its cool woodland native environment. It is low-growing to around 8 in (20 cm), usually frost-resistant, and produces a carpet of bright flowers in spring. The flattish flowers are pale yellow with dark eyes (but the garden forms come in every color), and bloom singly on hairy stems above rosettes of crinkled, lance-shaped, serrated leaves.

RUDBECKIA

Coneflower

These North American annuals, biennials and perennials are popular for their bright, daisy-like flowers with a prominent dark-colored central cone (hence their common name). Plants range from 24 in–6 ft (60 cm–2 m) tall, depending on species, and spread up to 3 ft (1 m) wide.

Cultivation

Grow in moist soil in a sunny position. Start from cuttings in spring. Propagate from seed or by division in spring or autumn.
Flowering time Summer–autumn.
Zone 6.

Rudbeckia fulgida 'Goldsturm'

This upstanding perennial bears flowerheads like daisies, yellow with

Rudbeckia fulgida 'Goldsturm'

central black cones. Growing 24 in (60 cm) high with a spread of 12 in (30 cm) or more, the plant has narrow lanceolate green leaves. Both sunny and shaded locations are suitable. It is very fashionable for massed plantings in meadow-style gardens but may need staking if too much shade is provided.

SALPIGLOSSIS SINUATA

Painted tongue

Offering a variety of flower colors including red, orange, yellow, blue and purple, this annual from Peru and Argentina blooms in summer and early autumn. The 2 in (5 cm) wide, heavily veined flowers are like small flaring trumpets, while the lanceolate leaves are light green. A fast grower, it reaches a height of 18–24 in (45–60 cm) and a spread of at least 15 in (38 cm). It is frost tender and dislikes dry conditions.

Cultivation
Plant in full sun in rich, well-drained soil. Deadhead regularly. It is best sown directly from seed in early spring in the place it is to grow as seedlings do not always survive transplanting. They are prone to attack by aphids.
Flowering time Summer, early autumn (mostly grown as an annual). *Zone 8–11.*

Salpiglossis sinuata

Salvia elegans 'Salsa Burgundy'

SALVIA

Blue sage

This large and widely distributed genus of annual and perennial herbs and shrubs includes species whose leaves are used as edible herbs as well as for a host of folk remedies. The leaves of most species are aromatic, and many produce decorative garden displays with spikes of small thimble-shaped flowers.

Cultivation
Establish these species in fertile well-drained soil in a sunny location. Propagate annuals from seed and perennials by division in spring or from softwood cuttings in spring and summer.
Flowering time Summer–autumn.
Zone 8–11.

Salvia elegans
syn. *S. rutilans*
Pineapple-scented sage

A smell of pineapples comes from this perennial's oval leaves, which are toothed and hairy. Growing to a height and spread of 3 ft (1 m), the half-hardy species blooms in summer and autumn producing scarlet flowers in spiral clusters.

Salvia leucantha
Mexican bush sage

This Mexican and tropical central American native is a woody subshrub grown for its seemingly endless display of downy purple and white flowers on long, arching spikes. The foliage is soft and gray-green. It will reach 3–4 ft (1–1.2 m) in height and spread, making it suitable for the middle of the border; it is often used as a flowering hedge in mild-winter regions.

Salvia splendens
Scarlet sage

This native of Brazil, which is grown as an annual, produces dense terminal

Salvia leucantha

spikes of scarlet flowers in summer through early autumn. The leaves are toothed ellipses. It grows to 12 in (30 cm) with a similar spread. In hotter climates, give it a little shade. *S. splendens* is half-hardy.

SCABIOSA

Scabious

This genus of annuals and perennials, found widely in temperate climates, produces tall-stemmed, honey-scented flowers ideal for cutting. Blooms of multiple florets with protruding filaments, giving a pincushion-like effect, are a feature. Flower colors range from pinkish white to deep purple.

Cultivation

Most species will thrive in full sun in well-drained, alkaline soil. Propagate annuals from seed in spring; perennials from cuttings in summer, seed in autumn, or by division in early spring. *Flowering time* Summer–early autumn. *Zone 6.*

Scabiosa atropurpurea

This bushy annual produces flowers from summer through to early autumn, provided blooms are cut or dead-headed.

Scabiosa atropurpurea

Scabiosa caucasica

The fragrant, dome-shaped flowerheads are 2 in (5 cm) wide, mainly crimson but also in white, pink, purple and blue. Sizes vary from 19 in (50) cm for dwarf forms, up to 3 ft (1 m) high. This fully hardy species has lobed, lance-like foliage.

Scabiosa caucasica

Pincushion flower

Flat, many petaled flowerheads in pink, red, purple or blue hues, with centers like pincushions, often in a contrasting color, make these summer-flowering annuals popular for borders and cottage gardens. A busy plant with lobed mid-green leaves, it reaches a height and spread of 19–24 in (50–60 cm). The native species is from the Caucasus, and there are many fully hardy cultivars.

STACHYS BYZANTINA

syn. *S. lanata, S. olympica*

Lamb's ears, lamb's tongue

The leaves give this perennial its common name: tongue-shaped, they are thick and whitish. Unfortunately their woolly surface turns mushy if rained on heavily. Frost also does damage. Nonetheless it makes a good ground cover or

Tagetes patula

Stachys byzantina

border plant, growing 12–19 in (30–50 cm) high, with a 24 in (60 cm) spread. Nip the buds at the onset of blooming to keep the foliage looking lush.

Cultivation
Establish in well-drained soil in full sun.
Flowering time Summer. *Zone 8.*

TAGETES

Marigold
These annuals are used in beds or for edges.

Cultivation
Plant seed in spring. To prolong flowering, cull the dead-heads. Watch out for attack by botrytis and slugs.
Flowering time Summer–early autumn. *Zone 9.*

Tagetes patula
French marigold
The double flowerheads produced in summer and early autumn by this bushy annual resemble carnations. They bloom in reds, yellows and oranges. The leaves are green and aromatic. This fast-grower reaches 12 in (30 cm) in height and spread.

THALICTRUM

Meadow rue
This genus is known for its fluffy, showy flowers. The branches of their slender

Thalictrum delavayi

upstanding stems often intertwine, and the leaves are finely divided. The flowers have four or five sepals and conspicuous stamen tufts. They serve well in borders and in the margins of woodland gardens.

Cultivation
Propagate from seed when fresh or by division in spring.
Flowering time Spring–summer. *Zone 6.*

Thalictrum delavayi
syn. *T. dipterocarpum* of gardens
Lavender shower
Rather than fluffy heads, this species bears a multitude of nodding, lilac flowers in loose panicles, their yellow

Tropaeolum majus

stamens prominent. Flowering time is from the middle to the end of summer. The finely divided leaves give the mid-green foliage a dainty appearance. Reaching 4 ft (1.2 m) high, this species has a spread of 24 in (60 cm).

TROPAEOLUM

Nasturtium

Bright flowers are the attraction of this genus of annuals, perennials and twining climbers, whose natural territory extends from Chile to Mexico.

Cultivation

Frost-hardy to frost-tender, most species prefer moist, well-drained soil and a sunny or semi-shaded location. Propagate from seed, basal stem cuttings or tubers in spring. Watch out for aphids and the caterpillars of the cabbage moth. *Flowering time* Spring–summer. *Zone 6.*

Tropaeolum majus

Garden nasturtium, Indian cress

The stem is trailing and climbing on this fast-growing, bushy annual. Its leaves are rounded and textured with radial veins. It blooms in summer and autumn, its 5-petaled flowers spurred, open and trumpet-shaped, in many shades of red or yellow. It grows to a spread of 12 in (30 cm) and a height up to twice that. Avoid fertilizing this plant, which is resistant to frost but not to drought, and let it have sun. There are several varieties with single or double flowers and compact or trailing habit. 'Alaska' has single flowers and prettily variegated leaves.

VERBENA

Verbena

Because of a susceptibility to mildew, these biennials and perennials are considered best grown as annuals. Originating in Europe, they have characteristically small, dark, irregularly shaped and toothed leaves. Half-hardy, they do best in areas where winters are not severe. An agreeably spicy aroma is associated with most verbenas.

Cultivation

Establish in medium, well-drained soil, in sun or at most semi-shade. To propagate, use seed in autumn or spring, stem cuttings in summer or autumn, or division in late winter. You can also propagate in spring using young shoots that appear at the crown of the plant. *Flowering time* Summer–autumn. *Zone 8.*

Verbena × hybrida

Verbena × hybrida

This trailing perennial bears slightly hairy leaves. It blooms in summer to autumn, its fragrant flowers appearing in dense clusters, many showing off white centers among the hues of red, mauve, violet, white and pink. Use this species in summer beds and containers. Avoid being heavy handed with fertilizers or the plants will yield more leaves than flowers.

VERONICA

Speedwell

These perennials are widespread through temperate regions. Although their flowers are usually blue, they encompass a wide variety of foliage and of size, with a height range from 12 in (30 cm) to over 4 ft (1.2 m). Some are evergreens, some semi-evergreens. The different species range from frost-resistant to fully hardy.

Cultivation

Establish them in well-drained, fertilized soil in sun. To propagate, use seed in autumn or spring, division in early spring or autumn or either softwood or semi-ripe cuttings in summer.
Flowering time Summer. *Zone 6.*

Veronica spicata

Digger's speedwell

A European species, this fully hardy perennial reaches a height of 24 in (60 cm) and a spread of up to 3 ft (1 m). Its stems are erect, hairy and branching. Spikes of small star-shaped blue flowers bloom in summer. The leaves of this species are mid-green, linear to lanceolate in shape.

VIOLA

Violet pansy

Although the sweet violet (*V. odorata*) gives one of the best loved of flower perfumes, many of the other species are less fragrant. Their leaves can be solitary or in clumps, lightly to heavily textured, kidney to heart-shaped. The annuals are suited to spring bedding, although big beds of them are needed if you want sufficient yield to pick. The perennials and sub-shrubs are good in beds and rock gardens. Some species have runners and are invasive.

Cultivation

Most species do best in lean or fertile soil that drains well and retains moisture, with some preferring an acidic pH. Grow them in sun or shade. They range from half- to fully hardy.
Flowering time Late winter–spring.
Zone 7.

Viola hederacea

syn. *V. reniformis, Erpetion reniforme*

Australian native violet

The tiny 5-petaled, scentless flowers that bloom on short stems on this creeping perennial from the southeast of Australia are lilac, white and solitary. They appear in spring, summer and autumn. The plant's stems are prostrate, suckering and mat forming, spreading widely but reaching only 2 in (5 cm) in

Veronica spicata

Viola odorata

Viola × wittrockiana

Viola hederacea

height. Its leaves are rounded and kidney-shaped, deep green and with irregular edges. Partially shade this frost-resistant but drought-tender species. Propagate *V. hederacea* by division in spring or autumn.

Viola odorata

Violet, sweet violet

A sweet perfume wafts from the flowers on this spreading, rhizomatous perennial from Europe, which grows 2½ in (6 cm) high over 19 in (50 cm) or more in spread. Its dark green leaves are a pointy kidney shape with shallow toothed edges. Spurred, flat-faced flowers in violet, white or rose, bloom from late winter through early spring. Boasting many cultivars, this fully hardy species self-seeds readily and can be propagated by division in autumn. The plants like well-composted, moist soil and a well-protected location in semi-shade.

Viola* × *wittrockiana

Pansy, viola

This group of predominantly bushy perennials are almost always grown as biennials or annuals. Offering flowers of a great many hues, the species bloom in late winter through spring and possibly into summer in cooler climates. The flowers grow up to 4 in (10 cm) across and have 5 petals in a somewhat flat-faced array. Its mid-green leaves are elliptical, sometimes with toothed margins. Sedate growers, these plants reach about 8 in (20 cm) in spread and height. Propagate from softwood cuttings in spring. Pansies usually have black blotches, violas none, but there are now intermediate types with pale-colored markings.

ZINNIA

Zinnia

Found through Mexico, Central and South America, this genus is an excellent source of cut flowers. The flowerheads on these half-hardy annuals are like the flowerheads of dahlias.

Cultivation

Establish them in fertile soil that drains well in a sunny position. They need frequent dead-heading. Sow seed under glass early in spring.

Flowering time Summer–autumn. *Zone 9.*

Zinnia elegans

Youth-and-old-age

This sturdy annual from Mexico is the best known of the zinnias. The flowerheads are purple, and bloom in summer to autumn. It grows fairly rapidly to 24–30 in (60–75 cm), with a smaller spread. Its deep green leaves are linear to lanceolate. Zinnia hybrids offer lovely hues of white, red, pink, yellow, violet, orange or crimson. Grow them in rich, loamy soil in an open, sunny location.

Zinnia elegans

SHRUBS

Shrubs are the workhorses of the garden. They can act as screens for privacy, soften the lines of the house, or be given starring roles by virtue of their flowers, fruit or handsome foliage. They provide detailed interest for less expense and work than any other plant. Shrubs should be valued as much for their habit and foliage as for their flowers. It can be very effective to set some small, rounded shrubs in front of a tall, arching one; to set dense foliage against shrubs which feature an open tracery of branches; to contrast an upright grower against one of spreading, prostrate habit. Some shrubs can be clipped to form hedges, while others can be trained flat against a wall.

Abutilon × *hybridum* 'Orange Queen'

Abelia × *grandiflora*

ABELIA × *GRANDIFLORA*

This hybrid between *Abelia chinensis* and *A. uniflora* grows to 6–8 ft (1.8–2.4 m) tall and wide. It has arching reddish brown canes and small, glossy dark green leaves. Small mauve and white flowers appear in early summer, usually with a second flush at summer's end. The dull pink calyces persist on the shrub after the flower falls, contrasting with the leaves which turn purplish bronze. The cultivar 'Francis Mason' has yellow or yellow-edged leaves but it has a tendency to revert to plain green.

Cultivation

Abelias prefer sun or light shade, and need a well-drained soil with regular water in summer. They are easily propagated from cuttings and can withstand heavy pruning, for example, when used for low hedging.
Height 6–8 ft (1.8–2.4 m). *Zone 7–10.*

ABUTILON

Chinese lantern, flowering maple

Grown for the beauty of their often variegated, maple- or heart-shaped leaves as much as for their delightful, colorful flowers, these leggy evergreen or semi-evergreen shrubs are grown in glasshouses in cold conditions or in the open in warmer areas. Often raised as indoor plants, they bloom best when they are rootbound. Popular with metallic flea beetles and aphids.

Cultivation

They prefer full sun or part-shade and a rich, moist, fertile and well-drained soil. Improve the flower yield by regular pinching back to ensure branching and hence budding. If necessary, tie to a support if lax. Raised from seed sown at any time, *Abutilon* will germinate within 3 weeks or less and should flower within 12 months.

Abutilon × *hybridum*

Flowering maple

These open, soft-wooded shrubs have green, heart-shaped leaves with a furry texture. They bear bell-shaped flowers, in shades of white, cream, pink, yellow, orange and red (often veined in contrasting tone), from spring to autumn. In the growing season, young plants may need tip pruning to promote bushy growth. Mature specimens should have the previous season's stems cut back hard annually in early spring. Propagate from softwood or semi-ripe cuttings from

summer to winter. Slightly tender, they are best grown as greenhouse plants in cold climates. 'Orange Queen' is a free-flowing hybrid with luminous blooms.
Height 8 ft (2.4 m). *Zone 9–11.*

AESCULUS PARVIFLORA

Bottlebrush buckeye

This many-stemmed shrub, native to south-eastern USA, grows 6–10 ft (1.8–3 m) tall, spreading into a broad clump by new growth from the roots. The 5 large, strongly veined leaflets have downy undersides. In late summer it produces spikes of spidery flowers with small white petals and long, pinkish stamens. This species likes a hot, humid summer, deep, moist soil and a sheltered position.

Cultivation

Although most are frost hardy, they perform best in those cool climates where seasons are sharply demarcated and summers are warm. They are propagated from seed or, in the case of selected clones and hybrids, by bud grafting.
Height 6–10 ft (1.8–3 m). *Zone 7–10.*

Aesculus parviflora

ARCTOSTAPHYLOS MANZANITA

Common manzanita

Native to California, the common manzanita (Spanish for 'little apple') reaches 8 ft (2.4 m) in height and spread or sometimes much larger. A slow-growing, stiff, woody shrub, it has thick, oval leaves coated in a whitish covering when young; the striking, reddish brown bark is sometimes hidden by peeling strips of duller, older bark. Tight clusters of small, urn-shaped, deep pink flowers in early spring are followed by ½ in (12 mm) red-brown berries. It tolerates long dry periods in summer.

Cultivation

They need full sun or part-shade and moist but well-drained, fertile, lime-free soil. The seed, enclosed in a small fleshy fruit, is difficult to germinate, which explains why manzanitas are propagated from tip cuttings hardened off in winter; treatment with smoke may assist germination.
Height 8 ft (2.4 m). *Zone 8–10.*

Arctostaphylos manzanita

ARONIA ARBUTIFOLIA

Red chokeberry

Native to eastern North America, where it is a common understory plant, this species grows to 6 ft (1.8 m) with many vertical stems forming spreading clumps. White flowers in spring are followed by bright red berries in autumn and early winter, popular with birds. Narrow, oval leaves turn bright red in fall—this is best in 'Brilliant' (sometimes listed as 'Brilliantissima').

Cultivation

Frost hardy and not demanding as to soil, they will grow well in part-shade but respond to full sun with more profuse fruit and brighter autumn foliage. Cut the oldest stems to the ground to encourage new growth. Propagate from seed or cuttings. The foliage is prone to disfigurement by the pear and cherry slug, the larva of a sawfly.

Height 6 ft (1.8 m). *Zone 4–9.*

AUCUBA JAPONICA

Japanese laurel, gold-dust tree, spotted laurel

Thriving in shade, while producing colorful fruits under a dense cover, this cool-climate mountain native of Japan grows in all but the most barren of soils. A bushy evergreen, it has stout, green shoots and glossy, dark green, oval leaves, heavily splashed with gold. Small, purple, star-shaped flowers are followed by red, egg-shaped berries, but only if at least one male plant is grown to every two females (the females are the ones that bear fruit).

Cultivation

Cut old shoots back in spring to restrict growth. Hardy to frost-hardy, it grows to 10 ft (3 m) in spread. Propagate the plant from semi-hardwood cuttings in autumn.

Height 6–10 ft (1.8–3 m). *Zone 7–10.*

BANKSIA

Banksia, bush honeysuckle

Named after the botanist, Sir Joseph Banks, who discovered this evergreen in 1770, banksias are found in every state of Australia, particularly in the south-western regions. Foliage and habit vary, but all species are characterized by colorful flowerheads, odd, woody follicle fruits, and adaptation to harsh conditions. The slender, tubular flowers arranged in neat, parallel rows along a spike usually appear in spring. Banksias

Aucuba japonica

Aronia arbutifolia

are closely related to the *Protea* genus found around the Cape of Good Hope, and scientists cite this phenomenon as evidence that the continents were once joined as part of the supercontinent Gondwanaland.

Cultivation

They prefer well-drained and sandy soil (free of nitrates and phosphates), and do best in full sun or part-shade conditions. Frost-hardy to frost-tender. Containerized plants need moderate watering during growth periods, but little water at other times. Propagate from seed in early spring or autumn. Do not allow potted seedlings to become rootbound before they are planted.

Banksia ericifolia

Heath banksia

This wiry, freely branching shrub has fine, glossy foliage and an upright, copper to orange, bottlebrush spike about 4–10 in (10–25 cm) long. It flowers in autumn to winter. It is found freely in coastal, sandstone ridges, but adapts to inland conditions.
Height Up to 16 ft (5 m). *Zone 8–11.*

BERBERIS

Barberry

Species from this genus of evergreen, semi-evergreen and deciduous shrubs from Europe, Asia and the Americas are among the most popular for cool climate gardens. The leaves are shiny, sometimes saw-toothed, and the flowers, which are like very small daffodils, are a delight, especially when offset against the red or purple foliage, which may change color in late summer or autumn.

Cultivation

They prefer sun or part-shade, any soil except waterlogged, and are fully frost-hardy. Smaller species are excellent in rock gardens, while taller species make good, dense hedges. They can be propagated from seed in autumn.

Berberis thunbergii

This deciduous species from Japan has pale to mid-green, oval leaves which turn orange-red in autumn. Small, red-tinged, pale yellow flowers erupt in mid-spring. Bright red, egg-shaped fruits follow. It is fully hardy. 'Atropurpurea Nana' is a very neat, bun-shaped plant, only 12–18 in (30–45 cm) high.
Height 5 ft (1.5 m). *Zone 3–10.*

Banksia ericifolia

Berberis thunbergii 'Atropurpurea Nana'

Buddleja davidii 'Royal Red'

Buxus sempervirens

BUDDLEJA

Butterfly bush

The spicy, fragrant blooms of *Buddleja* attract butterflies from far and wide—hence the common name. Found in Asia, Africa and the Americas, there is hardly any variation in the foliage between species—all have pointed, crepe-textured, large leaves, but the bloom varies—the tubular florets may be arranged in whorls, globes, single spikes or branched racemes.

Cultivation

Most do best in fertile, well-drained soil, and are fully hardy to frost-tender. Propagate these arching deciduous shrubs and trees from semi-ripe cuttings in summer.

Buddleja davidii
syn. *B. variabilis*
Butterfly bush, summer lilac

This deciduous or semi-evergreen arching shrub is the most widely known. It has dark-green, long, lance-shaped leaves with white-felted undersides. Small, honey-scented, purple, lilac or white flowers appear in long panicles in summer to autumn. It is a fully hardy species from China. 'Royal Red' has strongly fragrant panicles of purple red. *Height* Up to 14 ft (4 m). *Zone 7–10.*

BUXUS

Box

These densely foliaged evergreen shrubs are native to Mediterranean Europe, Japan and Central America. The flowers are insignificant but the foliage is ideal for hedging, edging and topiary.

Cultivation

They thrive in sun or semi-shade and any soil that is not waterlogged. They are best set out (use semi-ripe cuttings) in early spring or late summer, watered regularly and, as they grow (which is very slowly), pinched to shape. Trim and shear regularly as separate plants grow together. Promote new growth by cutting back stems to 12 in (30 cm) or less in late spring.

Buxus sempervirens

This is almost identical to *B. microphylla* but grows to twice the height. However, the form most often seen, 'Suffruticosa', grows to only about 30 in (75 cm) and is the type used to make clipped edgings in formal Italian or French style gardens. *Height* 10 ft (3 m). *Zone 6–10.*

CALLICARPA AMERICANA

American beauty berry

Not as commonly grown as it deserves, this deciduous species from southeastern

Calycanthus floridus

and central USA makes a low, spreading shrub to 3–6 ft (1–1.8 m) in height. It has broad, strongly veined leaves with downy undersides. The pink to violet-purple flowers are small but the brilliant mauve-magenta fruit are showy, borne in tight clusters and persist well into winter.

Cultivation

Callicarpa species do best in full sun and fertile soil. Cut back older branches in late winter to encourage strong flowering canes. Propagate from tip cuttings. *Height* 3–6 ft (1–1.8 m). *Zone 7–10.*

CALLUNA VULGARIS

Scottish heather, ling

A familiar sight as natural cover on moors and heaths in northern Europe, this bushy evergreen is a native of Europe and Asia Minor. A densely spreading bush, its small leaves are arranged in pairs. It has spikes of bell- to urn-shaped, single or double flowers, usually pink, mauve or white, which appear from mid-summer to autumn. The shrub does well in rock gardens and where mulched with pebbles.

Cultivation

Salt, wind and drought resistant, it makes good ground cover, preferring a gritty, well-drained, acid soil with regular water. Grows to a width of 19 in

Callicarpa americana

Calluna vulgaris 'Robert Chapman'

(50 cm). Propagate from autumn cuttings. Several cultivars, including 'Robert Chapman', are available, with foliage turning orange red in winter. *Height* 24 in (60 cm). *Zone 3–9.*

CALYCANTHUS FLORIDUS

Carolina allspice, sweet shrub

A shrub from southeastern USA, this grows to about 6–9 ft (1.8–2.7 m) and has broad, glossy, pale green leaves with downy undersides. Its 2 in (5 cm) wide, early summer flowers consist of many petals that are dull brownish red, often with paler tips.

Cultivation

Undemanding shrubs, they flower best in a sunny but sheltered position in

fertile, humus-rich, moist soil. Propagation is usually by layering branches, or from the seeds which are contained in soft, fig-like fruits.
Height 6–9 ft (1.8–2.7 m). *Zone 6–10.*

CAMELLIA

Camellia

Most species in this genus of evergreen, woody shrubs and trees are from mainland China and the Indo-Chinese peninsula. They grow in mountainous, subtropical areas, in partial shade. In Japan these lush plants are grown in part for the oil content of their seed capsules, but elsewhere most camellias are cultivated for their luxurious flowers and shiny foliage. Over 30 000 varieties now exist, and most of these are descended from *C. japonica.*

Cultivation

They prefer semi-shade in the open and a well-drained, neutral to acid soil. During frost or snow periods, move in containers to the shelter of evergreen trees. White or pink varieties need to be screened from direct sun or their flowers will discolor. Propagate from cuttings in late summer or mid-winter, or graft in spring or winter. Prune camellias during or immediately after flowering.

Camellia reticulata 'Dr. Clifford Parks'

Camellia japonica

Native to Japan, Korea and eastern China, this evergreen shrub contains much variation in habit, foliage, floral form and color. The flowers may be single to very double, in shades from white to red. It flowers in winter in temperate conditions and in spring in very cold areas. Prefers a cool soil, adequate moisture and a protected environment. Watering is essential in dry areas, or the buds will fail to open.
Height 14 ft (4 m). *Zone 7–11.*

Camellia reticulata

With its upright habit and handsome, serrated foliage, this is a favorite among enthusiasts. Found naturally in the

Camellia japonica cultivar

Camellia sasanqua 'Paradise Belinda'

forests of southern China, the species bears large, saucer-shaped, single, rose-pink and red flowers in spring; the cultivars, such as 'Dr. Clifford Parks', have large double flowers in shades of pink or red. 'Captain Rawes', the oldest, has been joined by many in recent years. Less cold-hardy than *C. japonica*, it is a taller, more open grower.
Height 16 ft (5 m). *Zone 8–10.*

Camellia sasanqua
This upright native of southern Japan is a lovely evergreen and the most sun-tolerant of all camellias. It is a fast-growing, slender and dense species, which produces an explosion of fragrant, single, white (occasionally red or pink) flowers in autumn. These flowers are usually quite short-lived. 'Paradise Belinda' has large, semi-double, glowing pink flowers.
Height 16 ft (5 m). *Zone 7–10.*

CEANOTHUS
California lilac

Originating in Mexico and the western states of the USA, this genus of over 50 species of evergreen or deciduous shrubs prefers cooler areas. *Ceanothus* species thrive in many parts of England, Europe and also in the cooler southern states of Australia. Despite the name, members of this genus are not lilacs. They bloom in much greater varieties of shades of blue, violet, mauve, pink and purple than true lilacs. The small, densely clustered flowers develop in showy terminals or panicles.

Cultivation
Half-hardy, all species do best in a sheltered spot in an open sunny position, preferring a light, gravelly, well-drained soil. To prune, cut deadwood from evergreens in spring, and trim side shoots after flowering. Propagate from seed in spring or from leafy, semi-hardwood cuttings taken in summer.

Ceanothus × delilianus
This hybrid makes a sturdy, vigorous, deciduous shrub with mid-green leaves that are broad and oval. It originated as a cross between the New Jersey tea *(Ceanothus americanus)* of eastern USA and the tropical *C. coeruleus* from Mexico and Guatemala, which has sky blue flowers. It includes some fine cultivars, the best known being 'Gloire de Versailles', a 12 ft (3.5 m) shrub with erect, loose panicles of pale blue scented flowers from mid-summer to early autumn.
Height 12 ft (3.5 m). *Zone 7–9.*

Ceanothus impressus
This evergreen, bushy shrub does best in full sun and well-drained soil. Frost-

Ceanothus × delilianus 'Gloire de Versailles'

Ceanothus impressus

Cistus × purpureus 'Brilliancy'

Cistus salviifolius

hardy, it bears deep blue flowers which appear in clusters from mid-spring to early summer. The leaves are small, dark green and crinkled. It has a spread of about 10 ft (3 m).
Height 6 ft (1.8 m). *Zone 8–10.*

CHIMONANTHUS PRAECOX

Wintersweet

This twiggy, deciduous shrub, native to China and Japan, bears dainty, brown and pale yellow flowers with purple centers. These appear on the bare wood of the branches during milder periods in mid-winter. It has rough, glossy, oval, dark green leaves. The fruits of *C. praecox* are yellowish brown when ripe.

Chimonanthus praecox

Cultivation

It needs constant moisture to thrive, preferring full sun and a fertile, well-drained soil. Prune lightly to shape. Propagate from seed in late spring and early summer, and by layering in autumn. It grows to 10 ft (3 m) in spread.
Height 8 ft (2.4 m). *Zone 6–10.*

CISTUS

Rock rose

This genus of spreading evergreens is famous for its drought resistance and ability to thrive in poor or sandy conditions, such as exposed banks or seaside cliffs. Equally, it does badly in moist, humid conditions. Native to the shores of the Mediterranean, *Cistus* species produce freely borne flowers, with crinkled petals in shades of pink, purple or white. These last only a day, but are quickly replaced. In cold areas they need shelter and are frost-hardy.

Cultivation

They do not transplant easily. Regular pinching back will maintain shape—cut out deadwood in spring, but do not prune hard. Propagate by seed in autumn or by softwood or greenwood cuttings in summer (cultivars and hybrids by cuttings in summer only), and grow the young plants in pots.

***Cistus × purpureus* 'Brilliancy'**

This straggling cultivar has a 3 ft (1 m) spread. In summer it bears little rose-pink

Cornus alba

flowers with crimson blotches near the central stamens, which are set off by elliptic, gray-green leaves with downy undersides. It likes well-drained sandy soil and full sun.
Height 4 ft (1.2 m). *Zone 7.*

Cistus salviifolius
This is a bushy, dense, evergreen bearing white flowers in late spring and early summer. Slightly smaller than *C. ladanifer*, its flowers have yellow blotches at the center.
Height 3 ft (1 m). *Zone 8–10.*

CORNUS ALBA
Red-barked dogwood, Tatarian dogwood
Shiny red branches and twigs, brightest in winter or late autumn, are the feature of this northeast Asian deciduous shrub. It makes a dense thicket of slender stems 6–10 ft (1.8–3 m) high and often twice that in spread, with lower branches suckering or taking root on the ground. In late spring and summer it bears small clusters of creamy yellow flowers, followed by pea-sized white or blue-tinted fruit. It thrives in damp ground and is effective by lakes and streams.

Some popular cultivars include 'Elegantissima', with gray-green leaves which are partly white on their margins; 'Sibirica', with bright red leaves and stems; and 'Spaethii', with brilliantly gold-variegated leaves.

Cultivation

This plant does best in sun or very light shade, and a rich, fertile, well-drained soil. It can be cut back annually almost to ground level to encourage new growth, which has the best color. Propagate from seed or rooted layers stuck in a moist sand-peat mixture. *Height* 6–10 ft (1.8–3 m). *Zone 4–9.*

Cotinus coggygria

Cotoneaster dammeri 'Coral Beauty'

COTINUS COGGYGRIA

syn. *Rhus cotinus*

Venetian sumach, smoke tree, wig tree

This tall-growing, deciduous shrub, found in southern Europe and in Asia, is grown chiefly for its splendid autumn color and unusual flowers. Its rounded leaves, normally oval and light green, turn a glorious yellow-red in autumn, more so in colder areas. Its fruits are unimpressive, as are its flowers—masses of tiny flower stalks forming pale gray clusters from late summer. The tiny stems left after the flowers fall give the appearance of puffs of smoke.

Cultivation

It does best in fertile soil that is not too rich. It needs full sun or semi-shade and is fully hardy. It grows to a spread of 10–14 ft (3–4 m). Prune back to growth buds by two thirds in winter. Propagate from greenwood or softwood cuttings in summer, or from seed in autumn. There are purple-leaved forms available, but they are not bright in full color. *Height* 10–14 ft (3–4 m). *Zone 6–10.*

COTONEASTER

Cotoneaster, rockspray

This genus of mostly evergreen bushes comes from Europe, North Africa and northern Asia. They are from the same family (Rosaceae) as the quince; the Greek *kotoneon* and *aster* together mean 'like a quince', and the genus name is pronounced 'kotonee-aster', not 'cotton-easter'. Cotoneasters are perhaps the most popular of berry-bearing shrubs and can tolerate almost any kind of soil condition (except waterlogged soil). They do thrive a little better, however, when the soil is dry and alkaline.

Cultivation

They are very drought resistant, and are fully frost-hardy. They are eminently suitable for use as an arching, specimen shrub, but may be used for hedging or for ground cover. Evergreen species do well in either sun or semi-shade, but deciduous varieties and cultivars prefer full sun. Propagate from cuttings in summer or seed in autumn.

Cotoneaster dammeri

This trailing, evergreen shrub has a spread of 3 ft (1 m). In summer it bears striking white flowers with purple anthers, followed in autumn by red fruits. *C. dammeri* is frost-hardy. 'Coral Beauty' is a ground-hugging cultivar with an open spreading habit. *Height* 24 in (60 cm). *Zone 5–10.*

CYTISUS SCOPARIUS

Common broom, Scotch broom

Widely distributed in central and western Europe including the United Kingdom, this is one of the taller and most vigorous species of *Cytisus*, reaching 6–8 ft (1.8–2.4 m) in height and making a great show of golden-yellow blossoms in late spring and early summer. The black seed pods may be abundant, ripening in midsummer and scattering their seed with a sharp, cracking sound in hot, dry weather. In cooler areas of some southern hemisphere countries it has become a troublesome weed. 'Pendulus' is a rare cultivar with pendulous branches.

Cultivation

Generally easy garden subjects, they flower well under most conditions except deep shade, tolerating both dry and boggy soils, fertile or quite infertile. They are easily propagated from seed, cuttings or, in the case of some named cultivars, by grafting.
Height 6–8 ft (1.8–2.4 m). *Zone 5–9.*

DAPHNE

Daphne, spurge laurel

Found everywhere except the tropics, these evergreen, semi-evergreen or deciduous shrubs are grown for their fragrant, tubular flowers that appear in winter and spring. The genus is named after the nymph in Greek mythology, who, rather than face the unwanted

Cytisus scoparius 'Pendulus'

Daphne odora

Daphne × burkwoodii

affections of the sun god Apollo, turned into a flowering shrub.

Cultivation

They thrive in semi-shady conditions and prefer a slightly acid, fertile, peaty soil that is well-drained but not too dry. Water lightly and use a small amount of complete fertilizer after flowering. Excessive watering will cause collar rot. Transplanting is not recommended, so choose the site carefully. It is best to grow daphnes in a raised spot, with the root junction above soil level. Between summer waterings allow the soil to dry out.

Daphne × burkwoodii
Burkwood's daphne

The dense clusters of fragrant, white and pink flowers of this upright, semi-evergreen shrub appear in late spring, and sometimes for a second time in autumn. Its leaves are pale to mid-green and lance-shaped. Fully hardy, it prefers a sunny spot with well-drained soil.
Height 3 ft (1 m). *Zone 6–9.*

Daphne odora
syn. *D. indica*

The most popular of the genus, this moderately frost-hardy, evergreen, bushy shrub from China grows to a spread of 5 ft (1.5 m). It bears fragrant, white to purplish pink flowers from mid-winter to early spring and has glossy, dark green, oval leaves. As a cut flower, it lasts well indoors. The form with yellow-margined leaves is said to be more tolerant of cold.
Height 3 ft (1 m). *Zone 8–10.*

DEUTZIA
Wedding bells, bridal wreath

These deciduous, arching bushes appear fairly nondescript until late spring or early summer, when a profusion of flowers appears—white, pink or bicolored depending on the species. Related to *Philadelphus*, which it also resembles, the genus *Deutzia* is a native of China, Japan and the Himalayas.

Cultivation

The shrubs prefer fertile, moist but well-drained soil and do best in full sun, although they require semi-shade in warmer areas. Give fertilizer in early

Deutzia × rosea

spring to encourage a full flower yield. Prune heavily to encourage bloom — remove about half the old wood. They can be propagate from softwood cuttings in summer.

Deutzia × rosea

This compact, bushy, arching shrub, a cross between *D. purpurascens* and *D. gracilis*, produces massed clusters of beautiful, bell-shaped, pale pink flowers in spring and early summer. Its leaves are dark green, oval and deciduous and it grows to a spread of 30 in (75 cm). This shrub is fully hardy, and prefers a moist soil and partial shade.
Height 3 ft (1 m). *Zone 7–10.*

ERICA

Heath, heather

This genus of evergreen shrubs is native to southern Africa, parts of northern Africa and much of western Europe. Related to azaleas and rhododendrons, it boasts some of the most popular flowering plants, partly because of the long flowering season. The different species bear tubular, waxy flowers of varying lengths, and small linear leaves grouped around a stem.

Erica carnea 'March Seedling'

Cultivation

Erica species are very particular, and require an acid soil that is porous and left constantly moist with unpolluted rainwater — if there is any hint of lime in the soil they will do badly. Avoid animal manure. Propagate from seed — kept moist and sheltered — or from tip cuttings taken in autumn or early winter. *Erica arborea* supplies the 'briar' (bruyère) from which tobacco pipes are made, but this species is rarely grown in gardens.

Erica carnea

syn. *E. herbacea*

This evergreen, spreading shrub makes an excellent ground cover. From early winter to late spring, it bears bell-shaped to tubular flowers in shades of red and pink (sometimes white). It has mid- to dark green leaves which are arranged in whorls. The cultivar 'March Seedling', which is shown in the photograph, has a spreading habit. It can also be grown in a container.
Height 12 in (30 cm). *Zone 8–9.*

Erica tetralix
Cross-leafed heath

This species from western and northern Europe usually has grayish green foliage, but the best forms are quite silvery. The leaves are in regular whorls of 4, hence both botanical and common names. The light pink or white flowers are large for a European erica, and appear in summer and autumn. A small shrub around 12 in (30 cm) high and wide, it does very well in moist soil in rockeries. 'Pink Star' bears lilac-pink flowers arranged in star-shaped patterns.
Height 12 in (30 cm). *Zone 3–9.*

Erica tetralix

Erica vagans
Cornish heath

This vigorous, spreading, European species, 30 in (75 cm) high and wide, has

Erica vagans

Fatsia japonica

deep green foliage and rounded, bell-shaped, pink, mauve or white flowers in clusters in summer and autumn. 'St. Keverne' has clear pink flowers in profusion.
Height 30 in (75 cm). *Zone 5–9.*

FATSIA JAPONICA

syn. *Aralia japonica, A. sieboldii*

Japanese aralia

Japanese aralia is one of the world's most loved house plants. It may also be cultivated as a spreading bush, or trained into a single-stemmed tree. It bears splendid, large, rounded, deeply lobed, glossy, dark green leaves under almost any conditions. There is also a variegated form. Dense clusters of tiny, white flowers are followed by small, black berries.

Cultivation

It does best in sunny or shaded areas and prefers a well-drained, fertile soil. Frost-hardy, it prefers shelter from cold winds. Cut back hard if it gets too leggy. Propagate by semi-ripe cuttings in summer or from seed in autumn or spring.
Height 6 ft (1.8 m). *Zone 8–11.*

Forsythia × *intermedia* cultivar

FORSYTHIA

Golden bells

The profuse blooms of golden yellow flowers are the principal attraction of this handsome genus of deciduous shrubs. They make excellent cut flowers.

Cultivation

Vase-shaped and deciduous, they are easy to grow in rich, well-drained soil. They prefer regions where winter is frosty—they are very frost-hardy. Propagate by division or from semi-hardwood cuttings that are taken in summer.

Forsythia × *intermedia*

Masses of bright yellow blooms carried on bare branches in the early spring make this a favorite shrub in country gardens in cold climates. Growing to a spread of 6 ft (1.8 m), its branches arch upwards from a basal trunk. As flowers are borne on last season's wood, the shrub should be pruned immediately after flowering.
Height 8 ft (2.4 m). *Zone 5–9.*

Fothergilla gardenii

FOTHERGILLA GARDENII

Witch alder, dwarf fothergilla

A small bushy shrub 24–36 in (60–90 cm) high from coastal plain areas of eastern USA, this species thrives in a cool climate with moist, well-drained soil. It produces fragrant white flowers 1½ in (35 mm) long in early spring, and the 2–3 in (5–8 cm) long leaves that follow develop brilliant autumn colors.

Cultivation

Frost hardy, they do best in humus-rich, moist but well-drained, acidic soil in sun or light shade and can be trimmed to shape after flowering if necessary. Propagate from seed or cuttings or by layering.

Height 24–36 in (60–90 cm). *Zone 5–10.*

FREMONTODENDRON CALIFORNICUM

This is the best known and hardiest species, ranging along California's Sierra Nevada foothills and coast ranges. It can reach 30 ft (9 m), but is usually a sparse, crooked shrub 20 ft (6 m) tall with dark brown bark. It produces a succession of 2 in (5 cm) wide golden flowers from mid- to late spring. *Fremontodendron californicum* subsp. *decumbens* has a dwarf habit and orange-yellow flowers.

Cultivation

Frost hardy, these plants are not difficult to grow in a sheltered, sunny position with neutral to alkaline, well-drained soil, but they tend to be short lived. Plant out in spring when the danger of frost has passed. They do not perform

well in climates with hot, wet summers. Propagate from seed in spring or cuttings in summer.
Height 20 ft (6 m). *Zone 8–10.*

FUCHSIA

Fuchsia, ladies' eardrops

Native to the rainforests of South America, these exotic evergreen and semi-evergreen shrubs and trees are grown for the splendid, pendulous, tubular flowers. These hang from axils, most heavily at the ends of arching branches. Each flower consists of 4 reflexed sepals and 4 or more petals, often in a contrasting color.

Cultivation

Fuchsias prefer a partially shaded, sheltered position and will thrive in almost any soil, as long as it contains plenty of organic matter, and is well-drained. They require plenty of water (sometimes twice a day in summer)—but avoid watering in full sun. Prune back drastically to prevent the plant from becoming too woody, and to maintain shape. They are moderately frost-hardy to frost-tender. Propagate from softwood cuttings in any season. Red spider mite may cause problems; also guard against leaf-eating caterpillars or looper, rust and gray mold.

Fremontodendron californicum

Fuschia magellanica

Fuchsia magellanica

With their attractive pendulous flowers, these shrubs are well worth growing. Innumerable large-flowered hybrids are available. Prune back to maintain shape. *Height* 8 ft (2.4 m). *Zone 8–10.*

Hamamelis mollis

HAMAMELIS MOLLIS

Chinese witch hazel

This upright, open shrub has extremely fragrant, golden-yellow flowers, borne on bare branches from mid-winter to early spring. It grows to a height and spread of 10–15 ft (3–4.5 m) and the large, thick leaves are mid-green above and downy underneath; they turn deep golden yellow in autumn. There are some popular cultivars —'Coombe Wood' with slightly larger flowers; and 'Pallida' with dense clusters of large, sweetly scented sulfur-yellow flowers and yellow leaves in autumn.

Cultivation

Hamamelis are good shrubs for cool-climate gardens, preferring an open, sunny position (although they will tolerate semi-shade) in fertile, moist but well-drained, loamy, acid soil. It can be propagated from seed, but germination may take a full year. Check for coral spot and honey fungus.
Height 10–15 ft (3–4.5 m). *Zone 4–9.*

HEBE

Veronica, shrub speedwell

Most of these evergreen shrubs are native to New Zealand but some species are to be found naturally in Chile and New Guinea. They are all grown for the luxurious, dense spikes of tiny, 4-petaled, purple, white or cerise flowers. Resistance to salt and sea winds make them eminently suited to coastal areas. They are good as dense hedges or thick ground covers.

Cultivation

Half-hardy, they require well-drained soil and full sun or semi-shade. Cut back in spring to shape and tidy, or to restrict growth. Propagate from semi-ripe cuttings in summer.

Hebe ochracea

A whipcord species with olive-green to golden brown stems, it is most often represented by 'James Stirling', a bright golden cultivar. The shrub grows to about 3 ft (1 m) wide. The inflorescences of about 10 white flowers are rarely seen in cultivation. Unnecessary pruning of this species may lead to dieback.
Height 3 ft (1 m). *Zone 8–9.*

Hebe ochracea 'James Stirling'

Hebe speciosa 'Alicia Amherst'

Hebe speciosa

This desirable species boasts deep green foliage and purple brushes of flowers that appear in terminal clusters in summer and winter to spring. It is half-hardy. Numerous, brightly colored cultivars exist, such as 'Alicia Amherst', which has purple flowers.
Height 3 ft (1 m). *Zone 8–10*

HELIOTROPIUM ARBORESCENS

syn. *H. peruvianum*

Cherry pie, heliotrope

This shrub has clusters of fragrant, purple to lavender flowers from late spring to autumn. A native of South America, it grows very quickly. It is a branching, evergreen species with dark green, wrinkled leaves.

Cultivation

Tender to frost, it needs rich, fertile, well-drained soil and full sun. In very dry areas, it is best raised in a semi-shady position and the soil kept moist. Potted specimens should be regularly watered in full growth, but moderately at other times. Cut back to half in early spring to promote a bushy look. Propagate from seed in spring or semi-ripe cuttings in early autumn.
Height 30 in (75 cm). *Zone 9.*

Heliotropium arborescens

Hibiscus rosa-sinensis cultivar

HIBISCUS

Rose of China, rose mallow, rose of Sharon, shrub althea

These beautifully exotic, flowering, evergreen or deciduous shrubs, perennials and annuals hail from all continents, but particularly the countries around the Indian ocean—eastern Africa, Madagascar and Malaysia—as well as the Pacific Islands, Australia and China. Popular in warm to tropical gardens, they bear showy flowers, many of which last as little as one day—longer in colder conditions. The genus is the floral emblem of Hawaii, where some of the most stunning hybrids are grown, and several beautiful species grow wild.

Cultivation

They thrive in full sun, in a well-drained, rich, slightly acid, sandy soil. Water regularly and fertilize during flowering. Trim after flowering to maintain shape. Propagate from cuttings taken in spring and summer. Potential pests include aphids, caterpillars, whitefly, tip borer and the hibiscus beetle.

Hibiscus rosa-sinensis

Rose of China, shoeflower

Native to China, this tall shrub bears coral-red flowers virtually all year in a frost-free climate. The wild form is less often seen in gardens than the numerous dazzling cultivars, many bred in Hawaii, which come in single or double and every color but blue. Plants range in height and spread and have evergreen, glossy leaves. They prefer full sun in tropical or subtropical climates where they are as important in gardens as roses are in temperate climates. In cold climates they can be grown in tubs in a greenhouse or as indoor plants. Water freely in summer, prune in spring after the cold weather is over, and propagate from cuttings in summer. The common name 'shoeflower' comes from a West Indian custom of polishing black shoes with the crushed flowers of the hibiscus.

Height 14 ft (4 m). *Zone 10–12.*

Hibiscus syriacus
Althea, rose of Sharon
This colorful, upright, deciduous shrub is the hardiest of the genus. It flowers freely in summer in varying shades of white, pink, soft red, mauve and violet-blue. The single, semi-double and double flowers are bell-shaped. It has small, glabrous leaves and a spread of 3–6 ft (1–1.8 m). Prune hard in winter to keep it healthy.
Height 14 ft (4 m). *Zone 6–10.*

HYDRANGEA
Hydrangea
These lush, popular, deciduous and evergreen shrubs are native to China, Japan and North America and they grow profusely in the summer months. Hydrangeas are grown for the striking and attractive, domed fertile flowers. Each head consists of small flowers surrounded by larger petal-like sepals.

Cultivation
They are fully to frost-hardy. They need constant watering, as they transpire heavily from the stems and large, saw-toothed leaves. The sun damages their foliage, so always position them in the shade, or in full sun only in areas that are frequently cloudy. Prune immediately after flowering—this encourages strong, vigorous growth for the following season. Propagate from softwood cuttings in summer.

Hydrangea macrophylla
Hortensia
This deciduous, bushy shrub from Japan flowers in mid- to late summer, the color depending on the pH of the soil. In soils with a pH of up to about 5.5, blue or purple flowers bloom; above this level they are pink. White flowers are unaffected by soil pH. There are two types: hortensias, with dense, domed heads; and lacecaps, with flat, open heads. Trim winter-damaged growth back to new growth and in summer, remove spent flowers. It is frost-hardy, has oval, serrated, green leaves and grows to a spread of 6 ft (1.8 m).
Height 6 ft (1.8 m). *Zone 6–10.*

Hydrangea quercifolia
Oak-leafed hydrangea
The dark green foliage of this deciduous, bushy shrub turns a brilliant red and purple in autumn. *H. quercifolia* bears

Hydrangea macrophylla

Hibiscus syriacus

Hypericum frondosum

Hydrangea quercifolia

white flowerheads from mid-summer to mid-autumn. Frost-hardy.
Height 6 ft (1.8 m). *Zone 5–10.*

HYPERICUM FRONDOSUM

Golden St. John's wort

A rounded deciduous shrub from the southeastern United States, golden St. John's wort grows up to 4 ft (1.2 m) tall with a similar spread. The many stems are upright and densely clothed with curving, oblong leaves that are a blue-green color with a powdery bloom. In summer clusters of showy, bright yellow

Ilex verticillata

flowers are produced. The cultivar 'Sunburst' is an improvement on the species and worth seeking out.

Cultivation

Mostly cool-climate plants, they prefer full sun but will tolerate some shade. They do best in fertile, well-drained soil, with plentiful water in late spring and summer. Remove seed capsules after flowering and prune in winter to maintain a rounded shape. Propagate from seed in autumn or from cuttings in summer.
Height 4 ft (1.2 m). *Zone 5–10.*

ILEX VERTICILLATA

Winterberry, black alder, coral berry

From eastern USA, this deciduous shrub grows 6–10 ft (1.8–3 m) high and has a spread of 4–10 ft (1.2–3 m). The toothed leaves are purple-tinged in spring and turn yellow in autumn. The bright red berries stay on the bare branches for a long period, persisting until spring. This shrub tolerates wet conditions. Cultivars include 'Cacapon', a female which produces abundant berries when grown with a male; 'Nana' (syn. 'Red Sprite'), a dwarf female which reaches 4 ft (1.2 m) tall and has a spread of 5 ft (1.5 m); and 'Winter Red', an extra vigorous female with a height and spread of 10 ft (3 m) and good crops of bright red berries when grown with a male plant.

Cultivation

Hollies grow well in deep, friable, well-drained soils with high organic content. An open, sunny position is best in cool climates. Water in hot, dry summers. Hollies do not like transplanting. Prune carefully in spring to check vigorous growth. Propagate from seed or cuttings. Check for signs of holly aphid and holly leaf miner.

Height 6–10 ft (1.8–3 m). *Zone 2–9.*

Juniperus communis

JUNIPERUS COMMUNIS

Common juniper

Ranging widely through northern Europe, North America and western Asia, this is either an upright tree growing to 20 ft (6 m) or a sprawling shrub with a height and spread of 10–15 ft (3–4.5 m). It has brownish red bark and grayish green leaves. Fleshy, greenish berries take 2 to 3 years to ripen to black and are used for flavoring gin. Hardiness varies considerably depending on the subspecies or cultivar. Among popular cultivars are 'Compressa', a dwarf, erect form suitable for the rock garden, growing to 30 in (75 cm) tall and 6 in (15 cm) wide with silvery blue needles; 'Depressa Aurea', a dwarf form growing to 24 in (60 cm) tall and 6 ft (1.8 m) wide with bronze-gold foliage; and 'Hibernica', growing 10–15 ft (3–4.5 m) tall and 2–4 ft (0.6–1.2 m) wide, forming a dense column of dull, blue-green foliage when young but becoming broader and conical with age.

Cultivation

Easily cultivated in a cool climate, they prefer a sunny position and any well-drained soil. Prune to maintain shape or restrict size, but do not make visible pruning cuts as old, leafless wood rarely sprouts. Propagate from cuttings in winter, layers if low-growing, or from seed; cultivars can be propagated by grafting.

Height 10–15 ft (3–4.5 m). *Zone 2–9.*

KALMIA LATIFOLIA

Mountain laurel

The charm and fragrance of this American native make it a favorite among shrub enthusiasts. In late spring and early summer, it bears clusters of distinctive, bright pink buds that open to heads of small, pale pink flowers with stamens arranged like umbrella ribs. It grows to a spread of 12 ft (3.5 m).

Cultivation
Fully hardy, it thrives in a moist, peaty, acid soil and prefers sun or semi-shade. Propagate by layering in summer, otherwise (with more difficulty) from softwood cuttings in summer, or seed in autumn.
Height 6 ft (1.8 m). *Zone 3–9.*

LAVANDULA
Lavender
These fragrant, flower-bearing plants come from southern Europe. Cultivated commercially for the perfume industry, they are also grown for their evergreen foliage and attractive bloom.

Cultivation
They prefer full sun and fertile, well-drained soil that is not too rich in nitrates and phosphates. Fully to half-hardy, lavender tend not to bloom profusely in warm conditions. Excellent as hedges, lavender need a light trimming in spring to keep their habit neat. Propagate in summer from semi-ripe cuttings.

Lavandula angustifolia 'Munstead'

Kalmia latifolia

Lavandula angustifolia
syn. *L. officinalis, L. spica*
English lavender
This dense, bushy, evergreen shrub is native to the Mediterranean countries of southern Europe. It has long-stemmed heads of mauve, scented flowers that appear from spring to autumn. It bears small, furry, gray leaves that turn green as the plant ages. Fully hardy, it makes an excellent hedge; trim it in spring to maintain the shape. There are a number of selected cultivars of which 'Munstead' and the dwarf 'Hidcote' are outstanding.
Height 24 in (60 cm). *Zone 6–10.*

Lavandula dentata
French lavender
The dense spikes of tubular, mauve-blue flowers of this bushy, evergreen shrub appear in autumn to late spring. Its aromatic leaves are serrated, fern-like and gray-green. Frost-hardy, *L. dentata* is drought resistant and will adapt to most soils.
Height 24 in (60 cm). *Zone 6–10.*

Lavandula stoechas
Spanish lavender, bush lavender
This evergreen, dense, bushy shrub is frost-hardy and grows to a spread of 24 in (60 cm). In late spring and summer, it bears terminal spikes of fragrant,

Leucothoe fontanesiana

Lavandula dentata

Lavandula stoechas

deep purple flowers. The leaves are aromatic and silver-gray.
Height 24 in (60 cm). *Zone 8–10.*

LEUCOTHOE FONTANESIANA

syn. *Leucothoe catesbaei*

Pearl flower, drooping leucothoe

Indigenous to the southeastern states of the USA, this evergreen shrub grows 3–5 ft (1–1.5 m) tall. The arching stems bear leathery, long-pointed dark green leaves and pendulous spikes of small bell-shaped white or pinkish flowers through spring. 'Rainbow' (or 'Golden Rainbow'), is a very popular cultivar, with cream and pink-mottled green leaves.

Cultivation

These shrubs prefer moist, acidic, well-drained soil and a sheltered position in sun or part-shade. Propagation is from seed, cuttings or from the suckering root sections of the plant, or by division.
Height 3–5 ft (1–1.5 m). *Zone 6–10.*

MAHONIA

Oregon grape, holly grape, mountain grape

Useful as hedges or windbreaks, these evergreen shrubs are also grown for their dense panicles of open, yellow flowers. These are followed by blue-black fruits that make excellent jam. Low-growing species are also useful for ground cover.

Mahonia aquifolium

Myrica californica

Cultivation
Plant in fertile soil that is well-drained but not too dry. In cold conditions, they require full sun; in warmer climates, partial shade will see them thrive. Propagate from seed in autumn or from semi-ripe cuttings in summer.

Mahonia aquifolium
Oregon grape, holly grape
From western North America, this dense, bushy species grows 6 ft (1.8 m) high and wide. Its 8 in (20 cm) long deep green pinnate leaves each consist of 5 to 9 holly-like leaflets; in the cooler months, these develop purple tones. Clustered heads of small, bright yellow flowers appear in spring, before the fruit. 'Compacta' is a more compact form growing to about half the size of the species.
Height 6 ft (1.8 m). *Zone 5–10.*

MYRICA CALIFORNICA
Pacific wax myrtle
An evergreen shrub or small tree, this native of the West Coast of the USA has dark green leaves and a decidedly upright habit, except where sheared by coastal winds. *Myrica californica* grows 25 ft (8 m) or more in height, less in spread.

Cultivation
Moderately frost hardy to frost tender, they thrive in part-shade, but will not grow in alkaline or chalky conditions, and must never be allowed to dry out. Propagate from seed or cuttings, or by layering in summer.
Height 25 ft (8 m). *Zone 7–10.*

NANDINA
Sacred bamboo, heavenly bamboo
Not a true bamboo, the stems of these evergreen and semi-evergreen shrubs from China and Japan will grow to a height of nearly 10 ft (3 m) but with a spread of only about 3 ft (1 m). This makes the genus popular with landscape gardeners, who also grow the species for the handsome, reddish foliage which appears in autumn and winter. Small, yellow-centered, white flowers are followed by red fruits.

Cultivation

Frost-hardy, they prefer a sheltered, sunny position, and fertile, well-drained, but not too dry soil. In spring, prune untidy, aging stems to the base. Propagate from semi-ripe cuttings or seed in summer.

Nandina domestica

Sacred bamboo, heavenly bamboo

This upright evergreen shrub is a native of Japan and China. In summer, it bears small, white, upright, star-shaped flowers in sprays; these are followed (on female plants) by red berries. It has narrow, lance-shaped, sheathing leaves that turn purplish-red in winter. Frost-hardy, it prefers a moist soil and sunny position, although it will grow in light shade. Thin out the older branches every few years.
Height 6 ft (1.8 m). *Zone 5–10.*

***Nandina domestica* 'Nana'**

This dwarf shrub is particularly popular, probably because it colors so strongly in winter. A semi-evergreen or evergreen, it grows to a spread of 14 ft (4 m). Frost-hardy, it rarely flowers. Given sufficient direct sun, its bright green leaves will turn scarlet in autumn to winter. *N. domestica* 'Nana' is very suitable for a mixed border or rock garden.
Height 12–24 in (30–60 cm). *Zone 5–10.*

NERIUM

Oleander, rose-bay, rose laurel

These evergreen shrubs are grown for their delightful flowers, which bloom in a variety of colors—pink, white, red and cream. They have dark, glossy, spear-shaped leaves.

Cultivation

Although they do best in full sun and a well-drained soil, they do extremely well in a variety of conditions—dry, semi-arid; salty coastal areas; and in soil with poor drainage—and flourish from tropical to warm-temperate climates. Ideally the shrub should be pruned to promote branching, and when potted, should be watered regularly when in full

Nandina domestica

Nandina domestica 'Nana'

Nerium oleander 'Punctatum'

Phormium tenax 'Variegatum'

Philadelphus coronarius

growth. Propagate from semi-ripe cuttings in summer, or from seed in spring. The plant is poisonous, and so bitter that even goats will not eat it.

***Nerium oleander* 'Punctatum'**

syn. *N. o. 'Monsieur Belaguier'*

This upright, evergreen shrub bears clusters of delightful, pale pink, single flowers from spring through to autumn. It is frost-tender.

Height 10 ft (3 m). *Zone 9–10.*

PHILADELPHUS

Mock orange, syringa

These suckering, deciduous shrubs come from Europe, Asia and the Americas and are among the most popular of flower-bearing shrubs because of their delightful orange-blossom fragrance. Very versatile plants, they are ideal besides pathways, in open borders or as wall shrubs. Hardiness varies considerably among the species.

Cultivation

They need sun and a fertile, well-drained soil. Thin out after blooming, and propagate from softwood cuttings in summer. Keep warm and moist until the roots establish themselves. Aphids may be a problem. The name 'syringa' is now the genus name for the lilac.

Philadelphus coronarius

Mock orange

This species is a native of Europe and Southeast Asia. Fully hardy, it grows

to a height and spread of 6 ft (1.8 m). It bears terminal clusters of fragrant, creamy white flowers in spring. Its oval, bright green leaves are slightly hairy on the undersides. Prune after flowering.
Height 6 ft (1.8 m). *Zone 2–10.*

PHORMIUM TENAX

New Zealand flax

Although really a perennial, New Zealand flax makes an ideal accent plant. It has stiff, upright green foliage that arises from a central base. Among the many cultivars is 'Variegatum' which has striped, pale yellow and white leaves.

Cultivation

Any reasonable soil will suit these hardy plants, but they appreciate watering in dry times. They enjoy cool to temperate climates and tolerate coastal conditions or the margin of water courses where they can form very large clumps but can be divided for propagation purposes. Alternatively, seed can be gathered from the spent flowers held on long straight woody stems often reaching 10–14 ft (3–4 m) high.
Height 10 ft (3 m). *Zone 8.*

PIERIS

Andromeda, pearl flower, lily-of-the-valley bush

These fairly dense, bushy, evergreen shrubs, native to the colder regions of North America and Asia, are related to the *Azalea* and are grown for their small, urn-shaped flowers.

Cultivation

Slow growing, they do best in a mildly acid soil that is well-drained and rich with leaf mold. They prefer a sheltered spot in shade or semi-shade and are fully to frost-hardy, although young plants may be killed by frost in spring. They also like a humid atmosphere, which

Pieris japonica

maintains the color of the foliage. Deadhead after flowering to improve the growth. Propagate from semi-ripe or soft tip cuttings in early summer.

Pieris japonica

Japanese pearl flower

This rounded, bushy, dense, evergreen shrub is a native of Japan. In spring it bears dense sprays of pendent, white flowers that resemble lily-of-the-valley. Though flower buds develop in autumn, they do not open until spring. When young, the small, glossy leaves are oval, turning bronze as the plant matures. Fully hardy.
Height 6 ft (1.8 m). *Zone 4–10.*

PINUS MUGO

Mountain pine, Swiss mountain pine

In the mountains of Europe this small tree grows slowly to 12 ft (3.5 m). Its windswept appearance reflects its habitat, making it an interesting bonsai and rock-garden specimen. Its pairs of 2 in (5 cm) long, bright green needles develop from resinous buds. The oval, dark brown cones are 1–2 in (2–5 cm) long. This species does not tolerate extreme heat or dry conditions. 'Aurea' has golden foliage. 'Gnom', a compact bush 6 ft (1.8 m) high with a similar spread, produces whitish new shoots against rich, black-green mature growth. 'Mops' matures to 5 ft (1.5 m) over 10 years.

Pittosporum tenuifolium 'Silver Magic'

Pinus mugo 'Mops'

Cultivation

Most pines are easily grown in a wide range of conditions, though their tolerance of both cold and warmth varies and each species has its optimum climate. They are mostly very wind resistant and will thrive on soils of moderate to low fertility, but may need a symbiotic soil fungus to assist nutrient uptake on poorer soils—these fungi are likely to be already present in the pines' native regions, but a handful of decaying needles from a pine forest can be added if planting pines where none have grown before. The majority of pines require well-drained soil. Propagate from seed. *Height* 12 ft (3.5 m). *Zone 2–9.*

PITTOSPORUM

Mock orange, pittosporum

These handsome, evergreen, fragrant shrubs and trees, found in China, Japan, Africa, New Zealand, Australia and the Pacific are grown for their fragrance and ornamental foliage. They make good screens and windbreaks.

Cultivation

They like a leaf-rich, well-drained soil and regular moisture. They are frost-hardy to frost-tender and do best in mild climates. Some species prefer sun, others sun or partial shade. Propagate from seed in autumn or spring, or from semi-ripe cuttings in summer.

Pittosporum tenuifolium

Kohuhu

This evergreen tree has a spread of 20 ft (6 m). A native of New Zealand, it bears glossy, oval, mid-green leaves with undulating margins, and bears dark purple, honey-scented flowers in spring. It is half-hardy. The smaller growing, variegated cultivars, such as 'Silver Magic', are popular garden shrubs. *Height* 20 ft (6 m). *Zone 9–10.*

POTENTILLA FRUTICOSA

Bush cinquefoil

This dense, deciduous shrub, found in many parts of the temperate northern hemisphere, grows to over 3 ft (1 m) tall with a spread of 4 ft (1.2 m) or more. From early summer to autumn garden varieties bear 1 in (25 mm) wide flowers in shades from white to yellow and orange, the orange ones often fading to salmon pink in the sunshine. The flat, mid-green leaves comprise 5 or 7 narrow elliptical leaflets arranged palmately. 'Tangerine' has golden orange flowers; 'Goldstar' is an upright shrub with large, deep yellow flowers; 'Maanleys' grows up to 4 ft (1.2 m) tall with blue-green foliage and pale yellow flowers; and 'Red Ace', a low grower with small leaves and bright orange-red flowers, is inclined to be untidy and short lived.

Cultivation

Plant in well-drained, fertile soil. Lime does not upset them. Although it thrives in full sun in temperate climates, the colors of pink, red and orange cultivars will be brighter if protected from very strong sun. Propagate from seed in autumn or from cuttings in summer. *Height* 3 ft (1 m). *Zone 2–9.*

Prunus laurocerasus

Potentilla fruticosa

PRUNUS LAUROCERASUS

Cherry laurel, laurel cherry

Both the botanical and common names of this handsome evergreen reflect the resemblance of its foliage to that of the true laurel (*Laurus nobilis*) and the two plants are sometimes confused. Native to the Balkans, Turkey and the Caspian region, it has been grown in western Europe since the sixteenth century. It is commonly grown as a hedge, but if unclipped can reach as much as 50 ft (15 m) in height. The shiny, bright green leaves are 6 in (15 cm) or more long; in mid- to late spring it bears upright

Pyracantha coccinea

sprays of small, sweetly scented white flowers, followed by red berries that ripen to black in autumn. One of the toughest of evergreens, cherry laurel tolerates alkaline soils and will grow in shade.

Cultivation

Plant in moist, well-drained soil in full sun but with some protection from strong wind for the spring blossom. Keep the ground around base of trees free of weeds and long grass and feed young trees with a high-nitrogen fertilizer. Propagate by grafting or from seed—named cultivars must be grafted or budded onto seedling stocks. Pests and diseases vary with locality.
Height 50 ft (15 m). *Zone 6–10.*

PYRACANTHA COCCINEA

Scarlet firethorn

This species, originally from southern Europe, Turkey and the Caucasus, produces a spectacular display of fiery scarlet fruit that resemble tiny apples. Both fruit and foliage become darker if grown in cool climates. It grows to 15 ft (4.5 m) with arching branches spreading to 6 ft (1.8 m). Its narrow leaves are up to 1½ in (35 mm) long, held on slender stalks. Young leaves and twigs are finely downy. 'Kasan' carries striking orange-red fruit. 'Lalandei', developed in France in the 1870s, is a vigorous plant with erect branches that display abundant fruit which ripen to bright orange-red.

Cultivation

These temperate-climate plants adapt to a wide range of soils. Firethorns need a sunny position for the brightest berry display, and adequate moisture in dry weather. Propagate from seed or cuttings. Pruning is often necessary to control size, but bear in mind that fruits are produced on second-year wood. They can be espaliered and also make dense, informal hedges and screens. They tend to naturalize and become invasive in favorable conditions. Check for fireblight and scab.
Height 15 ft (4.5 m). *Zone 5–9.*

RHODODENDRON

Rhododendron, azalea

The rhododendrons are a huge genus of some 600 species and countless cultivars, native mainly to the temperate regions of Europe, North America and Asia, although with representatives in the highlands of tropical Southeast Asia and one species *(R. lochae)* in Australia. The genus is divided into some 40 'series', but horticulturally there are three most important divisions. First, there are the azaleas, formerly given a genus of their own (azaleas usually have 5 stamens, the rest of the genus 10 or more); then the subtropical species and

Rhododendron catawbiense

their hybrids, mostly of the series Vireya and usually called vireya rhododendrons or simply vireyas; and the rhododendrons proper, which are variable in habit, from dwarfs growing 10 in (25 cm) high or less to small trees, and prefer a cooler climate than the other two groups do. Most of them share a dislike of lime, but where soils suit they are among the most desirable of all flowering shrubs.

Cultivation

As a general rule, they like a shaded to semi-shaded position with a cool root run and acid, perfectly drained soil with abundant humus; none can be called drought resistant. No regular pruning is required, although they can be cut back quite severely in early spring if needed. Propagation is by layering, from cuttings, or by grafting, most species being fairly slow to strike. Their usually shapely habit and compact root systems make them first rate subjects for container growing, and they are among the easiest of all shrubs to transplant, even when mature. Red spider, lace bug, thrips, caterpillars and leaf miners can cause problems, usually when the shrubs are in dry conditions.

Rhododendron catawbiense

Catawba rhododendron, mountain rosebay

This shrub from eastern USA is one of the most influential species in the development of frost-hardy hybrids. It grows to around 10 ft (3 m) tall and develops into a dense thicket of shiny, deep green foliage. Its cup-shaped flowers, which open from late spring, are pink, rosy pink, lilac-purple or white and carried in trusses of up to 20 blooms. 'Album' is a heat-resistant form with white flowers that open from pink buds.

Height 10 ft (3 m). *Zone 4–9.*

***Rhododendron* Hardy hybrids**

The most widely grown of the rhododendrons, the Hardy hybrids are mostly large, domed shrubs with large, dull

green leaves. They flower spectacularly in spring, bearing many almost spherical clusters of wide open flowers in shades of white, pink, red or purple; very rarely cream or yellow. There are many named cultivars, varying a little in hardiness, from frost-hardy to fully hardy. The usual conditions of cultivation for rhododendrons apply.
Height Up to 14 ft (4 m). *Zone 4–9.*

Rhododendron Kurume azalea hybrid, as a bonsai

Rhododendron Kurume azaleas

These are mainly derived from the Japanese *R. obtusum*, and are the most frost-hardy of the evergreen azaleas. They are very slow growers. The foliage is dark green and oval, and the densely bushy plants are so smothered in bloom in their spring season that the leaves are virtually obscured. The attractive individual flowers are small, about 1½ in (35 mm) across. They are single or double, and come in every shade from white through pink to red and purple.
Height 3 ft (1 m). *Zone 8–10.*

Rhododendron 'Cilpinense', a Hardy hybrid

Ribes sanguineum

Rhododendron degronianum* subsp. *yakushimanum
This upright, dense native of Japan bears rounded terminal clusters of expanding, tubular flowers in late spring. It has deep green, wrinkled leaves. It has been the parent of many hybrids, which retain its shapely and compact growth, as well as its beautiful flowers. It is perhaps the most desirable of the rhododendrons for small gardens in temperate to cool climates.
Height 3 ft (1 m). *Zone 9–11.*

Rhododendron schlippenbachii
Royal azalea
This deciduous azalea from Korea, Manchuria and nearby parts of Russia is a 6–15 ft (1.8–4.5 m) tall shrub with 4–6 in (10–15 cm) long leaves in whorls of five. Its 3- to 6-bloom trusses of 3 in (8 cm) wide flowers, which are usually lightly scented and open in mid-spring, vary from white flushed pink to rose pink, often with brown flecks. The foliage colors well in autumn. It prefers light shade.
Height 6–15 ft (1.8–4.5 m). *Zone 4–9.*

Rhododendron degronianum subsp. *yakushimanum*

RIBES SANGUINEUM
Red flowering currant, winter currant, flowering currant
This prickle-free, deciduous shrub from western North America has aromatic, lobed leaves that are held on 12 ft (3.5 m) stems. The deep pink or red flowers, appearing in late spring, are borne on

Rosa 'Golden Wings'

erect to drooping spikes. Bluish black berries follow in summer. There are several named cultivars, including 'King Edward VII' which bears carmine flowers; 'Brocklebankii' with golden leaves and pink flowers; 'White Icicle' has pure white clusters of flowers; and 'Pulborough Scarlet' which carries a mass of deep red flowers.

Cultivation

Unisexual species such as this must be planted in groups to ensure vigorous flowering and fruiting. Fully frost hardy, they need moist, rich soil and full sun to semi-shade. Some species host white pine blister rust. Propagate from seed or cuttings.
Height 12 ft (3.5 m). *Zone 6–10.*

ROSA

Rosa

The rose is perhaps the best loved of all flowers. Gardeners have developed many thousands of hybrids and garden cultivars, which are arranged in a variety of flower forms, and in every shade of red and pink, white, yellow, orange, mauve, purple, coral; everything that is but true blue. Many cultivars feature blends and variegations of two or more colors. Scent is variable, some cultivars offering intense fragrance, others virtually none. The plants range from only a few inches tall to giant, long limbed plants. The names of roses come and go from the catalogs with alarming speed.

Cultivation

Some of the Chinese species and their hybrids are half-hardy, but most roses are fully hardy. They all prefer sun and rich, well-drained soil. Pruning consists of removing weak or elderly branches and shortening the rest, and is carried out either immediately after bloom (for spring-only types) or in winter (for

Rosa 'Peace'

'repeat-flowering' types). Aphids, caterpillars, scale insects, mildew, black spot, rust, and various virus diseases may prove bothersome, and it is important to seek the guidance of an experienced grower as to which varieties are most resistant in your local conditions. Roses are normally propagated by budding in summer, although many grow readily from cuttings taken in late summer or autumn.

Rosa 'Golden Wings'

A shrub rose of garden origin, 'Golden Wings' has a remontant (repeat flowering) habit. The single, clear yellow blooms deepen in tone towards the center and fade somewhat as they age. The brownish central stamens provide contrast. Long, pointed buds open to flattish cup-shaped scented blooms. Growth is relatively open and also rather stiff.

Height 6 ft (1.8 m). *Zone 8.*

Rosa 'Peace'

Released by the French rose breeder Meilland in 1945, this rose is known as 'Madame A. Meilland' in France, but elsewhere as 'Peace'. It is a vigorous grower with glossy deep green leaves which seem to repel disease. Known as a large flowered hybrid tea rose, the rounded, double pale yellow blooms are flushed pink and usually held one to a stem. Flowers in spring and in autumn.

Height 4 ft (1.2 m). *Zone 8.*

SANTOLINA CHAMAECYPARISSUS

Cotton lavender, lavender cotton

This low-spreading, aromatic shrub is native to mild, coastal areas of the Mediterranean. It bears bright yellow, rounded flowerheads on long stalks, set among oblong, grayish green leaves.

Cultivation

Cotton lavender is hardy and does best in a sunny spot in soil that is well drained but not too rich. Dead-head continually. Straggly old plants should be pruned in early spring. Propagate from semi-ripe cuttings in summer. *Height* 19 in (50 cm). *Zone 7.*

SKIMMIA JAPONICA

Japanese skimmia

This fully frost-hardy shrub from Japan, China and Southeast Asia grows to about 20 ft (6 m) high and wide. It has 4 in (10 cm) long, glossy, deep green, leathery, oval leaves. In spring terminal clusters of slightly fragrant, creamy white flowers are borne, followed by ½ in (12 mm) long, bright red berries. Both male and female plants are required to obtain berries. 'Rubella' has red-margined leaves and dark red flower buds. *Skimmia japonica* subsp. *reevesiana* 'Robert Fortune' is a hermaphrodite with pale green leaves margined in dark green.

Cultivation

Skimmias are plants for shade or part-shade and grow very well with rhododendrons, azaleas and camellias. Like them they prefer moist, humus-rich, well-drained soil. They can be raised from seed in autumn but are most commonly grown from cuttings in late summer.
Height 20 ft (6 m). *Zone 7–10.*

Santolina chamaecyparissus

Spiraea japonica 'Anthony Waterer'

SPIRAEA

Spirea, maybush, garland flower, bridal wreath

Native to the northern hemisphere, these thick, often arching, deciduous or semi-

Skimmia japonica

evergreen shrubs are grown for their beautiful springtime bloom of pink, white or crimson flowers.

Cultivation
Fully hardy, they do best in a fertile, moist, well-drained soil in full sun. A layering of manure in autumn and early spring will help bring out the best quality bloom. Cut back spent heads to the old wood. Propagate from softwood cuttings in summer.

***Spiraea japonica* 'Anthony Waterer'**
This fully hardy, upright, deciduous shrub bears crimson-pink flowers from late spring to early summer. It grows to a spread of 3 ft (1 m). The red foliage turns green as the shrub ages.
Height 5 ft (1.5 m). *Zone 9.*

SYMPHORICARPOS ORBICULATUS

Indian currant, coral berry
This tough, adaptable shrub from the USA and Mexico grows to about 6 ft (1.8 m) high and wide. It is very dense and twiggy, with oval leaves around 1½ in (35 mm) long. The fruit are small, under ¼ in (6 mm) in diameter, but abundant and a conspicuous bright pink. The berries last long after the leaves have fallen. A hot summer will yield a heavier crop of berries.

Cultivation
They are easily grown in any moist, well-drained soil in sun or shade and are usually propagated from open-ground winter hardwood cuttings. Being resistant to shade, poor soil and pollution, they are very suitable for city gardens.
Height 6 ft (1.8 m). *Zone 3–9.*

SYRINGA

Lilac
These vigorous, open, deciduous bushes, native to Europe and northeastern Asia, are much loved. They are grown for the delightful fragrance of their flowers, which form in dense panicles in any shade of red, pink, white, mauve, purple, or even yellow, most being cultivars of the Turkish *S. vulgaris*. The leaves are oval and medium sized.

Cultivation
Lilacs are fully hardy, and require cold, dormant winter conditions to bloom the

Symphoricarpos orbiculatus

Syringa vulgaris 'Souvenir de Louis Spaëth'

following spring. They do best in a deep, fertile, well-drained, preferably alkaline soil, in full sun. Prune after flowering to maintain the shape. Dead-head for the first few years. Propagate by grafting or from softwood cuttings in summer. Grafted plants should be set with the graft union well below the soil surface. This ensures that the upper grafted section of the plant will root.

***Syringa vulgaris* 'Souvenir de Louis Spaëth'**

In late spring, this lilac shrub bears long, thin panicles of sweet-smelling, single, purple-red flowers among dark green, heart-shaped leaves. Its width nearly matches its height.

Height Up to 16 ft (5 m). *Zone 2–9.*

TAXUS × MEDIA

These hybrids between the English and Japanese yews offer a range of sizes and shapes for the garden. 'Brownii', a male form, and 'Everlow' are low and rounded, eventually reaching 8 ft (2.4 m) tall and wide. 'Hatfield' is the broad, upright male form, while 'Hicksii' is narrow, upright and female; both are good for hedging.

Cultivation

These frost-hardy trees tolerate a wide range of conditions, including heavy shade and chalky soil. However, they do not enjoy warm winters or hot, dry summers. Propagate from seed or cuttings or by grafting.

Height 8 ft (2.4 m). *Zones 5–9.*

Taxus × media 'Everlow'

Teucrium chamaedrys

TEUCRIUM CHAMAEDRYS

Wall germander

This hardy, evergreen alpine species of subshrub is native to Europe and south-western Asia. It grows 1–2 ft (30–60 cm) tall with a spread of 2–3 ft (60–90 cm). The toothed, ovate leaves are glossy deep green above and gray beneath. It is suitable for walls, steep banks and edging, and has long been used as a medicinal herb. Spikes of pale to deep rosy purple flowers are produced in summer and autumn.

Cultivation

Mostly fairly frost hardy, they prefer light, well-drained soil and sun. Propagate from cuttings in summer.
Height 1–2 ft (30–60 cm). *Zone 5–10.*

Thuja occidentalis 'Ericoides'

THUJA OCCIDENTALIS

American arbor-vitae

There are over 140 cultivars of this species, ranging from dwarf shrubs to large trees. 'Ericoides', 19 in (50 cm) tall, has soft, loose, bronze juvenile foliage which becomes brownish green as it matures.

Cultivation

Fully hardy, it tolerates most types of soil. All cultivars need full sun. Prune to shape or to restrict size. Propagate from hardwood cuttings taken from a young plant and strike in humid conditions, between late autumn and winter.
Height 3–6 ft (1–1.8 m). *Zone 4–9.*

Viburnum × burkwoodii

Viburnum dilatatum 'Iroquois'

VIBURNUM

Snowball tree, cranberry bush, guelder rose, laurustinus

These deciduous or evergreen shrubs and trees are grown for their fragrant flowers, fruits and beautiful autumn foliage. Prolific flowering can be expected in all suggested zones, however, foliage colors best in colder areas.

Cultivation

Fully to frost-hardy, the hundred-odd species and many more varieties grow best in sun or semi-shade in a rich, moist, well-drained soil. Remove spent flowerheads regularly and prune annually to maintain shape. Propagate from cuttings in summer or from seed in autumn. Mildew and spider mite may cause problems.

Viburnum × burkwoodii

Burkwood viburnum

A hybrid between *Viburnum carlesii* and *V. utile,* this 8–10 ft (2.4–3 m) high semi-evergreen shrub has glossy, deep green, pointed oval leaves to about 3 in (8 cm) long. They are pale sage green on the undersides and those that drop in autumn develop bright yellow and red tones. From early to late spring ball-shaped clusters of small, starry, fragrant flowers open; they are pink in the bud, opening white. 'Anne Russell', the result of a backcross with *V. carlesii,* has clusters of fragrant flowers. 'Park Farm' has a more spreading habit and larger flowers.

Height 8–10 ft (2.4–3 m). *Zone 5–10.*

Viburnum dilatatum

Linden viburnum

From Japan and China, this 10 ft (3 m) tall deciduous shrub has coarsely toothed, hairy oval leaves. Its flowers are white and abundant and carried in heads 4–6 in (10–15 cm) wide; bright red fruit follow. 'Iroquois' is slightly smaller and bushier than the species with flowers more of a creamy white.

Height 10 ft (3 m). *Zone 5–10.*

Viburnum plicatum
'Pink Beauty'
In late spring and early summer, this bushy, deciduous shrub bears large, rounded heads of flowers with white bracts. It is fully hardy.
Height 10 ft (3 m). *Zone 5–10.*

YUCCA FILAMENTOSA

Adam's needle-and-thread
The leaves on this plant form basal rosettes and are edged with white threads. Up to 3 ft (1 m) long, they are thin-textured and a slightly bluish gray-green. The nodding, white flowers are 2 in (5 cm) long, borne on erect panicles to 6 ft (1.8 m) tall in summer. It is native to eastern USA and frost hardy.

Cultivation
Yuccas do best in areas of low humidity; they prefer full sun and sandy soil with good drainage. Depending on the species, they are frost hardy to frost tender. Propagate from seed (if available), cuttings or suckers in spring.
Height 6 ft (1.8 m). *Zone 4–10.*

Yucca filamentosa

Viburnum plicatum 'Pink Beauty'

TREES

Trees are the most important plants in any garden. They grow bigger and live longer than any others, and they are the main creators of the form and structure of your garden. They enhance your garden and the entire street. According to the type and how you place them, they can also provide shade, shelter or privacy. Deciduous trees give summer shade and winter sun; evergreens are good for backdrops and screening. Some trees branch high enough to walk under, while others sweep to the ground. Scale is important when choosing trees for your garden. If you garden on a grand scale, you can think of forest giants; in small gardens, small trees are more appropriate.

Acacia baileyana

Abies concolor var. *lowiana*

ABIES

Silver fir, balsam

These 40 diverse species of conical conifers are cold-climate evergreens. Prized for their aromatic wood and sap, their usefulness to the timber and pharmaceutical industries has threatened many species with extinction. Some

Abies pinsapo

attain majestic heights, growing 3 ft (1 m) a year. In autumn the spiral branches show seed-bearing cones, not pendent but growing upright, which distinguishes *Abies* from similar conifers like the spruces. The soft, spindle-shaped leaves are flat and round-edged, often bearing two parallel silver lines on the underside. Most species are too large for the average garden, being better suited to a country property.

Cultivation

Fully hardy, they prefer moist soil, partial shade and a cool climate. Prune in late winter to encourage shape and limit size; propagate from seeds from ripened cones. The classic European Christmas tree belongs to this genus.

Abies concolor

Colorado fir, white fir

This species grows wild in the Rocky Mountains of the western USA, where it reaches 150 ft (45 m), with a taller race,

Abies concolor var. *lowiana* (Pacific fir), found closer to the coast in Oregon and northern California. The needles, which are bluish green on both sides and blunt tipped, exude a lemon scent when bruised. Cones range from deep dull purple to pale brown. A fine ornamental fir, it is also hardy and vigorous. Seedlings vary in the blueness of their foliage. *Height* 150 ft (45 m).

Abies pinsapo
Spanish fir

A handsome column-shaped tree reaching 100 ft (30 m), often with multiple leaders and densely crowded branches, this fir adapts to a wide range of soils and climates. Purple pollen cones on the lower branch tips are pretty in spring. *Height* 100 ft (30 m). *Zone 5–9.*

ACACIA
Wattle, acacia

This extremely diverse genus contains over 1000 short-lived evergreen, semi-evergreen and deciduous species, mostly native to Australia and Africa. They are valued for their beautiful dense golden blossoms and rapid growth. Most species have flat, spindle-shaped stalks (phyllodes) instead of conventional leaves. A few develop pinnate, fern-like fronds or compound leaves. The fruit is a long, legume-like pod. Heat-treated seeds may be used for propagation, mimicking the way seeds are released in brushfires.

Cultivation

Renowned for their ability to survive drought, acacias grow best in warm climates with well-drained soil and full sun; few can be described as more than half-hardy. To extend their life, completely remove dead branches and prune soon after flowering ends. Watch for borers, leaf miner and acacia scale.

Acer palmatum

Acacia baileyana
Cootamundra wattle

Native to Australia, this is an elegant, half-hardy evergreen. In late winter to early spring, balls of golden blossom appear on drooping branches. The foliage is silver-blue pinnate leaves, rather than phyllodes, 2 in (5 cm) long. Ugly circular swellings may appear on the limbs as a result of gall wasp; remove and burn affected limbs.
Height 20 ft (6 m). *Zone 8–11.*

ACER
Maple

Originating in the cool-temperate zones of the northern hemisphere, these deciduous trees and shrubs are prized for their decorative bark and magnificent foliage. Hand-shaped leaves with pointed fingers color dramatically in autumn. Some species produce little flowers followed by 2-winged fruit (samaras) which 'fly' long distances on the wind.

Cultivation

Maples prefer cool or temperate climates with rich, well-drained soil and will not flourish in dry heat or tropical conditions. Provide full sun or partial shade; shelter from the wind to avoid leaf burn. A neutral to acid soil encourages the best in leaf colors. Prune and graft cultivars in late winter. Propagate the species from seed in autumn, budding in summer.

Acer palmatum
Japanese maple
There are many cultivars of this popular species, both trees and shrubs, and all have striking foliage. A deciduous, shapely tree with a bushy head, it grows 10–16 ft (3–5 m) in mild-winter areas and can reach 50 ft (15 m) in cool-temperate zones. The 5-pointed leaves are lobed. They turn from mid-green to bronze in spring and reddish orange in autumn. Avoid pruning and protect from the wind.
Height 14 ft (4 m) or more. *Zone 6–10.*

Acer palmatum 'Dissectum Atropurpureum'
Japanese maple
Usually grown as a grafted standard, this plant is one of the most popular cultivars of the Japanese maples. Deciduous, it has deep reddish purple spring foliage, fading during summer and coloring again in autumn. Best grown in a position with afternoon shade.
Height 3–6 ft (1–2 m). *Zone 6–10.*

AESCULUS × CARNEA

syn. *A. rubicunda*
Redhorse-chestnut, buckeye
This deciduous hybrid between the Indian and European horse-chestnuts is valued for its beautiful foliage and well-rounded shape. It grows slowly and is fully hardy. The dark green, divided leaves are prone to leaf spot when immature. Large, upright clusters of rich pink blossoms appear in late spring to early summer, followed by the fruit.

Cultivation
This species prefers a cold winter to cool-temperate climate. Suitable for parks or large gardens, it needs a rich, moist, well-drained soil and full sun or partial shade. Leaves burn easily. Propagate from seed in autumn; by grafting in late winter. Pruning is generally unnecessary but the tree may be lopped in winter. The white species *A. hippocastanum* is larger than the red.
Height 25 ft (8 m). *Zone 6–9.*

Acer palmatum 'Dissectum Atropurpureum'

Aesculus × carnea

ALBIZIA

Silk tree

This genus comprises over 100 species of deciduous trees and shrubs, which are mainly quick growing, native to the tropical and subtropical areas of Asia, Africa and Australia, with one species in Mexico. They are distinguished from their close relatives in the *Acacia* genus by their stamens, which are knitted together. Trees vary in height, and are noted for their very unusual foliage: opposing pairs of bipinnate leaves form along central stalks and fold up at night. Clusters of small flowers, spiky or downy, form large, globular crowns similar to bottlebrushes. Plants gradually refuse to bloom in pots but are still worthwhile for their foliage.

Cultivation

They prefer full sun with protection from the wind. Plant in a light, compost-enriched soil and propagate from seed in late autumn to early spring.

Albizia julibrissin

Pink silk tree

Found in the area between Iran and Japan, this is a squat tree with a broad crown. Sometimes reaching a height of 30 ft (9 m), it has large, pale to mid-green pinnate leaves. An abundance of translucent pink, downy blossom appears in late spring to early summer. The species is very cold tolerant and is valuable as the only fern-leaved tree for cool-temperate climates. Plant in a rich, well-drained soil. Propagate from seed in autumn; sucker and root cutting in winter.
Height 16 ft (5 m) or more. *Zone 8–10.*

Albizia julibrissin

Amelanchier arborea

AMELANCHIER ARBOREA

syn. *Amelanchier canadensis* of gardens

Downy serviceberry

Occurring naturally in the eastern USA, this easily grown tree has a narrowish crown and drooping lower branches. The finely toothed, pointed leaves are covered with white down as they emerge in spring. Profuse flowers, in short upright sprays, are followed in early summer by small fleshy fruit. In autumn the foliage turns red, orange or yellow.

Cultivation

They do best in moist, fertile soil in a grassy glade in the shelter of other trees but receiving ample sun. Propagation is normally from seed or by layering.
Height 20 ft (6 m). *Zone 4–9.*

Arbutus unedo

Arbutus menziesii

ARBUTUS

This genus contains some 20 species of frost-hardy, evergreen trees and shrubs. They have attractive, dark green leaves and decorative bark, and are native from California to the Mediterranean. Bell-shaped flower clusters bloom in spring, followed in summer by small orange-red spherical fruit, which may take up to a year to mature. *Arbutus* do well in both cool and warm-temperate climates. They are attractive planted in tubs, where root constriction causes earlier blooming and fruiting.

Cultivation

Plant in a well-drained, slightly acid soil; protect from sea breezes and full sun. Propagate from seed in spring, cuttings in summer and layering in autumn or spring. *Arbutus* is Latin for 'strawberry', but the hard, reddish yellow fruit is edible but tasteless. It is used to make wine and jam in Italy and Spain.

Arbutus menziesii

Madrone

Native from California to British Columbia, the madrone is the giant of the genus, reaching 100 ft (30 m) in height and 6 ft (1.8 m) in diameter. It has beautiful, smooth, orange-brown bark and smooth-edged, glossy green leaves with whitish undersides, and produces large clusters of pure white flowers and profuse small, orange-red fruit.
Height 100 ft (30 m). *Zone 7–9.*

Arbutus unedo

Irish strawberry tree, cane apple

A native of Ireland and southern Europe, this small tree is valued for its attractive foliage and its bark, used for tanning. Pink or white flowers form in clusters of 30 to 50 in autumn and early winter. A species with a shrubby habit, it is suitable for hedges and backdrops. It is a hardy tree and will tolerate neglect but responds to better conditions. It dislikes shade and damp ground.
Height 16 ft (5 m). *Zone 7–10.*

AZARA MICROPHYLLA

This fairly erect small tree reaches greater heights in the wild in its native Chile and western Argentina. A vigorous grower, it has fine foliage, rather like a box *(Buxus)* though much more open in habit. In late winter it produces numerous small flower clusters, dull gold and delightfully fragrant, half hidden under the leaf sprays. The leaves of the cultivar 'Variegata' are attractively variegated with cream.

Cultivation

Plant in a sheltered position to protect from both wind and frost damage. It prefers a deep fertile soil with ample moisture. Prune after flowering and propagate from semi-hardwood cuttings in summer.
Height 20 ft (6 m). *Zone 7–9.*

Azara microphylla

BETULA

Birch

This genus contains over 35 species, native to the northern hemisphere. These fully hardy, elegant, deciduous trees have slender, weeping branches, shimmering foliage and broad serrated leaves that turn gold in autumn. Pendent fruit contains winged seeds. Gray, red-brown, white or yellowish black bark is shed in long strips.

Cultivation

Birches will grow in any well-drained soil, provided they receive plentiful water and full sun. Pruning is unnecessary. Propagate from seed, by grafting in late winter or from softwood cuttings in early summer.

Betula papyrifera

Betula papyrifera

Paper birch, canoe birch

Famed for its tough papery bark, once used by Native Americans for their light but strong canoes, the paper birch is one of the most wide-ranging North American species and is extremely cold hardy. The largish leaves are broadly heart-shaped or egg-shaped. The white or cream bark peels off in thin, curling layers, exposing new bark of a pale orange-brown. Its chief ornamental value is in the bark.
Height 60 ft (18 m). *Zone 2–9.*

CARPINUS BETULUS

Common hornbeam, European hornbeam

Ranging from Asia Minor across Europe to eastern England, this species can grow to 80 ft (24 m) although 30 ft (9 m) is an average garden height. It has a broad, rounded crown and pale gray bark, fairly smooth and often fluted. The ovate leaves are ribbed and serrated, downy when young, and change from dark green in summer to yellow in autumn. Inconspicuous flowers in early spring are followed by clusters of pale yellow winged fruit. *Carpinus betulus* likes cool, moist conditions.

Cultivation

It grows best in well-drained, moderately fertile soil in a sunny or partly shaded position. Propagation is normally from seed except for certain named clones, which must be grafted.
Height 30 ft (9 m). *Zone 6–9.*

Catalpa bignonioides

Carpinus betulus

CATALPA BIGNONIOIDES

Indian bean tree, cigar tree

This deciduous North American tree is valued for its dense foliage and flowers. It spreads broadly in later life and has small heart-shaped leaves that are pale green or yellow, which are grouped in threes. Bell-shaped and perfumed, the flowers are white, pink or lemon, variegated with purple and yellow. They appear in summer in thick upright clusters, 6–12 ft (15–30 cm) tall, later replaced by drooping tubular seed pods.

Cultivation

This tree likes full sun, shelter from the wind and rich, well-drained soil. It is best grown alone. Propagate from seed in autumn, cultivars by budding and cuttings in summer.
Height 25 ft (8 m). *Zone 8–10.*

CEDRUS

Cedar

This genus of conifers, native to Africa and India, contains four species of tall, conical trees valued for their timber. The spiraled foliage is gray-green and needle-shaped. They have woody, egg-shaped cones that bear seed scales.

Cultivation

These fully hardy trees prefer cool temperatures, full sun and rich, well-drained soil. Too large for the average garden, they are better suited to country properties. Propagate from seed; some cultivars by grafting. Cedars have an ancient lineage; their timber was used for King Solomon's temple and it was greatly valued by the Greeks and Romans.

Cedrus atlantica
Mt. Atlas cedar
Originating in North Africa, this fast-growing species has pale green or blue-gray, spindly foliage, which is distinctively short at 1 in (25 cm). The bark is dark and scaly. Erect, light green to purple flowers bloom in summer. The barrel-shaped, brown male and pale green female cones take 2 years to mature. While young, this tree may be grown in a tub. This species is popular for ornamental effect in cool climates.
Height 25 ft (8 m) or more. *Zone 6–9.*

Cedrus deodara
Deodar, Indian cedar
The largest of its genus, this magnificent Himalayan native has tiered branches which droop slightly at the extremities where the silvery gray leaves develop. Male and female cones grow on separate branches and the 2–4 in (5–10 cm) cones have flat tops. This species will grow in various climates, from very dry inland to cooler mountain areas. Height is determined by soil quality and the amount of water the tree receives. In cultivation, it makes fast early growth. Suitable for pots, it may be replanted when up to 6 ft (1.8 m) tall.
Height 40 ft (12 m). *Zone 7–10.*

CEANOTHUS ARBOREUS
Tree ceanothus, island ceanothus
One of the largest-growing evergreen species, *Ceanothus arboreus* from islands off the south Californian coast makes an evergreen tree of up to 30 ft (9 m) but in gardens it is normally only half that, developing a thick, low-branching trunk. The leaves have downy undersides and are larger than in most species and the flowers, ranging from very pale blue to deep blue, are in loose clusters carried just above the leaves in spring and early summer.

Cedrus deodara

Cedrus atlantica

Ceanothus arboreus 'Mist'

Cultivation
This tree requires full sun and prefers shelter, particularly from strong winds, in well-drained soil. Propagate from seed, often freely produced in small round capsules, or from cuttings. *Height* 30 ft (9 m). *Zone 8–10.*

CELTIS OCCIDENTALIS

American hackberry
This species comes from the eastern USA, the Mississippi Basin and eastern Canada. In its preferred habitat of forests in deep, rich, alluvial soils, it can reach a very large size, but when planted in the open it makes a shapely, spreading tree of 40–60 ft (12–18 m). The bark, smooth on saplings, becomes rough as the tree matures. The pea-sized fruit ripen through red to dull purple. The

Celtis occidentalis

foliage turns pale yellow in autumn; it can become a pest along riverbanks and channels in some countries.

Cultivation
In cool climates, this frost-hardy tree likes dry soil and full sun; in warm areas it likes rich, moist, well-drained soil and part-shade. Propagate from seed in fall. *Height* 40–60 ft (12–18 m). *Zone 3–10.*

CERCIDIPHYLLUM JAPONICUM

In cultivation in the West *Cercidiphyllum japonicum* is known as a small, rather slender tree to about 40 ft (12 m) high, but in Japan and China it is the largest native deciduous tree—ancient specimens up to 130 ft (40 m) tall, with trunks over 15 ft (4.5 m) in diameter, are known. The trunk often forks at a narrow angle and the short branches spread horizontally in tiers. The heart-shaped leaves are mostly under 3 in (8 cm) wide, but larger in *C. j.* var. *magnificum*; the Chinese *C. j.* var. *sinense* has slightly different leaves and flowers.

Cercis canadensis

Cultivation

This tree prefers rich, moist but well-drained soil in a sunny or partly shaded position. It is fully frost hardy but the spring foliage is easily damaged by late frost, very dry conditions or drying winds. Propagate from seed or cuttings. *Height* 40 ft (12 m). *Zone 6–9.*

CERCIS

Redbud, Judas tree

This genus consists of 7 ornamental trees and shrubs native to North America, southern Europe and Asia. They have beautiful, pea-like flowers. Deciduous species reach 40 ft (12 m) with fine multiple branches. It is straight out of these limbs that the pink, white or purple stalkless flowers appear at the end of winter. Numerous flat seed pods, 4 in (10 cm) long, follow the blooms and endure until the following winter.

Cultivation

These trees prefer rich porous soils and full sun. They do not like being moved, so transplant when young. Propagate from seed in autumn and bud cultivars in summer. According to legend, Judas Iscariot hanged himself from the bough of one of these trees after betraying Jesus Christ.

Cercidiphyllum japonicum

Cercis canadensis

Eastern redbud

Native to eastern and central USA, this tree can reach 40 ft (12 m) in the wild and is strikingly beautiful in flower. In gardens it rarely exceeds 12 ft (3.5 m), branching close to the ground. The leaves are heart-shaped with a distinct point, and appear after the flowers. The buds are deep rose, and the paler rose flowers are profuse and showy; flowering may continue from spring into early summer. 'Forest Pansy' has purple-colored leaves. *Height* 12 ft (3.5 m). *Zone 5–9.*

CHAMAECYPARIS

False cypress

Native to the USA and eastern Asia, the 8 conifers that make up this genus may be shrubby and small, or erect and tall.

Their small leaves vary considerably in color, from green to grayish blue. Branches may be stiff or arching, tiered or constant. All species are easily propagated, withstand transplanting and do not require pruning—hence their popularity as possibly the most commonly cultivated genus of evergreens.

Chamaecyparis lawsoniana 'Winston Churchill'

Cultivation

They prefer cool-temperate conditions and full sun. Propagate from seed; cultivars by cuttings. Once classified as true cypresses, they were placed in their own genus early this century.

Chamaecyparis lawsoniana

Lawson cypress, Port Orford cedar

This native of the USA is prized for its quality timber and appearance. It has a triangular shape, later becoming open-crowned and columnar, and is variable in height. Tiny, deep green scales cover the slender, slightly arching branches, giving the tree a felty look. Narrow rectangular cones of both genders appear on the same tree. The species thrives in cool conditions and rich, damp soil. There are many garden varieties with narrower habit, or silvery or golden foliage, such as 'Winston Churchill'. *Height* 40 ft (12 m). *Zone 6–9.*

Chamaecyparis pisifera cultivar

Chamaecyparis pisifera

Sawara cypress

This fully hardy species has stiff branches and reddish brown bark with raised vertical lines. The deep green leaf scales have white margins. Cultivars are grouped into three main categories: Filifera, Plumosa and Squarrosa. *Height* 25 ft (8 m) or more. *Zone 5–10.*

CHIONANTHUS VIRGINICUS

American fringe tree

The individual flowers of this species are similar to those of *Chionanthus retusus*, but the leaves are larger and less shiny and the longer, drooping flower sprays appear among the foliage rather than standing above it. In its native forests of southeastern USA it grows in rich, moist soil close to streams, occasionally 30 ft (9 m) tall but often only a shrub. Away from its native regions it can be a shy bloomer, performing better in continental climates of central Europe than in the UK and not doing so well in climates warmer than that.

Cultivation
This cool-climate tree is easily grown but may be slow to increase in size and can take 10 years to flower. A sunny but sheltered position with good soil and drainage suits it best. Propagate from seed in autumn.
Height 30 ft (9 m). *Zone 5–9.*

CLADRASTIS LUTEA
syn. *Cladrastis kentukea*
American yellowwood
The natural range of this species is from North Carolina to Alabama and Missouri, in rich soils on hill slopes or along ravines near streams. There it grows to 60 ft (18 m) with a trunk diameter to 3 ft (1 m), forking not far above the ground with steeply angled limbs. In cultivation it rarely exceeds 30 ft (9 m). The leaves consist of 5 to 9 broad, veined leaflets that are a fresh, rich green in summer turning yellow in autumn. White flowers appear in early summer. Some trees flower only every second year.

Cultivation
Fully frost hardy, it prefers full sun and fertile, well-drained soil. It also needs protection from strong winds as the wood is brittle. Propagate from seed in autumn or from cuttings in winter.
Height 30 ft (9 m). *Zone 6–10.*

CORNUS
Dogwood
This is a large genus from the temperate northern hemisphere, with over 100 species varying from small shrubs to forest trees. They can be either evergreen or deciduous, and their attraction can be colored bark, autumn foliage or showy flowers, though the actual flowers are insignificant and the display comes from the 4 bracts which surround the flower cluster. In many species the flowers are followed by berries that are long lasting.

Chionanthus virginicus

Cladrastis lutea

Cornus florida

Cornus kousa var. chinensis

Cultivation

Fertile soil and drought-free, cool but not frosty climates are preferred.

Cornus florida

Dogwood

Originating in the USA, this slim or shrubby deciduous species grows slowly. It is valued for its abundant pink or white spring flowers and deep green, oval, large veined leaves, 3–4 in (8–10 cm) long, which turn vivid, reddish purple in autumn. It requires deep, rich, acid soil. *Height* 16 ft (5 m). *Zone 5–9.*

Cornus kousa

Japanese flowering dogwood, kousa

Occurring wild in Japan, China and Korea, *Cornus kousa* can reach 20 ft (6 m) or more at maturity with dense, deep green foliage and tiered lower branches. In early summer when the leaves have fully expanded, the flowerheads with large, pure white bracts appear, each bract tapering to an acute point. The small compound fruits are dull red. *Cornus kousa* var. *chinensis* has slightly larger 'flowers' and more vigorous growth.
Height 20 ft (6 m). *Zone 6–9.*

CRATAEGUS VIRIDIS

Green hawthorn

Making a small tree of up to about 30 ft (9 m), this species from the south-eastern USA has fairly broad, glossy dark green leaves that are toothed or lobed in the upper half; in late spring–early summer it bears white flowers in small and rather sparse clusters, followed by smallish red fruit. 'Winter King' is a superior cultivar with silvery bark, a vase-like form with relatively few thorns, good red autumn color and bright red fruit that lasts well into winter.

Cultivation

Hawthorns are robust, frost-hardy, deciduous trees, most of them compact enough even for quite small gardens. They are sun-lovers and not very fussy about soil type or drainage. Some hawthorns are prone to fireblight, controlled only by prompt removal and burning of affected branches. Foliage may also be disfigured by the 'pear and cherry slug' (larva of a sawfly); spray severe attacks with an insecticide. Propagate from cold-stratified seed, or by grafting of named clones.
Height 30 ft (9 m). *Zone 4–9.*

Crataegus viridis

CRYPTOMERIA JAPONICA 'ELEGANS'

Bronze Japanese cedar

This erect triangular Asian conifer is highly valued for its fascinating needle-like foliage that develops in soft feathery whorls and drapes to the ground. Leaves turn from deep green in summer to rich golden rust in autumn.

Cultivation

It prefers cool conditions but will survive in the heat with regular watering. Plant in cool, damp soil and shelter from cold winds; it will withstand transplanting up to a reasonable size. Propagate from cuttings.

Height 20 ft (6 m) or more. *Zone 7–8.*

Cryptomeria japonica 'Elegans'

CUPRESSUS

Cypress

Native to Europe, Asia, the USA and Central America, this diverse genus of evergreen coniferous trees and shrubs may be tall and slender or open and squat. They make symmetrical shade trees or hedges. Golden green or bluish gray, needle-like foliage changes to tiny leaf scales in maturity. They have globose, scale-covered cones.

Cultivation

They prefer cool to warm-temperate regions, can survive in very dry, sandy soil and are ideal for coastal locations. Prune frequently to promote fresh growth. Mature plants will not survive transplanting. Propagate from cuttings in winter or cold-treated seed from the end of autumn to late winter. The trees are susceptible to leafroller caterpillars, beetles, weevils and canker.

Cupressus sempervirens 'Swane's Golden'

Cupressus arizonica

Arizona cypress, rough-barked Arizona cypress

Originating in Arizona, and sometimes confused with *Cupressus glabra*, this pyramidal species will grow to 50 ft (15 m). Its mature foliage is gray-green and does not display the white spots of the smooth Arizona cypress. It has short-stalked, large, round cones, up to 1 in (25 mm) across, and a brown, stringy and furrowed bark. It is grown both as a specimen tree and as a hedge.
Height 50 ft (15 m). *Zone 7–10.*

Cupressus sempervirens

Mediterranean cypress, funereal cypress

C. sempervirens is a familiar sight in Italian gardens, with its green, pencil-slim spires. It is notable for having the largest cones of the genus. 'Swane's Golden', which originated in Australia, is admired for its yellow leaves and is more frost tender. Its spreading root system makes it unsuitable for smaller gardens. Take cuttings from good stock; avoid overfertilizing.
Height 30 ft (9 m). *Zone 8–10.*

DAVIDIA INVOLUCRATA

Dove tree, handkerchief tree

This native to China, the only species of its genus, is valued for its unusual white

Cupressus arizonica

Davidia involucrata

bracts. This deciduous ornamental develops a rounded appearance. Its broad, oval leaves up to 6 in (15 cm) long, are succeeded in late spring by small, deep-set, brownish red flowers. Two white bracts (commonly mistaken for petals) of unequal lengths surround the flower. The longer bract resembles a birch leaf or handkerchief; hence the common name. Purplish green, pear-shaped seed pods follow, each encasing a single nut.

Cultivation

Plant in full sun or partial shade in rich, porous soil and protect the bracts from harsh winds. It is frost-hardy. Propagate (with some difficulty) from cuttings or seed in spring.
Height 25 ft (8 m) or more. *Zone 8–9.*

EUCALYPTUS

Gum tree, eucalypt

This diverse genus of mainly Australian natives contains over 600 species of evergreen trees and shrubs, prized for their beauty, shade, oils, hardwood and honey. Foliage varies from linear to heart-shaped; young and adult leaves differ markedly, making identification difficult. All species have distinctively lidded flower buds with densely packed stamens, blooming in spring or summer in shades of white, red or yellow. Trees vary greatly from frost-hardy to frost-tender and differ in size, shape and habitat: some low, multi-trunked species are excellent sand-binders, able to survive for a year without rain in the arid inland; other gnarled, salt-resistant species thrive in swamps; others still, straight and tall, flourish in cool mountain areas.

Cultivation

Plant eucalypts in isolation with full sun in rich, well-drained soil; trees do not transplant well. Prune in spring and early winter. Propagate from seed in autumn and late winter.

Eucalyptus citriodora

Lemon-scented gum

This species is valued for its slender beauty. The long, narrow leaves have a lemony scent when crushed. The trunk is covered with smooth, pinkish gray bark that peels in patches. The deep green foliage is rough and downy when young, becoming lanceolate and smooth when mature. Flowers bloom in thick terminal clusters, 1 in (25 mm) across. It is half-hardy and fast growing. Shelter young trees from frost.
Height 40 ft (12 m). *Zone 9–11.*

Eucalyptus citriodora

Eucalyptus leucoxylon

Eucalyptus leucoxylon
Whitewood, white iron bark, red-flowered yellow gum

This erect evergreen has smooth, bluish white bark marked with yellow patches. Its rounded crown is covered with grayish green, lanceolate leaves of varying widths. White or pink flowers (according to variety) appear in long-stemmed triple clusters during winter and spring. The seed pods are 1 in (25 mm) long with pointed ends. This moderately frost-hardy species prefers a cool climate and rich, well-drained soil. *Height* 40 ft (12 m). *Zone 9–10.*

FAGUS

Beech

Native to Europe and North America, this small cool-climate genus includes some of the world's most popular deciduous trees. They are well rounded

Fagus sylvatica

with dense crowns, and are valued for their autumn foliage and timber. Foliage varies in shape, size and color, ranging from yellow to purple. Inconspicuous flowers bloom in late spring, followed in late autumn by the pyramid-shaped nuts in their prickly oval seed pods.

Cultivation

The purple-leaved trees like full sun; the yellow-leaved prefer partial shade. All species enjoy well-drained, alkaline soil.

Fagus sylvatica
European beech

Triangular in shape with a broad spreading crown and drooping branches, this tree grows quickly. Young foliage is oval, downy and light green, maturing to deep glossy green. Leaves turn a vivid golden orange in autumn. It prefers cold climates and partial shade and will do best in well-drained alkaline soils. Prune in summer and propagate from seed in autumn, budding in late summer.
Height 30 ft (9 m). *Zone 5–9.*

Fagus sylvatica f. purpurea
Copper beech

The name *purpurea* covers the purple and copper leafed forms of beech, which are usually selected seedlings rather than grafted named cultivars. The copper beech generally is a more slender tree than the species, bearing deep purple, somewhat glossy, heavily veined and unevenly margined leaves in spring and summer. These age to a rich purple brown in autumn and can be held on the tree for a long time during the winter.
Height 30 ft (9 m). *Zone 5–9.*

FRANKLINIA ALATAMAHA

The name is taken from the Altamaha River in Georgia, where this species was first discovered. It makes a small, spreading tree of about 15–20 ft (4.5–6 m), often multi-trunked. The glossy, bright green leaves turn scarlet in autumn, while the 3 in (8 cm) wide fragrant flowers open in late summer and early fall.

Franklinia alatamaha

Fagus sylvatica f. purpurea

Cultivation

Frost hardy, it prefers humus-rich, moist but well-drained soil and a sheltered, warm position in full sun. Growth is slow. Climates with long, hot, humid summers produce the best flowering. Propagate from fresh ripe seed.
Height 15–20 ft (4.5–6 m). *Zone 7–10.*

FRAXINUS

Ash

Native to the northern hemisphere, this well-known genus contains about 60 deciduous timber trees and shrubs. They are extremely variable in size. Dense flower clusters which are insignificant in most species appear in early spring, followed by distinctive feathery foliage up to 12 in (30 cm) long, divided into 3 to 13 leaflets. Decorative drooping clusters of small, winged seeds develop from the flowers.

Fraxinus pennsylvanica

Fraxinus americana 'Autumn Purple'

Cultivation

These fully hardy trees will endure a broad range of temperatures provided that they are planted in deep, fertile soil with sufficient moisture and full sun. Propagate from heat-treated seed in autumn, or by budding in summer.

Fraxinus americana

White ash

The most valued ash in North America, this species occurs naturally through the eastern USA and in southeastern Canada. In the wild it reaches about 80 ft (24 m) with a long straight trunk and furrowed gray-brown bark and a somewhat domed canopy. The pinnate leaves have 7 to 9 large, dark green leaflets with silvery undersides. The inconspicuous flowers appear before the leaves. Autumn color is most commonly a fine yellow. A number of forms are available including *Fraxinus americana* var. *juglandifolia*, which has a slender, columnar habit, and 'Autumn Purple' with leaves that turn reddish purple in fall.
Height 80 ft (24 m). *Zone 4–10.*

Fraxinus pennsylvanica

Red ash, green ash

Similar to *Fraxinus americana*, this tree is also a fast-growing native of North America but is not as large; it reaches 70 ft (21 m) in height with a similar spread. Its green leaves are divided into 5 to 9 leaflets and are sometimes hairy, resembling stalks. This species prefers a moist soil. 'Summit' has an upright, cylindrical habit with leaves turning yellow in autumn; *F. pennsylvanica* var. *subintegerrima* has long, narrow, sword-shaped leaves.
Height 70 ft (21 m). *Zone 4–10.*

GINKGO BILOBA

Maidenhair tree

The sole member of its genus, this important deciduous conifer has been found in fossils that are over 200 million years old. Native apparently to Europe, Asia, and two areas in America, it is now known in the wild only in China. Fortunately, it is widely cultivated. This hardy tree is valued for its rich autumn foliage and timber. Its triangular crown broadens out in maturity. The arching branches develop bright green, fan-shaped leaves, similar to the maidenhair fern but much larger, which turn deep golden yellow in autumn. Little yellow flowers sprinkle the mature trees in spring, followed by orange-yellow fruits about the size of a small plum. The female tree is not popular among some gardeners as the fallen seeds have an unpleasant odor.

Cultivation

This enduring tree survives both arid and wet climates and withstands urban pollution. The tree needs deep fertile soil and it should be propagated from seed or graft.

Height 25 ft (8 m) or more. *Zone 3–10.*

GLEDITSIA TRIACANTHOS 'SKYLINE'

Honey locust

The deciduous North American honey locust and its thornless form *inermis* has supported many cultivars including 'Ruby Lace', with reddish young growth turning dull bronze in autumn; 'Sunburst', with bright yellow young leaves; and 'Skyline'. This has fern-like pale green summer foliage composed of many leaflets which turn rich yellow in autumn. Its broad symmetrical crown is made up of ascending upper branches with lower and middle branches being of a more horizontal nature.

Cultivation

This form, as with all the *Gleditsias,* likes full sun in deep friable soil and although fully hardy likes protection from frost when young. Propagate by budding in spring or summer, while the species can be grown from seed sown in autumn.

Height 50 ft (15 m). *Zone 3–10.*

Gleditsia triacanthos 'Skyline'

Ginkgo biloba

Halesia carolina

Hamamelis virginiana

HALESIA CAROLINA

syn. *Halesia tetraptera*

Carolina silverbell

This ornamental, spreading tree grows 25–40 ft (8–12 m) high and somewhat wider. It flowers profusely, even when young, producing masses of drooping, bell-shaped white or pink-flushed flowers in mid- to late spring. The flowers are followed by 4-winged green fruit that ripen to pale brown. The mid-green leaves are downy when they first appear and turn yellow in autumn.

Cultivation

A cool-climate plant, it prefers a sheltered position in part- to full sun and grows best in well-drained, moist, neutral to acid soil. Propagation is from seed in autumn or from softwood cuttings in summer. Halesias have little trouble with pests and diseases. *Height* 25–40 ft (8–12 m). *Zone 3–9.*

HAMAMELIS VIRGINIANA

Virginian witch hazel, common witch hazel

This witch hazel has an open, upright habit and grows to a height and spread of 12–20 ft (3.5–6 m) but can be readily adapted to tree-like form by training to a single trunk in early years. Small, fragrant, curled and twisted yellow flowers appear in autumn as the leaves fall. The dark green, broadly oval leaves turn a bright buttercup yellow in autumn.

Cultivation

This plant prefers an open, sunny position (although it will tolerate semi-shade) in fertile, moist but well-drained, loamy, acid soil. It can be raised from seed, but germination may take a full year. Check for coral spot and honey fungus. *Height* 12–20 ft (3.5–6 m). *Zone 7–9.*

ILEX

The 400 or so evergreen and deciduous trees and shrubs that make up this large genus are grown for their foliage and clusters of small glossy berries. Hollies make excellent hedges, border plants, tub plants or screens for privacy according to their height. Male and female plants must be grown together to obtain the berries.

Cultivation

Hollies grow well in deep, friable, well-drained soil with high organic content.

Ilex aquifolium

They are fully to marginally frost hardy. An open, sunny position is best in cool climates. Prune carefully in spring. Propagate from seed or cuttings. Check for signs of holly aphid and holly leaf miner.

Ilex aquifolium
English holly
A valued ornamental, this is the parent plant of many cultivars. Evergreen, it is a popular Christmas decoration in the northern hemisphere with its glossy, spiny-edged dark green leaves and bright red winter berries. It has an erect, many-branching habit.
Height 50 ft (15 m). *Zone 5.*

Ilex opaca
American holly
The best known American species, this evergreen tree grows to a height and spread of about 30 ft (9 m); it has an erect habit and produces red berries in winter. The leaves are dull green above and yellowish underneath, with spiny or smooth edges. It prefers a sunny position

Ilex opaca

and acid soil, and does not do well near the sea.
Height 30 ft (9 m). *Zone 5–10.*

JACARANDA MIMOSIFOLIA
syn. J. ovalifolia
Jacaranda
Native to the high plains of Brazil, this fast grower is valued for its beautiful flowers, foliage and timber. It develops a broad, rounded crown. Vivid green, fern-like foliage is bipinnate, with 12 or more leaflets. Depending on climate, the leaves may be shed in winter or early spring before the flowers appear. These are very attractive, mauve-blue terminal clusters of tubular blossoms. Flat, leathery seed pods follow.

Cultivation
This half-hardy species prefers dry and temperate climates. Protect the young tree from frosts. Plant in rich, porous soil with full sun and do not over water. Do not prune as new shoots will spoil shape. Propagate from seed in spring.
Height 30 ft (9 m). *Zone 10–11.*

JUNIPERUS VIRGINIANA

Eastern red cedar, pencil cedar
From North America, this is the tallest of the junipers commonly grown in gardens, reaching 50–60 ft (15–18 m) high. It has a conical or broadly columnar habit and both scale- and needle-like, gray-green leaves. The berries are fleshy, small, glaucous and brownish violet. The wood is used in making pencils, hence the common name.

Cultivation
Easily cultivated in a cool climate, it prefers a sunny position and any well-drained soil. Prune to maintain shape or restrict size, but do not make visible pruning cuts as old, leafless wood rarely sprouts. Propagate from cuttings in winter, layers if low-growing, or from seed.
Height 50–60 ft (15–18 m). *Zone 2–9.*

KOELREUTERIA PANICULATA

China tree, golden-rain tree, varnish tree, pride of India
This deciduous Asian native has a broad convex crown and grows quickly. Its feathery bipinnate foliage grows up to 18 in (45 cm) long and turns from green to deep golden yellow in autumn, particularly in cooler climates. Large decorative clusters of golden yellow flowers develop in summer, followed by pinkish brown seed pods that are swollen with black seeds.

Jacaranda mimosifolia

Koelreuteria paniculata

Juniperus virginiana

Cultivation

This frost-hardy species survives arid inland conditions and enjoys full sun and strong alkaline soil. Propagate from seed in spring; root cuttings in winter. The flowers are used in Chinese medicine.
Height 30–50 ft (9–15 m). *Zone 4–10.*

LAGERSTROEMIA INDICA

Crepe myrtle, pride of India

Of neat appearance, this deciduous small tree or large shrub has an open, spreading, rounded head. In mid- to late summer it bears large clusters of frilly flowers in tones of white, pink, lilac or dark purplish red. In cooler areas the small, oval leaves turn shades of gold in autumn. Older plants are prone to attack by powdery mildew in areas of high humidity, but newer cultivars seem to be more resilient.

Cultivation

Grown mainly for its crepe-like flowers, this tree or large shrub produces glorious autumn foliage color and beautiful bark on its usually multistemmed trunk. Will produce larger flowerheads if pruned.
Height 27 ft (7 m). *Zone 6–9.*

LAURUS NOBILIS

Sweet bay, bay tree, bay laurel, laurel

An evergreen, broadly conical tree, this species is usually smaller in cultivation. Its glossy, dark green leaves are smooth and leathery and highly aromatic when crushed. It produces small, star-shaped, fragrant yellow flowers in spring, followed by small, round green berries that ripen to dark purplish black in autumn. This tree is particularly suited to clipping and shaping.

Cultivation

Grow in full sun in well drained, yet moisture retentive soil. Fertilize regularly in spring/summer for quick growth. This plant makes an ideal standard or pot specimen as it tolerates clipping.
Height 30 ft (9 m). *Zone 7–9.*

LIQUIDAMBAR

Sweet gum

This deciduous genus contains three species, one each from Asia, Asia Minor and North to Central America. All are valued for their splendid autumn foliage, which varies greatly in color. Conical in shape, the trees grow to varying heights. The leaves are palmate, resem-

Laurus nobilis

Lagerstroemia indica

Liquidambar styraciflua

Liriodendron tulipifera

bling the maple, with 5–7 deeply cut, serrated lobes.

Cultivation

Frost-hardy when fully grown, these trees can survive extremes in temperature. They prefer a warm moist location but are not salt-resistant. Nothing will grow near them as they are voracious feeders, sucking what goodness there is from the soil. Plant in deep, porous earth with full sun or partial shade. Propagate from seed in autumn; bud in spring.

Liquidambar styraciflua

Sweet gum, red gum, bilsted

This deciduous native of North and Central America has an erect conical shape that may spread in maturity. It grows quickly, depending on conditions. The lustrous foliage, with 5 or 7 lobes, is 4–6 in (10–15 cm) wide. Young leaves are pale green, maturing to deep green and turning vivid red-purple and orange-yellow in autumn. The branches develop corky shoots in winter. This frost-hardy tree survives hot weather with regular watering. Select seedling trees in autumn as color is variable.
Height 50 ft (15 m). *Zone 5–10.*

LIRIODENDRON TULIPIFERA

Tulip tree, tulip poplar, yellow poplar

This deciduous North American native is valued for its flowers and rich yellow autumn foliage. The tree grows quickly in a symmetrical pyramid; branches often do not start until halfway up. Distinctive, 4-lobed leaves have blunted middle teeth, giving the foliage a squarish appearance. In spring the tree bears green, scented flowers shaped like tulips, with orange bands encircling the stamens. These are followed by conical seed heads containing winged seeds.

Cultivation

This fully hardy species prefers cool climates and enjoys full sun and neutral to acid soil. It may be transplanted up to a good size and is propagated from seed in autumn, budding in summer.
Height 30 ft (9 m). *Zone 3–10.*

Magnolia grandiflora

MAGNOLIA

Magnolia

This genus comprises two groups: deciduous species, native to eastern Asia, and evergreens, native to Central America and southern USA. All are valued for their beautiful large flowers. The evergreen species have spreading crowns, and their elliptical leaves are lustrous green on top, pitted with brown underneath. The perfumed flowers with silky petals and densely packed stamens bloom on deciduous trees in spring, sometimes before the foliage; on the evergreens, in summer.

Cultivation

Trees prefer full sun or partial shade and rich, well-drained soil (slightly acid for deciduous species). Fertilize poor soil first with manure. Transplant with care: the roots are extremely fragile. Propagate from cuttings in summer, seed in autumn, graft cultivars in winter.

Magnolia grandiflora

Bull bay, southern magnolia, laurel magnolia

This evergreen species from southern USA varies broadly in size and habit.

Magnolia × *soulangiana* 'Brozzoni'

It may be compact and rounded or spreading and conical. It has thick, woody foliage of shiny mid- to deep green leaves, downy brown underneath. Cup-shaped white blooms with a strong citrus scent appear from mid-summer to early autumn, followed by red-brown cones. This moderately frost-hardy species prefers warm climates and moist soil.
Height 25 ft (8 m). *Zone 6–11.*

Magnolia* × *soulangiana

Saucer magnolia, Soulange-Bodin's magnolia

This deciduous tree develops slowly, frequently growing multiple trunks and a rounded crown. Tulip-like blooms precede the foliage in early spring, even on young plants. The flower's interior

Magnolia stellata

varies from snow white to light pink; the exterior is a deeper pink. The dull green foliage is up to 6 in (15 cm) long. This species prefers a temperate climate and requires shelter from hot winds. This hybrid was bred in 1820 by Étienne Soulange-Bodin. Of the many cultivars available, the fast-growing 'Brozzoni' flowers later in the season when the plant is fully clothed in new leaves.
Height 20 ft (6 m). *Zone 4–9.*

Magnolia stellata
Star magnolia
This many-branched, compact, deciduous shrub from Japan grows 10–15 ft (3–4.5 m) tall and wide, with aromatic bark when young, and narrow dark green leaves. Fragrant, star-like, pure white flowers open from silky buds in late winter and early spring, before the leaves. It flowers when quite young. There are several cultivars in shades of pink, including 'Rosea'. 'Waterlily', the most prolific flowerer, has more petals than the species and slightly larger white flowers.
Height 10–15 ft (3–4.5 m). *Zone 5–9.*

Magnolia virginiana
Sweet bay
From eastern America, this evergreen to semi-evergreen tree reaches a height of 20 ft (6 m) in gardens. In cooler climates it may become deciduous. Fragrant, creamy white, goblet-shaped flowers are produced in summer and are followed by red fruit 2 in (5 cm) long with scarlet seeds. The leaves of this species are smaller than those of most other magnolias.
Height 20 ft (6 m). *Zone 5–10.*

MALUS

Crab-apple, apple

Native to the northern hemisphere, this diverse genus contains 25 deciduous shrubs and trees, valued for their flowers, foliage and fruit. Foliage ranges from bronze, hairy and wide-lobed to deep green, linear and neat, while the spring blossom varies in color from deep purple to pure white. The acidic fruit also varies widely, from edible kinds that can be eaten cooked, to purely ornamental crab-apples.

Cultivation

Fully hardy, the trees like full sun and cold weather and tolerate any soil that is not too wet. Propagate by budding in summer or grafting in winter.

Malus floribunda

Magnolia virginiana

Oxydendrum arboreum

Malus floribunda

Japanese flowering crab-apple, showy crab-apple

The early spring buds of this expansive, thick-crowned tree are crimson red, blooming into light pink blossoms. The variable foliage is oval to rectangular, some types with heavily saw-toothed edges and 3 to 5 lobes. Small, reddish yellow, scented crab-apples appear in autumn. The oldest of the decorative crab-apples, this tree is thought to originate in Japan.

Height 20 ft (6 m). *Zone 3–9.*

NYSSA SYLVATICA

Sour gum, pepperidge, black gum, tupelo

Native to North America and Asia, this striking deciduous species is valued for its autumn foliage, its timber and honey. Its shape is a wide-based pyramid. Large leaves are almost diamond shaped and mid to deep green, turning vivid red and yellow in autumn; although away from its native home the colors are not always reliable (in some years it just turns yellow). Little clusters of flowers, while inconspicuous, contribute to some of the finest honey in the world.

Cultivation

This species likes temperate, humid conditions and relishes waterlogged, slightly acid soil. Plant in full sun or partial shade and avoid transplanting. Propagate from seed in autumn, cuttings in summer.

Height 30 ft (9 m). *Zone 3–10.*

OXYDENDRUM ARBOREUM

This cool-climate species tolerates frost better than it does dry conditions. The trunk is slender and the crown pyramid-shaped. Streamers of small white lily-of-the-valley-like flowers appear in late summer sometimes prior to, sometimes coinciding with, the display of deep scarlet foliage.

Cultivation

For the best autumn colors, it should be planted in an open position in sun or part-shade in moist soil. An occasional dressing of iron and/or ammonia after flowering may be required. Propagate from cuttings in summer or seed in autumn.

Height 20–40 ft (6–12 m). *Zone 3–9.*

PARROTIA PERSICA

Persian witch-hazel, parrotia, ironwood

Originating in Iran, *P. persica* is a spreading, short-trunked deciduous species, with flaking bark. It is valued for its decorative autumn foliage, and often has pendent limbs. Upright spirals of wiry crimson stamens appear without petals on leafless branches in early spring, followed by glossy, oval foliage. The leaves have undulating margins and turn vivid red, yellow and orange in autumn.

Nyssa sylvatica

Pinus strobus

Parrotia persica

Cultivation

The tree is fully hardy, though frosts may damage buds, and prefers a cool climate. Plant in a protected location in deep, rich soil: it withstands lime but shows the best leaf colors in a neutral to acid soil. Propagate from seed in autumn, cuttings in summer.
Height 20 ft (6 m). *Zone 3–9.*

PINUS

Pine

This northern hemisphere genus comprises 80 variable evergreen conifers. Many species are conical when immature, their crowns expanding in later life. The leaves, cylindrical needles up to 18 in (45 cm) long, are erect when young and develop in clustered whorls of 2, 3 or 5, depending on the species. Upright yellow-red male catkins and female flowers appear on the same tree. The latter develop into scaled seed-bearing cones, borne singly or in bunches depending upon type of pine.

Cultivation

Preferred habitats range from cold high altitudes to subtropical coasts, some fully hardy species growing in difficult positions such as windswept cliffs. All enjoy full sun. Prune young trees' candle-like young shoots if necessary to control shape; propagate from seed or by grafting. Pine trees are prone to leafroller caterpillars. They are greatly valued for their softwood, oil and resin.

Pinus strobus

Eastern white pine, Weymouth pine

Occurring naturally in eastern North America, where it is valued for its timber, this species grows to 200 ft (60 m) in the wild but to less than 80 ft (24 m) in cultivation. It is characterized by deeply fissured, grayish brown bark and whorled branches. The conical crown becomes flattish with age. Its fine, 4 in (10 cm) long, bluish green needles are soft and are carried in groups of five. The pointed cones, clustered at the branch ends, produce copious amounts of white resin. This species develops rapidly if grown away from a polluted environment and, though cold hardy, it is susceptible to dry conditions and windburn.

Height 80 ft (24 m). *Zone 3–9.*

PITTOSPORUM

Mock orange, tarata

This predominantly Australasian genus, valued for its scented blooms and decorative leaves, contains 75 trees and shrubs. The trees have an attractive triangular habit or a domed crown appearance. Their flowers have a strong citrus scent and the attractive seed pods of some species contain their seeds in a sticky resin.

Cultivation

All species of *Pittosporum* prefer temperate to tropical climates. Some of them like dryish, well-drained soil; others prefer damp locations. They are simple to propagate, from seed in autumn and spring; mature cuttings in summer; and several species from semi-ripe cuttings in summer.

Pittosporum undulatum 'Sunburst'

Pittosporum undulatum

Sweet pittosporum, Australian daphne

This popular Australian species reaches 20–40 ft (6–12 m) tall with a wide dome. The dense green leaves are lance-shaped with scalloped edges. Profuse clusters of creamy white, bell-shaped flowers in spring are followed by yellow-brown fruit. Marginally frost hardy, it prefers moderate to warm climates. Watch for white scale and sooty mold. 'Sunburst' is a popular cultivar.

Height 20–40 ft (6–12 m). *Zone 9–11.*

PLATANUS

Plane tree, sycamore

This is a diverse deciduous genus of wide-crowned species. The scaly yellow, brown and white trunks are often buttressed or multiple; the lower branches are arching and gnarled. The wide, maple-like foliage consists of 5 lobes and ranges from light green to dark green. Insignificant flowers are followed in autumn by hanging bunches of large, spherical fruit.

Cultivation

Trees vary from fully hardy to frost-hardy, growing in climates from cold to warm-temperate. All like full sun. Some species prefer rich, well-drained soil; others like arid conditions. Propagate from cuttings, or from seed in autumn.

Platanus × *acerifolia*

syn. *P.* × *hybrida*, *P.* × *hispanica*

London plane

This popular hybrid, from Asia's *P. orientalis* and North America's *P. occidentalis*, is robust and fast growing, reaching up to 80 ft (24 m) with a wide, spreading crown. Shiny, pale green leaves with 3 to 5 lobes are 10 in (25 cm) wide. Little red flowers appear in pendent clusters, followed by paired spherical fruit. This tree is able to withstand extremes in temperature. *Height* 80 ft (24 m). *Zone 3–10.*

PODOCARPUS

Fern pine, yellow-wood

This diverse ornamental genus of evergreen conifers for cool to warm-

Platanus × *acerifolia*

Podocarpus macrophyllus 'Maki'

temperate climates is native to Australia, New Zealand, South America and South Africa. Species vary from low and spreading to slender and erect. The dense foliage consists of very narrow leaves, long or short according to species. The spherical fruit, more like berries than cones, are borne individually on short stems (*Podocarpus* means 'footed stalk').

Cultivation

These trees like warm conditions, full sun or partial shade and grow in a range of soils from rich to poor. Propagate from seed or cuttings.

Podocarpus macrophyllus

Kusamaki, Buddhist pine, yew pine

From the mountains of Japan and China, where it grows to 70 ft (21 m) tall with a spread of 12 ft (3.5 m), this cold-tolerant species prefers moist, rich soil. It has long, thick, dark green leaves up to 6 in (15 cm) long and responds well to pruning, making a good thick hedge. It is often grown in Japanese temple gardens and is also a suitable container plant. The berries are small and black. 'Maki', rarely bigger than a shrub, has a distinctly erect habit with almost vertical branches.

Height 70 ft (21 m). *Zone 7–11.*

PRUNUS

Cherry, peach, plum

This large genus contains over 200 evergreen or deciduous shrubs and trees and thousands of cultivars. They are grown either for their fruit or for their ornamental foliage, flowers and bark. Their shape is often inversely conical. Members of the Rosaceae family, they bear sweetly scented single or double rose-like flowers with 5 petals ranging from white to scarlet.

Cultivation

All species are fully hardy and thrive in most well-drained soils. The evergreens like partial shade; prune in spring and propagate from cuttings in summer and autumn. Useful for hedges, deciduous types prefer full sun; prune after flowering and propagate from seed in autumn or cuttings in winter. Bud or graft cultivars in spring and autumn.

Prunus mume

Japanese apricot

This small deciduous tree comes from China, Korea and Japan. The species has white or pink blooms, but double-flowered cultivars in white or light or deep pink are popular, as is the semi-double 'Geisha'. This is the 'plum blossom' which is such a favorite subject with Chinese and Japanese painters because it flowers while snow is still on the ground. It is fast growing, and trees have gnarled trunks and branches. Frost-hardy, this species prefers climates that are cool temperate. *Height* 16 ft (5 m). *Zone 5–9.*

Prunus sargentii

Sargent cherry

This flowering cherry species is native to Japan, Korea and eastern Siberia, and is one of the tallest of the Japanese flowering cherry group, growing to as much as 80 ft (24 m), with dark chest-nut-colored bark. In mid-spring the

Prunus sargentii

Prunus mume 'Geisha'

Prunus serrulata cultivar

branches are covered with pink flowers with deeper pink stamens, accompanied by the unfolding leaves which are long-pointed and up to 5 in (12 cm) in length; in autumn they make a brilliant display of reddish bronze, turning orange and red. This species performs best away from polluted environments.
Height 80 ft (24 m). *Zone 4–9.*

Prunus serrulata
Japanese flowering cherry
Originating in east Asia, this deciduous species is the parent of many cultivars. It grows quickly, with a dome shape and spreading habit. Its scaly bark is a glossy reddish brown. The finely toothed glossy leaves turn from deep green to orange and yellow in autumn. Long-stemmed terminal clusters of white unscented flowers appear in spring. Many cultivars exist. It prefers cooler climates. Avoid pruning where possible as trees develop a naturally shapely habit.
Height 30 ft (9 m). *Zone 4–9.*

Prunus × *yedoensis* 'Shidare-Yoshino'

Prunus subhirtella 'Pendula'
Higan cherry, rosebud cherry
This deciduous spreading tree has a wide crown and arching branches. It develops sharply elliptical, serrated deep green leaves which turn yellow in autumn. Light pink flowers, predominantly single with 5 petals, appear from winter to early spring before the foliage. These are followed by little spherical brown-red fruit. This cultivar prefers cooler climates, while 'Autumnalis' is more reliably winter flowering.
Height 10 ft (3 m). *Zone 4.*

Prunus × _yedoensis_
Tokyo cherry
This Japanese hybrid is an elegant, fully hardy deciduous tree. It has a convex crown and pendent limbs. White or light pink flowers with an almond fragrance open in early spring, preceding the deep green foliage. This tree prefers a cooler climate with full sun and well-drained soil. 'Shidare-Yoshino' has a weeping

Prunus subhirtella 'Pendula'

Pyrus calleryana

habit and white flowers that appear in early spring.
Height 10 ft (3 m). *Zone 6.*

PYRUS

Pear

This genus contains deciduous species native to Europe, Asia and Africa. They are valued for their foliage, flowers and edible fruit. Foliage is diverse, from ovate and hairy to linear and smooth, and in many species assumes brilliant color in autumn. White flowers are followed by plump fruit in various shades of brown, yellow and green.

Cultivation

Species range from fully hardy to half-hardy and enjoy well-drained soil with full sun. Propagate these long-lived trees from seed in autumn; bud cultivars in summer, graft in winter.

Pyrus calleryana

Callery pear

Grown as an ornamental, this shapely semi-evergreen tree from China bears showy clusters of white flowers, which appear in early spring and are often followed by small, brown, inedible fruit. The grayish green, 3 in (8 cm) long

Quercus robur

leaves stay on the tree until late autumn, when they turn shades of rich purplish claret, red, orange or yellow. Tolerating heat, dry conditions, wind and poor soil, it makes an ideal street tree. It is resistant to fire blight but is not very long lived. 'Bradford' is a common cultivar that flowers profusely and grows well in poor conditions.
Height 60 ft (18 m). *Zone 5–9.*

QUERCUS

Oak

This extremely diverse genus contains some 450 species of evergreen or deciduous trees and shrubs, mostly native to the northern hemisphere. They range from small and shrubby to very tall and erect. Foliage varies from wide, multi-lobed and leathery to lustrous, thin and papery. All species bear acorns inside woody pods, which also differ from species to species: slender and sharp or stubby and flat; sleek-shelled or downy and rough. They are excellent shade trees for parks and large gardens.

Cultivation

Oaks prefer cooler weather and deep, damp, well-drained soil. Some like alkaline soils and full sun; others like semi-shade. Propagate from seed in autumn. Guard against oak-leaf miner.

Quercus robur

English oak, common oak

As a symbol of Britain, the English oak was widely planted throughout the British Empire. This fully hardy species grows quickly, with an expansive crown and large, heavy branches. The leaves, inverted ovals with 6 to 12 serrations and 2 small auxiliary wing teeth, turn from deep green to golden brown in autumn. Egg-shaped acorns are one-third covered by their cup and develop in small bunches on the slender stems.
Height 100 ft (30 m). *Zone 3–10.*

Robinia pseudoacacia 'Frisia'

ROBINIA

Black locust

This deciduous genus contains 20 species of trees and shrubs, native to North America but now common worldwide. They have a rounded shape and spreading habit. The scented flowers and fruit are typical of the Leguminoseae family, the peas resembling those of the locust tree (hence the common name). The species will survive in a broad range of temperatures and soils but dislikes saturated soil.

Cultivation

Plant in full sun and protect the fragile limbs from strong winds. Propagate from seed and suckers in autumn, cultivars by grafting.

***Robinia pseudoacacia* 'Frisia'**

This expansive deciduous cultivar is thornless and grows 30 ft (9 m) wide. Its feather-like foliage has rounded leaflets and changes from gold in spring to yellowish orange in autumn. Plant this fully hardy tree in well-drained soil with full sun.

Height 30 ft (9 m). *Zone 3–10.*

SALIX

Willow, osier

Originating in the northern hemisphere, these 250 deciduous species of trees and shrubs have convex crowns, rough, twisted trunks and weeping branches. Excellent shade trees, their narrow, tassel-like foliage often drapes along the ground. Pendent male and female catkins usually develop on different trees and may be either slender and soft or thick and leathery.

Cultivation

Trees vary from fully to frost-hardy and love waterside locations, where eroded banks benefit from their strong suckering habit. They will grow in all except very dry soils and require full sun, or partial shade in hot regions. Prune every two years; propagate from cuttings in summer and winter. Watch for caterpillars, gall mites and aphids.

Salix alba var. *sericea*

Salix alba

White willow

A very adaptable tree from Europe, northern Africa and central Asia, this species has erect branches, which weep somewhat at the tips and are clothed with 3 in (8 cm) long, narrow leaves that are bright green above with flattened silky hairs on the undersides. The white willow makes a good windbreak tree, albeit with invasive roots. 'Britzensis' (syn. 'Chermesina') has bright red stems; 'Chrysostela' has yellow shoots tipped with orange; *Salix alba* var. *caerulea* has blue-green leaves and is the willow from which cricket bats are made; *S. a.* var. *sericea* has silvery foliage; and 'Vitellina', the golden willow, has young growth of a brilliant clear yellow.

Height 80 ft (24 m). *Zone 2–10.*

Salix babylonica

Salix babylonica
Weeping willow, Napoleon's willow
This very attractive, popular tree is native to China. It has a broad dome and erect branches that support distinctively arching branchlets. The light green lanceolate leaves, brushing the ground, are slender and thinly lobed. This temperate species will grow in most conditions if planted by waterways. *Height* 40 ft (12 m). *Zone 4–10.*

SEQUOIADENDRON GIGANTEUM

syn. *Sequoia gigantea, Wellingtonia gigantea*
Big tree, mammoth tree, wellingtonia
This long-living evergreen conifer, native to Sierra Nevada, has an attractive triangular shape and the broadest trunk of all known trees. Like its redwood relative, this vigorous tree grows taller in the wild. Its bluish green needles mature to brown and drape along the ground during its first 50 years, after which it develops no new lower branches. This is one of the largest and longest lived of all trees; one specimen has been recorded as 3000 years old.

Sequoiadendron giganteum

Cultivation
These trees like cool climates, full sun and damp soil. Propagate from seed. *Height* 270 ft (80 m). *Zone 6–9.*

SOPHORA

This diverse and widespread genus belongs to the Leguminoseae (pea) family and contains semi-evergreen and deciduous species. They have thick fern-like foliage with differing numbers of oval leaflets. The pea-like flowers hang in thick terminal clusters during summer, generally in shades of white and yellow.

Cultivation
Plant in rich porous soil with full sun. Pruning is tolerated. Propagate deciduous species from seed or cuttings in autumn; semi-evergreens from softwood cuttings in summer.

Sophora japonica
Pagoda tree, scholar tree
Native to Japan, China and Korea, this deciduous species grows 20–50 ft (6–15 m) wide. Its round crown is composed of deep green foliage with up to 16 oval leaflets. Older trees bear big, open clusters of little yellowish white pea-like flowers in late summer, followed by green elliptical seed pods. This fully hardy species enjoys hot summers. The leaves of *S. japonica* are believed to have special medicinal qualities.
Height 25 ft (8 m) or more. *Zone 4–10.*

SORBUS

This genus, a member of the Rosaceae family, has semi-evergreen and deciduous species native to Europe, North America and temperate Asia. Shrubs or trees are valued for their foliage, timber and edible fruit. Leaves vary from green to plain deep purplish red, the deciduous species displaying intense autumn colors. Little, white 5-petalled flowers appear in spring, followed in summer by enduring pendent bunches of berries.

Cultivation

These cool-climate trees range from frost-hardy to frost-tender, preferring full sun or partial shade and rich, moisture-retentive soil. Propagate by grafting in winter, from buds and cuttings in summer or seed in autumn. Susceptible to fireblight. Some species' edible fruit is used to make cider.

Sorbus americana
American mountain ash
This is a vigorous tree with ascending reddish branches and red sticky buds. The pinnate leaves are bright green, turning bright golden yellow in autumn. Large dense bunches of small red berries follow. It comes from eastern North America.
Height 30 ft (9 m). *Zone 3–9.*

Sorbus aucuparia

Sophora japonica

Sorbus aucuparia
Rowan, mountain ash, quickbeam
Originating in Europe and Asia, this erect broad-crowned tree grows 20–40 ft (6–12 m) tall and is valued for its flowers, foliage and edible fruit. These

Stewartia pseudocamellia

Stryrax japonicus

green pinnate leaves comprise up to 15 leaflets and change to yellowish red in autumn. Big dense sprays of white spring blossoms are followed by a profusion of elliptical orange-red summer berries, turning golden yellow in autumn. The fruit is used to make Rowan jelly. This deciduous species is suited to most climates and should not be replanted until of considerable size. The cultivar 'Beissneri' has attractive greenish gold foliage.
Height 20 ft (6 m) or more. *Zone 2–9.*

STEWARTIA PSEUDOCAMELLIA

syn. *Stuartia pseudocamellia*

False camellia, Japanese stewartia

Indigenous to Japan (not Hokkaido) and Korea, this species can grow to 70 ft (21 m) high in the wild but is more commonly about 20 ft (6 m) in cultivation. It blooms from late spring to early summer and the white flowers are followed by small, spherical, nut-like seed capsules that are a prominent feature from mid-summer. It has attractive peeling bark and yellow, orange and red autumn foliage. *Stewartia pseudocamellia* var. *koreana* (syn. *Stewartia koreana)* hardly differs from the typical Japanese plants, the main distinction being that the petals spread more widely instead of being cupped and the leaves are broader and less silky when young.

Cultivation

This tree grows best in moist, humus-rich, well-drained, slightly acidic soil in sun or part-shade. Propagate from seed in autumn or from cuttings in summer.
Height 20 ft (6 m). *Zone 6–10.*

STYRAX JAPONICUS

Japanese snowbell, Japanese snowdrop tree

This species is a native of Japan, Korea and China. It flowers from mid-spring. Its branches, which are clothed with rather narrow, deep green shiny leaves, are held horizontally, creating a tiered effect. It prefers shade.

Cultivation
They prefer cool, moist, well-drained soil and cool, moist, summer climates. Usually raised from stratified seed in autumn, they can be grown from cuttings in summer. *Height* 25 ft (8 m). *Zone 6–9.*

TAXUS BACCATA

Yew
This long-living evergreen conifer originates in Europe, Africa and Asia. Its irregular conical shape becomes level-crowned in maturity. Its slender needles are deep green with a greenish yellow underside and develop in typical whorls. Small pollen-rich bunches of male flowers and green globular female flowers develop on separate trees. Unusually, this conifer has no cones; the female flower develops instead into an individual seed partly enclosed in a fleshy red case.

Cultivation
This frost-hardy tree likes full sun. It is greatly favored for hedging and topiary. It propagates simply from seed and cuttings in spring and is prone to scale insects. 'Fastigiata' is an upright cultivar. *Height* 16 ft (5 m). *Zone 4–9.*

Taxus baccata 'Fastigiata'

THUJA

Arborvitae
This small genus comprises 5 species of evergreen conifers, native to North America or Asia. They have heavily grooved trunks and flat compound foliage. Woody green seed-bearing cones of varying size mature to brown before releasing their seeds.

Cultivation
They will grow in most soils but prefer moderate climates and full sun. Propagate from seed or cuttings. Several species are among the world's most valuable softwood timber trees.

Thuja plicata
Western red cedar, giant arborvitae, western arborvitae
Native to an area spreading from California to Alaska, this species grows quickly. Triangular to columnar,

Thuja plicata 'Zebrina'

it has brownish red, scaly bark and upstretched limbs. Sprays of shiny green scales, backed with silver, hang from their extremities. Its very small, erect cones open like flowers to disperse their seeds. It is frost-hardy. 'Zebrina', one of many cultivars, has green foliage, which is attractively banded with gold.
Height 70 ft (21 m) or more. *Zone 5–9.*

TILIA 'PETIOLARIS'

syn. *Tilia petiolaris*

Weeping silver linden, pendent silver lime, weeping lime

Possibly no more than a form of *Tilia tomentosa*, this weeping tree has a spreading, conical form which expands with age. The pointed, cordate leaves are 2–4 in (5–10 cm) long, deep green on top and silver-felted underneath. Creamy yellow flowers bloom in terminal clusters and are followed by bumpy, nut-like seed pods.

Tilia 'Petiolaris'

Cultivation

Very frost hardy, it does best in cool climates and prefers full sun, neutral, well-drained soil and plenty of water in dry periods. Even quite large trees can be readily transplanted during their winter dormancy. Propagate from seed in autumn, from cuttings or by layering; selected forms and hybrids can be grafted in late summer.
Height 60–80 ft (18–24 m). *Zone 5–9.*

TSUGA CANADENSIS

Eastern hemlock, Canadian hemlock

From the cool northeast of North America, this slow-growing tree forms a broad pyramidal crown, and the thin branches have pendulous tips. The short, oblong needles are arranged in 2 rows and are grayish brown and hairy when young, maturing to dark green with 2 grayish bands on the undersides. Oval cones 1 in (25 mm) long are borne at the ends of the branchlets and disperse their seeds in autumn. 'Pendula' forms a semi-prostrate mound to 6 ft (1.8 m) tall and wide; its lime-green juvenile foliage becomes grayish green with age.

Cultivation

This frost-hardy tree tolerates shade and thrives in slightly acid, deep, well-drained soil containing plenty of organic matter. It does not enjoy urban environments or very exposed positions, and dislikes being transplanted. Propagate from seed in spring or cuttings in fall.
Height 80 ft (24 m). *Zone 2–9.*

ULMUS

Elm

This genus contains over 15 fully hardy species of deciduous trees and shrubs native to Asia, Europe and North America. The elliptical foliage of the majestic, round-crowned trees varies:

from slender, deep green and shiny to broad, mid-green and roughly textured; heavily or finely serrated; with or without prominent parallel ribs. Inconspicuous flowers with reddish stalks but no petals appear in early spring. Thick clusters of greenish white pods, containing single winged seeds, develop at the ends of branches in summer.

Cultivation
Plant these moderate-climate trees in rich, well-drained soil with full sun. Propagate from seed or cuttings or by grafting the numerous suckers. Many of England's finest specimens were destroyed by Dutch elm disease.

Ulmus parvifolia
Chinese elm, lacebark elm
Native to China and Japan, this elm has a spreading, sinuous habit and bark mottled with dark gray, reddish brown and cream. It is semi-evergreen in mild climates. The small, leathery, dark green leaves, smooth and shiny on top, have small, blunt teeth. The fruit mature in autumn. It is relatively resistant to Dutch elm disease. 'Frosty' is a shrubby, slow-growing form with small, neatly arranged leaves bearing white teeth.
Height 60 ft (18 m). *Zone 5–10.*

Zelkova serrata

ZELKOVA SERRATA
Japanese zelkova
This ornamental tree from Japan, Korea and Taiwan grows to a height of 80 ft (24 m) or more with a wide, spreading crown. It has smooth bark dappled gray and brown and new shoots are tinged purple. The pointed, oblong, sharply serrated leaves are light green and slightly hairy above, with shiny undersides. The foliage turns golden yellow to rusty brown in autumn. Cultivars include 'Village Green', and 'Green Vase' growing to 40 ft (12 m) tall in a graceful vase shape.

Cultivation
Although frost hardy, it prefers some shelter. It needs full sun and deep, fertile, well-drained soil and plenty of water during summer. Propagate from seed or root cuttings in autumn, or by grafting.
Height 80 ft (24 m). *Zone 3–10.*

Ulmus parvifolia

BULBS, CORMS & TUBERS

The history of bulbs and how they came to western Europe to be hybridized into the plants we grow today is fascinating. Most of the bulbs we think of as being indigenous to Europe can be traced back to their native habitat much further east in the mountainous regions of Asia Minor, while others were gathered initially from southern Africa. In horticultural terms, the word 'bulb' includes true bulbs (onions), corms (gladiolus and freesias) and tubers (dahlias and potatoes). As bulbs have differing flowering times, there is no limit to the type and number which can be included in the garden to provide for almost year-round color.

Allium christophii

Allium moly

ALLIUM

Garlic and onions belong to this large genus of over 700 species, native to Asia, Africa and America. There are many very attractive ornamental species as well as edible ones. Many species have a pungent onion or garlic scent but this is usually only noticeable when parts of the plant are bruised or crushed. They vary greatly in size: from 2 in (4–5 cm) to 3 ft (1 m) high. Smaller species are ideal in a rock garden.

Cultivation

Most are frost-hardy and easy to grow; some are so vigorous they can become difficult to control. Plant bulbs in autumn in well-drained soil, 2–4 in (4–10 cm) deep, depending on the size of the bulb. Propagate from offsets, which multiply freely, or from seed.

Flowering time Late spring–early autumn.
Zone 5–9.

Allium christophii

syn. *A. albopilosum*

This attractive, hardy species grows up to 24 in (60 cm) high. The broad leaves are green and shiny on top and white beneath. The sturdy stem bears a rounded umbel of flowers up to 12 in (30 cm) wide. The individual violet flowers borne in spring are star-shaped. They turn black as the seeds ripen and are very useful for dried flower arrangements. Bulbs should be planted in autumn 2½ in (6 cm) deep in well-drained soil. *A. christophii* grows best in full sun. Propagate by dividing offsets.

Allium moly
Golden garlic

Native to Spain, *A. moly* grows up to 15 in (38 cm). Broad, gray-green basal leaves surround stems which each bear an umbel of up to 40 flowers. The bright yellow, star-shaped flowers appear in summer. It is very hardy and can be planted in full sun or partial shade. Bulbs or seeds should be planted in autumn in well-drained soil. Propagate by division of bulbs. The Spanish once regarded this plant as a sign of prosperity if they discovered it in their gardens.

ALSTROEMERIA LIGTU HYBRIDS

These tuberous perennials from South Africa have colored flowers in shades of yellow, orange, salmon and pink, often streaked or spotted with another color. They make excellent cut flowers, reaching a height of 30 in (75 cm) and are borne in profusion over many months. They vary from other species of

Anemone coronaria 'St. Brigid'

Alstroemeria Ligtu hybrid

Alstroemeria in that their leaves are twisted and narrow and their flowers are more flared.

Cultivation

Plants will grow and flower well in sun or dappled shade when planted in well drained, friable soil. They are frost hardy but in really cold areas the dormant tubers can be protected by a thick mulch. Propagated by division or from seed, they will naturalize when conditions are to their liking.
Flowering time Spring–summer.
Zone 6–8.

ANEMONE

Windflower

This highly varied genus is mainly native to southern Europe and the Middle East. Size and flower color vary greatly, as do flowering times; the planting of tubers can be staggered to provide a succession of glorious blooms.

Cultivation

Most species are fairly hardy and do well in rich, well-drained soil in a sunny or lightly shaded situation. Take care that those planted from the tubers, such as *A. coronaria*, are not upside down. Grow from seed planted in summer, being careful to protect the seedlings from hot sun. Plant new tubers each year for best results, as they become weakened after blooming.
Flowering time Late winter–spring.
Zone 6–9.

Anemone blanda

Anemone blanda

Wood anemone

This delicate-looking species is frost-hardy. Native to Greece, it grows to 8 in (20 cm) with green, oval, toothed leaves. The star-shaped flowers which appear in spring can be white, pink or blue and are about 1½ in (35 mm) wide. *A. blanda* self-seeds freely and, given moist, slightly shaded conditions, should spread into a beautiful display of flowers.

Anemone coronaria

Wind poppy

Many hybrids have evolved from this fully hardy species, the most commonly planted anemone. It grows up to 10 in (25 cm). The poppy-like flowers are up to 4 in (10 cm) wide and can range in color from red to purple to blue. *A. coronaria* is usually treated as an annual. 'De Caen' is a single and 'St. Brigid' is a popular semi-double, with colors ranging from pink to purple to scarlet to blue. Excellent as a cut flower.

Canna × *generalis* 'Alfred Cole'

BEGONIA, TUBERHYBRIDA GROUP

These are the well-known tuberous begonias, sold in full bloom by florists and in an earlier era displayed in public conservatories designed especially for their needs. Their glorious large blooms come in almost every color of the rainbow except blues, as singles or doubles, with many variations of frills and ruffles. These beautiful hybrids are derived from a number of species native to the Andean region of South America. The tubers sprout in mid-spring, producing weak, brittle stems up to about 24 in (60 cm) long with rather sparse, mid-green leaves. The summer flowers can weigh down the stems, which may need staking. After flowering, plants enter their dormant stage and the tubers are normally lifted in mid-autumn and stored dry. 'Mandy Henschke' has a multiplicity of petals developed only in the male flower. The biggest flowers are obtained by removing buds, and sacrificing the smaller single female flowers that grow on either side of the central male.

Begonia, Tuberhybrida Group 'Mandy Henschke'

Cultivation

Tuberous begonias require special treatment: tubers must be forced into growth in early spring at a temperature of 65°F (18°C) in peat moss or sphagnum, and kept in a cool, well-ventilated greenhouse for the summer flowering season. After flowering, plants die back and tubers are lifted in mid-autumn and stored dry. Propagate from tubers. Begonias are susceptible to gray mold, powdery mildew and botrytis in the warmer part of the year if conditions are too damp. *Flowering time* Summer. *Zone 9–11.*

CANNA × GENERALIS

These hardy plants are invaluable for bold displays of both foliage and flowers. The wide, strap leaves emerge from a central base and are topped with flowers in many shades rainging from cream through yellows to bright orange and pale to deep pinks. Foliage can be green, bronze or red depending on the cultivar. 'Alfred Cole' is a vigorous, compact plant to 3 ft (1 m) tall with bronze foliage and showy flowers.

Cultivation

These thirsty plants require a fertile, moist soil in a sunny position with ample mulch to retain soil moisture. Rhizomes should be divided every couple of years to retain plant vigor and plants can be increased in this way during spring. *Flowering time* Spring–summer. *Zone 6–9.*

CLIVIA

Bush lily, fire lily

These South African natives produce a glorious display of funnel-shaped flowers in spring or summer. They are quite easy to grow in all but frost-prone areas. Plant in a sheltered position in rich, well-drained soil. Keep fairly dry in winter and increase watering in spring and summer.

Cultivation

Propagate by division after flowering. Seed can also be used but this can be slow to flower. In cooler areas they can be grown in pots; they flower best when quite potbound.
Flowering time Spring–summer.
Zone 8–9.

Clivia miniata

Fire lily, bush lily

This showy species grows up to 18 in (45 cm). A cluster of up to 12 funnel-shaped flowers appear in spring. The 3 in (8 cm) flowers are orange-red, paler at the throat. The foliage is glossy, thick and strap-like. It does well in a shaded area. Hybrids of *C. miniata* in yellow and cream are becoming more available.

COLCHICUM

Autumn crocus

This genus of flowering corms is native mainly to Europe and Asia. Masses of crocus-like flowers appear in autumn

Clivia miniata

Colchicum autumnale

Convallaria majalis

followed by the strap-like basal foliage. Frost-hardy, they are very easy to grow. However, they are not suitable for very hot areas.

Cultivation

Plant the corms in late summer in well-drained soil in sun or partial shade. Corms will also usually flower without any soil, so they can be kept inside for display and planted after flowering. Propagate from seed or by division in summer. The plants are poisonous, although their active ingredient, colchicine, is used in the treatment of certain forms of cancer.

Flowering time Autumn. *Zone 6–8.*

Colchicum autumnale

The best known of the species, *Colchicum autumnale* grows to 6 in (15 cm) and has rosy pink to white, goblet-shaped flowers up to 4 in (10 cm) long. Each corm produces masses of flowers and multiplies freely. There is also a double-flowered form.

CONVALLARIA MAJALIS

Lily-of-the-valley

Renowned for its glorious perfume, this beautiful plant is native to the northern hemisphere, and does best in cool climates. It is low-growing, up to 8 in (20 cm), with thick, oval to oblong, dark green leaves. The dainty, white, bell-shaped flowers appear in spring.

Cultivation

The rhizomes, or 'pips' as they are commonly known, should be planted in autumn in a partially shaded position in a cool or cold area. Soil should be rich and moist, and a dressing of mulch will give good results. Water well during the growing period. Given the right conditions, *C. majalis* spreads freely, sometimes becoming overcrowded, when it will need to be divided.

Flowering time Spring. *Zone 6–9.*

CROCOSMIA

Montbretia

These half- to fully hardy South African natives bear attractive displays of flowers in summer. Tall, pleated leaves form a fan of foliage, somewhat similar to a gladiolus. A branched spike of brightly colored flowers sits proudly atop the tall stem.

Cultivation
Plant the corms in winter in rich soil with adequate drainage in a position which receives morning sun. Water well through summer. They will multiply freely and should not be divided unless overcrowded. This should be done in spring if necessary.
Flowering time Summer. *Zone 7–9.*

***Crocosmia* 'Lucifer'**
This striking cultivar bears a tall flowering stem to 4 ft (1.2 m) topped with sprays of large, flame red flowers. They make excellent cut flowers.

Crocosmia 'Lucifer'

CROCUS
Crocus
Crocuses herald the beginning of spring in Europe and North America. The lovely goblet-shaped flowers vary greatly in color. The foliage is grass-like, with a silver-white stripe along the center of the leaf.

Cultivation
Fully hardy, they do best in a cool to cold area. In warm areas the corms may flower in the first season but may not flower again. They can be grown in pots in warmer areas, in a cool spot. Corms should be planted in early autumn in moist, well-drained soil in full sun or partial shade. Keep well watered until the foliage begins to die. They do not spread very fast but clumps can be divided if they are overcrowded. Seed can be planted in autumn, but plants grown from seed usually will not flower for three years.
Flowering time Winter–spring. *Zone 6–8.*

Crocus Dutch hybrid

***Crocus*, Dutch hybrids**
The Dutch hybrids are vigorous plants with large flowers up to 6 in (15 cm) long. The color range is varied, white to yellow to purple to blue. There are also some striped varieties. Many of these hybrids derive from *C. vernus*. They should be planted in autumn in well-drained soil at a depth of about 4 in (10 cm).

Crocus tomasinianus
This crocus grows to 4 in (10 cm) and has lavender to purple, sometimes white-throated, goblet-shaped flowers. One of the more easily grown species, it does well in a rock garden, or naturalized under deciduous trees. There is also a purple-maroon form.

Crocus tomasinianus

Cyclamen hederifolium

CYCLAMEN

Cyclamen

The flower of the cyclamen must be one of the most elegant of all plants. These winter-flowering natives of the Mediterranean region are often used in pots indoors but can also be grown in the garden. Florist's cyclamen (*C. persicum*) is usually bought already in flower for an indoor display. Keep it in good light but out of direct sun in an unheated room. It is frost-tender, although the other species are rated frost- to fully hardy.

Cultivation

Plant tubers in light, fibrous soil, rich in organic matter with excellent drainage in partial shade. Water regularly during growth but allow to dry out during summer. The tubers are best left undisturbed and should grow larger each year, flowering more abundantly each season. Propagate from seed in autumn. Plants should flower in a year.
Flowering time Autumn–winter.
Zone 8–9.

Cyclamen hederifolium
syn. *C. neapolitanum*
This autumn-flowering species can produce corms up to 6 in (15 cm) wide. Growing to 4 in (10 cm), it has dark green, marbled, ivy-shaped foliage. The flowers are white to rose-pink, darker at the base and some strains are perfumed.

DAHLIA × HORTENSIS 'BISHOP OF LLANDAFF'
The parents of modern dahlias were tubers brought back from South America to be used as a food source. As these proved to be too bitter for European tastes, hybridization for flowers began. The bronze foliage of this hybrid is in itself an asset in garden color scheming and when flowering the combination of the red and bronze makes a striking accent.

Cultivation
Dahlias do best in an open sunny position in rich, well-drained soil. They are heavy feeders so fertilize the position well and plant tubers about 4 in (10 cm) deep in early spring. To increase flowering, trim growing tips to encourage bushiness and dead-head spent flowers regularly to prolong the display. *Flowering time* Late summer–autumn. *Zone 6–9.*

FREESIA
Freesia
These South African natives are extensively grown for their brightly colored and deliciously scented spring flowers. They are rather tender but easily grown in most areas except those that suffer heavy frost. Slender, sword-shaped leaves surround wiry stems which bear spikes of goblet-shaped flowers. The weight of the flowers can be too much for the stems so they may need to be supported by twigs or wire.

Cultivation
Plant the corms in autumn in full sun in well-drained soil. Water well through the growing season but allow to dry out after flowering. The clumps are best left undisturbed for three years; they can then be divided in autumn. Seed should be sown in late summer. In cold climates, they grow well in pots in a greenhouse. *Flowering time* Spring. *Zone 7–9.*

***Freesia* Bergunden strain**
One of the newer hybrids, the Bergunden strain offers the gardener

Freesia Bergunden strain hybrids

Dahlia × hortensis 'Bishop of Llandaff'

Fritillaria imperialis 'Lutea'

a collection of richly colored, scented flowers in rose, white, blue, yellow and red, all of which feature lighter colored centers. Their sturdy stems, up to 18 in (45 cm) long, carry masses of long lasting blooms which make ideal cut flowers.

FRITILLARIA IMPERIALIS

Crown imperial

Native to Turkey, Iran, Afghanistan and Kashmir, this is the tallest of the species and the easiest to grow. The leafy stems up to 5 ft (1.5 m) high bear whorls of lance-shaped pale green leaves. Pendent clusters of up to 8 yellow, orange or red bell-shaped flowers appear in late spring and early summer. The flowers have an unpleasant odor. The popular garden form 'Lutea' bears bright yellow flowers.

Cultivation

Mostly quite frost hardy, they do best in areas with cold winters. Plant bulbs in early autumn in part-shade in rich, organic, well-drained soil. Water well through the growing season but allow to

Gladiolus, Grandiflorus Group 'Red Majesty'

Hippeastrum 'Cocktail'

dry out after flowering. In areas with high summer rainfall, lift bulbs gently and keep them out of the ground for as short a time as possible. Propagate from offsets in summer, but do not disturb clumps for a few years. Seed can be sown in fall but will take 4 to 5 years to bloom.
Flowering time Late spring–early summer. *Zone 4–9.*

GLADIOLUS, GRANDIFLORUS GROUP

These very large-flowering hybrids produce long, densely packed spikes of broadly funnel-shaped flowers in summer. The sometimes ruffled flowers are arranged in alternating fashion mostly on one side of a 3–5 ft (1–1.5 m) stem. They are regarded as too demanding for normal garden use, in terms of pest and disease control, as well as requiring support to keep upright. They are therefore grown mainly for exhibition or as commercial cut flowers. 'Red Majesty' has lightly ruffled red flowers.

Cultivation

Plant corms about 4 in (10 cm) deep in well-drained, sandy soil in a sunny position. In cool areas plant in early spring; in warm areas plant from autumn. Water well in summer and cut off spent flower stems. Tall stems may need staking. When picking for indoors, cut when the lower flowers open. Lift corms over winter in cold climates; lift large-flowered corms in all areas, especially those with high winter rainfall; store when perfectly dry. Propagate from seed or cormlets in spring.
Flowering time Summer. *Zone 7–10.*

HIPPEASTRUM 'COCKTAIL'

Amaryllis, Barbados lily

This spectacular trumpet-shaped tropical lily, indigenous to South America, is cultivated virtually everywhere as a potted plant. There are more than 80 species but it is the intensely developed hybrids that are most often grown. These have been bred mainly by the Dutch and are known as Dutch Hybrids; they include 'Apple Blossom' and 'Cocktail'. The flowers can be up to 12 in (30 cm) across and are borne, before the leaves develop, in clusters of 3 or 4 atop a large hollow stem. Colors include white, pink, red and pink, and red streaked with white. Hippeastrums normally flower at the end of spring, but in the northern hemisphere potted plants can be coaxed into flowering out of season to make colorful Christmas decorations. They generally grow to 24 in (60 cm) high and 12 in (30 cm) wide.

Cultivation

Hippeastrums grow outdoors in a frost-free, warm climate. Bulbs should be planted in autumn in well-drained soil rich in organic matter, with just the tip of the bulb exposed, in full sun or part-shade. Water and feed well through the growing season and allow the bulb to dry after the foliage dies down. Protect from snails.
Flowering time Late spring. *Zone 10–11.*

Iris Dutch Hybrid 'Blue Magic'

Hyacinthus orientalis

HYACINTHUS ORIENTALIS

Hyacinth

Popular with gardeners all over the world, the popular named varieties of hyacinth are cultivars of *H. orientalis* which originally comes from the Middle East and Mediterranean region. A spike of flowers is massed on top of a 12 in (30 cm) stem. The sweetly perfumed flowers vary enormously in color. 'King of the Blues' is a favorite, but many others are available in white, pale yellow, pink, red or purple. The glossy green foliage is strap-like.

Cultivation

Plant the bulbs in clumps in autumn in rich, well-drained soil in full sun or partial shade. Frost-hardy, hyacinths do best in cool areas, as well as in pots. It is best to buy new bulbs each year, as the flowers are never as magnificent as in that first spring; but, planted in a congenial spot, they will continue to bloom each spring for years.
Flowering time Spring. *Zone 6–9.*

IRIS

This wide-ranging genus of more than 200 species, native to the temperate regions of the northern hemisphere, is named for the Greek goddess of the rainbow and is valued for its beautiful and distinctive flowers. Each flower has 6 petals: 3 outer petals, called 'falls', which droop away from the center and alternate with the inner petals, called 'standards'. There are many hybrids. Irises are divided into 2 main groups, rhizomatous and bulbous.

Cultivation

Growing conditions vary greatly; however, as a rule rhizomatous irises are very frost hardy and prefer a sunny position; some of the beardless types like very moist soil. Bulbous irises are very

frost hardy, and prefer a sunny position with ample moisture during growth, but very little during their summer dormancy; plant in autumn. Bulbous irises are prone to virus infection and need to be kept free of aphids. Propagate irises by division in late summer after flowering, or from seed in fall.
Flowering time Spring–early summer.
Zone 3–9.

Iris, Dutch Hybrids

These bulbous irises of the Xiphium group derive their purity of color from the northern African *Iris tingitana;* their other main parent, *I. xiphium,* tends towards purple. They do well in temperate climates, and prefer sun and well-drained, slightly alkaline soil, but will also grow in acidic soil. They range in color from pale blue to almost violet. 'Blue Magic' has flowers in the middle of the color range. *Zone 6–8.*

***Iris* 'Mary Frances'**
Iris

'Mary Frances' is an outstanding popular bearded iris. Growing upwards to 30 in (70 cm), its sword-like leaves are complemented by lavender blue flowers.

Iris 'Mary Frances'

Iris ensata
syn. *Iris kaempferi*
Japanese flag, higo iris

Native to Japan and cultivated there for centuries, this beardless iris grows to 3 ft (1 m) tall. It has purple flowers with yellow blotches on each fall, which appear from late spring to early summer; the leaves have a prominent midrib. The many named varieties bear huge flowers, up to 10 in (25 cm) wide, in shades of white, lavender, blue and purple, often blending 2 shades and some with double flowers. These plants prefer part-shade in hot areas, rich, acid soil and plenty of moisture, and can even grow in shallow water provided they are not submerged in winter; the foliage dies down for the winter. *Zone 4–8.*

Iris sibirica
Siberian flag

Despite the name, this well-known species has a natural distribution across temperate Eurasia from France to Lake Baikal. It is one of the most popular beardless irises, usually found in gardens in one of its cultivars rather than its wild form.

Iris ensata

Leucojum aestivum

Iris sibirica 'Cleave Dodge'

Ixia maculata hybrid

The plants make strongly vertical clumps of slender bright green leaves 2–4 ft (0.6–1.2 m) high. In late spring or early summer, flowering stems rise above the foliage with narrow-petalled, blue, purple or white flowers, often veined in a deeper color. It prefers full sun to very light shade (particularly in hot areas), a moderately moist, rich soil that may be slightly acid and water during the hottest periods. It will grow in a wet soil and prefers cold winters. 'Cleave Dodge' has mid-blue flowers. *Zone 3–8.*

IXIA

African corn lily

The South African corn lily produces masses of delightful, star-shaped flowers on wiry stems. These flowers close in the evening and on cloudy days. The tallest species grows to about 24 in (60 cm). The leaves are usually long and slender. They are sensitive to frost but easy to grow in temperate to warm areas.

Cultivation

The bulbs should be planted in early autumn in well-drained soil. Blood and bone mixed into the soil before planting will help produce good blooms. A sunny position is ideal except in warm areas where they will need protection from hot sun. Water well through winter and spring but allow to dry out after flowering. Propagate from offsets in autumn. Seed can be used and this should flower in the third year.

Flowering time Spring. *Zone 7–9.*

Ixia maculata

Yellow ixia

This is the most commonly grown species. The stems grow to about 18 in (45 cm), with small flowers clustered along the top, with brown centers, and orange to yellow petals, sometimes with pinkish red undersides. There are white, yellow, pink, orange or red garden forms.

LEUCOJUM AESTIVUM

Snowflake

These dainty bulbs are native to Europe and Asia. They multiply freely year after year and large clumps of the bell-shaped, nodding blooms make a glorious display. The fragrant white flowers have a green spot near the tip of each petal and are borne in clusters atop 12 in (30 cm) stems.

Cultivation

Frost-hardy, the small bulbs should be planted in autumn in a sunny position, but need protection from hot sun in warm areas. Under a deciduous tree is ideal. The soil should be rich, moist and well-drained. Propagate from seed or the freely forming offsets in autumn or spring, but clumps are best left undisturbed for a few years.
Flowering time Late winter–early spring.
Zone 8–9.

LILIUM

Lily

Many plants are commonly called lilies but the 'true' lilies are the many species and hybrids of the magnificent *Lilium* genus. The elegant flowers possess a breathtaking beauty often accompanied by a glorious perfume. The flowers have 6 petals arranged in a variety of ways, and 6 stamens. In recent years, many hybrids, easier to grow than most true lilies, have been created, and have become very popular. The most important groups are the Asiatic or Mid-Century hybrids, the Trumpet hybrids, the Aurelians which have trumpet or bowl shaped flowers, and the spectacular Oriental hybrids. They need lime-free soil, although *L. regale* and *L. lancifolium* can tolerate a little lime.

Cultivation

The scaly bulbs should be planted in autumn but in cold areas they are best planted in spring. The soil should be rich with excellent drainage and the bulbs planted fairly deep as they like a cool root run. A dressing of mulch in spring helps keep the roots cool. A partially shaded position is best as the flowers need protection from hot afternoon sun. Dead flowers should be removed but leaves and stems should not be cut back until autumn. Clumps are best left undisturbed for a few years; they can then be lifted and divided.
Flowering time Spring–summer.
Zone 7–9.

Lilium lancifolium

***Lilium* 'Conneticut King'**

Derived from mixed parentage, 'Conneticut King' is a fine example of an Asiatic hybrid. This early flowering lilium grows to 3 ft (1 m) tall and holds many upward facing golden yellow flowers towards the uppermost section of the stem. Individual stems may need staking if plants are grown in an open position.

Lilium lancifolium

syn. *L. tigrinum*

Tiger lily

One of the most popular species and one of the oldest in cultivation, the tiger lily grows to about 5 ft (1.5 m). It produces masses of bright orange, trumpet-shaped, sharply reflexed flowers. The large blooms are spotted with purple and are usually pendent. The tiger lily can harbor viruses without showing any ill effects and for this reason is best grown away from other lilies. It is grown in its native China for the edible bulbs.

Lilium 'Conneticut King'

Lilium regale

Lilium regale

Regal lily

Growing up to 8 ft (2.4 m), this easily grown lily from western China bears from 3 to 20 fragrant blooms on each stem. The trumpet-shaped flowers appear in summer. The inside of the petals is white, while the outside is carmine.

MUSCARI

Grape hyacinth

The popular grape hyacinths are natives of the Mediterranean region. A short spike bears grape-like clusters of bright blue or white flowers.

Cultivation

Fully to half-hardy, they need a rich, well-drained soil. Plant the bulbs in autumn in a sunny position, but protect from hot sun. The slender, strap-like leaves appear soon after planting, as the summer dormancy period is very short. The clumps should spread freely and are best left undisturbed for a few years. Divide the bulbs if they become overcrowded. They can also be grown from seed.
Flowering time Early spring. *Zone 6–9.*

Muscari armeniacum

Grape hyacinth

Growing to about 2 in (5 cm), this is one of the best loved of spring bulbs. The

Muscari armeniacum 'Heavenly Blue'

flowers may be blue or white, and there are several named cultivars of which 'Heavenly Blue' is the best known.

NARCISSUS

Daffodil, jonquil, narcissus

The sunny yellow flowers of the daffodil are popular all over the world. They are easy to grow, multiply freely and bloom year after year. Native to the northern hemisphere, the genus is extremely varied, but all flowers have 6 petals which surround a cup or corona. They are grouped into 10 'divisions' or classes, the most important of which are: the Trumpet narcissi (Div. 1) which have trumpets as long as the outer petals or perianth, the Large-cupped narcissi (Div. 2), with trumpets from one-third to two-thirds as long; Small-cupped narcissi (Div. 3), with trumpets less than one-third the length of the petals; and Double-flowered narcissi (Div. 4) with double flowers, either one or several per stem. The remaining groups cover hybrids of important species such as *N. tazetta*, *triandrus*, *cyclaminius* and *poeticus*;. Div. 10 is miscellaneous species.

Narcissus bulbocodium

Cultivation

They are usually fully hardy and grow best in cool areas. Bulbs are usually planted in autumn, 4–6 in (10–15 cm) deep in rich, well-drained soil. Full sun is fine in cool areas, but they will need some shade in warmer areas. Water well during growth and allow to dry out once the leaves die down. Remove spent flowers but let the leaves die off naturally. Clumps will multiply freely and should be left undisturbed for a few years. Lift and divide them in autumn. *Flowering time* Spring. *Zone 6–9.*

Narcissus bulbocodium

Hoop-petticoat daffodil

This species grows to 6 in (15 cm) and has many forms. Bright yellow flowers, with a long corona and shaped like a petticoat hoop, appear in spring. The petals are usually insignificant.

Narcissus jonquilla

Jonquil

This species grows up to 14 in (35 cm). Three to six flowers are borne in a cluster, the yellow petals are star-like and the corona is green to gold. The fragrant flowers appear in spring. *N. jonquilla* is very easy to grow.

Narcissus jonquilla

Narcissus poeticus var. *recurvis*

Nerine bowdenii

Narcissus 'Silver Chimes'

Narcissus poeticus
Poet's daffodil
This species grows to about 12 in (30 cm). The fragrant flowers appear in late spring. The petals are usually white and the small cup is pale yellow, fringed with green or red. It is a highly variable species and includes var. *recurvis*, a form with petals recurved away from the central cup or corona.

***Narcissus* 'Silver Chimes'**
This fine hybrid of *N. triandrus* can grow to 10 in (25 cm). The fragrant flowers appear in late spring, up to 10 per stem. The star-shaped petals are creamy white and the small cup is white also. A good cultivar for warm areas, it is much more widely available than the species *N. tazetta* itself, which is very similar but smaller.

NERINE

Guernsey lily
These are actually native to South Africa. They were originally found in Guernsey, but these were the result of bulbs washed up onto the island after a shipwreck. The pretty, spider-like flowers are borne in clusters at the top of tall stems, usually in autumn. The foliage is strap-like.

Cultivation
The bulbs should be planted in sandy soil with good drainage in a sunny position. Water well during growth but allow to dry out over the summer dormancy period. They are not suitable for areas with high summer rainfall or severe frosts. They can be propagated from seed or offsets, but the plants do not like being disturbed and may take a couple of years to flower. They are good plants for pots and can be brought inside when in flower. Half-hardy, they need a

Nerine flexuosa 'Alba'

Rhodohypoxis baurii

warm, sheltered spot in cool climates.
Flowering time Autumn. *Zone 8–9.*

Nerine bowdenii

Pink spider lily, large pink nerine

A sturdy stem of 24 in (60) cm bears up to 12 pink blooms. The flowers are like trumpets but the narrow petals are split and reflexed. They have a crimson rib running along their center and the edges are frilled. There is also a white form.

Nerine flexuosa 'Alba'

A sturdy stem up to 24 in (60 cm) bears a cluster of up to 15 white flowers. The trumpet-shaped flowers have narrow, reflexed petals. The foliage is narrow and strap-like and appears before the flowers.

RANUNCULUS ASIATICUS

Persian buttercup

This frost-hardy native of the Mediterranean region is parent to many hybrids and cultivars popular all over the world. Masses of single or double flowers are borne on 14 in (35 cm) stems. The blooms are available in many colors.

Cultivation

The claw-like tubers should be planted in autumn in a sunny position in well-drained soil enriched with organic matter. Water well through the growing season and allow to dry out after flowering. The tubers are usually lifted after flowering and should be stored in a cool dry place. Propagation is by division or from seed sown in spring.
Flowering time Spring. *Zone 8–9.*

Ranunculus asiaticus

RHODOHYPOXIS BAURII

Red star

This charming dwarf plant comes from the mountains of South Africa and is frost-hardy, although it appreciates a warm spot in cold areas. It produces masses of star-shaped flowers. Each small stem bears one, 6-petaled, red, pink or white flower.

Cultivation

Plant in early spring in rich, acidic, well-drained soil in full sun. It needs plenty of water during the growing season but must be kept dry in winter. Propagate by division or from seed in spring.
Flowering time Late spring–early summer. *Zone 8.*

SCHIZOSTYLIS COCCINEA

River lily

Growing from a small corm, this plant with its grass-like foliage and slender spikes of rich red flowers is a valuable addition to the moist garden because of its late flowering habit. It grows to around 12–15 in (30–40 cm) tall.

Cultivation

Growing naturally along river banks in South Africa, this plant appreciates a moist, yet sunny position and will naturalize if given the optimum conditions. Plant in a permanent position and leave undisturbed for best results.
Flowering time Autumn. *Zone 7–8.*

Sparaxis tricolor

Schizostylis coccinea

SPARAXIS TRICOLOR

Velvet flower, harlequin flower

This frost-tender native of South Africa is easily grown in warm areas. The 12 in (30 cm) wiry, drooping stems bear a spike of up to 5 funnel- to star-shaped blooms in spring. The 2 in (5 cm) flowers are red to pink or orange. The center is usually yellow, outlined in black. The flowers close at night and on dull days.

Cultivation

Plant corms in autumn in a sunny spot in well-drained soil. Water well during the growing season, but allow to dry out when dormant. The corms should be lifted in areas which have wet summers. Propagate from the freely produced offsets or from seed in early autumn
Flowering time Spring. *Zone 9.*

TIGRIDIA PAVONIA

Tiger flower, jockey's cap lily

This brightly colored Mexican native blooms in summer. The triangular flowers are short-lived, often lasting for only a day, but a succession of new blooms will keep appearing for weeks. The 5 in (13 cm) flowers are usually red with a yellow center spotted with purple, and borne on 24 in (60 cm) stems. The foliage is iris-like, sword-shaped and pleated.

Cultivation
Plant in spring in a sunny position in rich, well-drained soil. Water well during the growing season, but allow to dry out when dormant. Lift in cool areas or those with high winter rainfall. Propagate from offsets, or seed sown in spring.
Flowering time Summer–early autumn. *Zone 9.*

TULBAGHIA VIOLACEA
Sweet garlic, wild garlic
This South African native is delightful to look at but smells strongly of garlic. A tall, 24 in (60 cm) stem bears a round cluster of tubular, star-shaped, mauve flowers.

Cultivation
The rhizomes should be planted at the end of winter in rich, moist soil in partial shade. It is half-hardy and could be grown in a pot in cold areas. Clumps are best left undisturbed for a few years. Propagate by division in late winter or by sowing seed in spring.
Flowering time Spring–autumn. *Zone 8–9.*

TULIPA
Tulip
The elegant flower of the tulip has made it one of the most popular bulbs in the world. Tulips originated in the Middle East and Asia and have been cultivated for hundreds of years. The genus contains about 100 species, but the most commonly grown tulips are the highly developed cultivars grouped under *T. gesneriana* which vary in color, shape and flowering time. There are many cultivars which were formerly grouped into a large number of classes. Recently the classification has been simplified, the main groups being: Single Early, Double Early, Single Late, Double Late, and the Parrot tulips. The Single Late tulips are themselves subdivided, and there are also important groups of garden varieties derived from *T. fosteriana*, *greigii* and *kaufmanniana*. The other species are grouped as 'botanical tulips'.

Cultivation
Tulips do best in cool areas but can be grown in pots in warm climates. Plant the bulbs in late autumn, in a sunny spot in rich, limed, and well-drained soil. Water well during the growing season. Spent flowers can be removed but allow the leaves to die off naturally. Lift the bulbs in areas with a wet summer, and store in a cool, well-ventilated spot. Propagate by division in autumn.
Flowering time Spring. *Zone 3–9.*

Tigridia pavonia

Tulbaghia violacea

Tulipa 'Apeldoorn'

Vallota speciosa

Tulipa saxatilis

Tulipa, Parrot Group 'Flaming Parrot'

***Tulipa* 'Apeldoorn'**

Arguably the most popular of all tulips, 'Apeldoorn' is a Darwin hybrid of clear scarlet red with a black base. Tall growing, it has strong upright stems arising from wide, strap-like foliage.

Tulipa saxatilis

syn. *T. bakeri*

Rock tulip

A species originating in Crete, it does well in warmer climates. The 45-cm stems bear up to 3 goblet-shaped flowers which eventually open out almost flat. The purple-pink flowers have bright yellow centers. It flowers in early spring.

***Tulipa*, Parrot Group**

This is a group of rather strange, often bizarrely colored, single-flowered cultivars with laciniate, curled and twisted petals. Mainly late flowering and with stems of variable length, they may have very big flowers with deeply cut, fringed petals on long but weak stems. 'Flaming Parrot' has an exterior of barium yellow, lighter to the edge and flamed crimson, primrose yellow inside flamed glowing red, a base of primrose yellow and black-purple anthers. *Zone 5–7.*

VALLOTA SPECIOSA

syn. *Cyrtanthus purpureus*

Scarborough lily

This beautiful plant, with its showy red flowers, is originally from South Africa. The stout stem bears up to 5 orange-red, trumpet-shaped blooms. The flowers are about 4 in (10 cm) wide. It has thick, green leaves and is half-hardy.

Watsonia beatricis

Cultivation

Plant the bulbs in late winter in rich, well-drained soil, and in partial shade in very warm areas. Water well through the growing season but allow to dry out over winter. Remove spent flowerheads. The small offsets can be removed from the parent bulb and planted out in late winter. *Flowering time* Summer–autumn. *Zone 9–10.*

WATSONIA

These natives of South Africa produce fragrant flowers. They appear quite similar to the gladiolus and have lance-shaped leaves and a tall flowering spike.

Cultivation

The corms should be planted in autumn in light, well-drained soil in a sunny spot. They like plenty of water during the growing season. They are half-hardy. Clumps are best left undisturbed and they should spread freely. They can be propagated from seed or by division when clumps become overcrowded. *Flowering time* Spring–summer. *Zone 8–9.*

Watsonia beatricis

Beatrice watsonia

This evergreen species grows to 4 ft (1.2 m). The flower spike bears tubular, star-shaped flowers which are salmon pink. The green foliage is sword-shaped. Hardier than other species, it can withstand some frost. There is some doubt about whether this plant, common in nurseries under this name, is the true wild species, which is now correctly known as *W. pillansii.*

Zantedeschia aethiopica

ZANTEDESCHIA AETHIOPICA

White arum lily, lily of the Nile

Although normally deciduous, in summer and early autumn this species can stay evergreen if given enough moisture. It can also be grown in water up to 6–12 in (15–30 cm) deep. This species reaches 24–36 in (60–90 cm) in height and spread, with large clumps of broad, dark green leaves. The large flowers, produced in spring, summer and autumn, are pure white with a yellow spadix.

Cultivation

This genus includes frost-tender to moderately frost-hardy plants; most are intolerant of dry conditions and prefer well-drained soil. Propagate from offsets in winter.
Flowering time Spring, summer, autumn. *Zone 8–10.*

LAWNS, GROUND COVERS & ORNAMENTAL GRASSES

The universal favorite for flooring the main part of a garden is a lawn. It is soft and quiet underfoot, it doesn't reflect glare, and its greenness is a flattering backdrop for plants and flowers. The finest lawns are the result of careful blending. Every area has its own particular lawn grass species, and these are the ones you should choose. You may, however, decide to dispense with a lawn and carpet the ground with low-growing, easy-care plants, such as spreading evergreen perennials or low-growing shrubs. Ornamental grasses can be placed anywhere in the garden, including with more orthodox annuals and perennials.

ARCTOSTAPHYLOS UVA-URSI

Bearberry, kinnikinnick

Found in the wild in the colder regions of the northern hemisphere, this species is best known as a completely prostrate form that can cascade over walls or embankments to form curtains of neat, dark green foliage that develops intense red tones in autumn and winter. In late spring it bears small clusters of dull pink, almost globular flowers, followed by green berries that ripen to red.

Cultivation

It needs full sun or part-shade and moist but well-drained, fertile, lime-free soil. The seed, enclosed in a small fleshy fruit, is difficult to germinate, which explains why they are propagated from tip cuttings hardened off in winter; treatment with smoke may assist germination. *Planting time* Winter. *Zone 4–9.*

Arctostaphylos uva-ursi

Calamagrostis × acutiflora

CALAMAGROSTIS × ACUTIFLORA

Feather reed grass

A hybrid between the Eurasian species *Calamagrostis arundinacea* and *C. epigejos*, this clump-forming grass has a strong, upright habit with thin, arching leaves up to about 3 ft (1 m) long. The somewhat silky, brown seed heads are borne on erect, much branched panicles 3–5 ft (1–1.5 m) tall, and persist into winter.

Cultivation

Almost any moist soil in full sun or part-shade suits these plants. If conditions are to their liking, some may become invasive so are best given ample space, for example, beside a pond. Regular division of clumps serves to keep growth in check. Seed heads and old leaves can be cut back to ground level in early winter. Propagate by division of clumps. *Planting time* Autumn. *Zone 6–9.*

CAREX ELATA 'AUREA'

Golden sedge

A perennial with a mound forming habit, it has grass-like pendant leaves. Blackish brown flower spikes form in summer.

Cultivation

Plant in a full sun position in fertile soil. It doesn't mind wet soil, which makes it useful for the edges of water features. Cut back hard at the end of winter. *Planting time* Spring. *Zone* 8.

Carex elata 'Aurea'

CORTADERIA SELLOANA

syns *Cortaderia argentea, Gynerium argenteum*

Pampas grass

Native to Argentina and southern Brazil, this stately grass grows to a height of 10 ft (3 m) and similar spread, the pale green foliage forming a dense clump about 6 ft (1.8 m) high. In summer and autumn plume-like panicles appear above the leaves on pole-like stems, consisting of vast numbers of small silky spikelets varying in color from creamy white to purplish pink. In some regions this species has become very invasive.

Cultivation

Pampas grass is easily grown in any open sunny position, in almost any soil as long as moisture is adequate. It tolerates exposure to strong winds and even to salt spray. With age a clump will build up unsightly dead leaves and old flowering stems; if circumstances allow, these can be disposed of by setting fire to the clump in autumn or winter, otherwise it should be cut back 12 in (30 cm) or so high. Propagate by division of selected forms.

Planting time Autumn. *Zone 6–10.*

CYPERUS PAPYRUS

Paper reed, papyrus

The papyrus of the ancient Egyptians is one of the stateliest of all water plants for mild climates. It is rampant, growing 5–8 ft (1.5–2.4 m) tall with an indefinite spread. In summer its long, sturdy, leafless stems carry great starbursts of fine branchlets that carry the tiny brown flowers. It will grow in very shallow water and prefers a sunny position.

Cultivation

Grow in rich compost and water well. Direct sunlight is tolerated. Repot when the plant fills the container. If the tips turn brown, the atmosphere may be too dry, while a lack of new stems may indicate too little light. Propagate from seed or by division.

Planting time Summer. *Zone 10–12.*

FESTUCA

Fescue

A native of Asia and temperate Europe, this genus provides good grassed areas in cold through moderate climates. They grow deep roots and form tufts with short rhizomes and green leaves.

Cultivation

The turfs have a loose texture, wear well and tolerate semi-shade. They also withstand drought and frost well.

Planting time Autumn, early spring. *Zone 8.*

Festuca scoparia

Cortaderia selloana

Hedera helix 'Silver Queen'

Iberis sempervirens

Festuca scoparia

Beargrass, bearskin grass

This fully hardy evergreen grows into tufts that form a dark green, spiky ground cover, which needs regular grooming to keep tidy and dense. Spreading widely, the species reaches only 6 in (15 cm) high. Establish in well-drained soil in full sun.

HEDERA HELIX

Common ivy, English ivy

This very frost-hardy species from Europe will produce a dense, dark green cover. It is often used as a ground cover. 'Silver Queen' (syn. 'Tricolor') has shallowly lobed, triangular leaves that are gray-green with cream markings.

Cultivation

In sun or shade ivies are adaptable to a wide variety of conditions, soils and climates. Regular pruning is recommended so that no flowers are produced. If the mature growth, which produces tiny green flowers in autumn followed by black berries, is struck as cuttings, the resultant plants remain as shrubs. Propagate from cuttings or rooted stems. Pests afflicting ivy include spider mites, scale, thrips and aphids.

Planting time Autumn. *Zone 4–11.*

IBERIS SEMPERVIRENS

Candytuft, evergreen candytuft

A low, spreading, evergreen subshrub, this species from southern Europe is ideal for rock gardens. It has narrow, dark green leaves and dense, rounded heads of unscented white flowers in spring and early summer. It is frost hardy, and grows 6–12 in (15–30 cm) high with a spread of 18–24 in (45–60 cm). Lightly trim after flowering.

Cultivation

Fully to marginally frost hardy, they need a warm, sunny position and a well-drained, light soil, preferably with added lime or dolomite. Propagate from seed in spring or autumn or cuttings in summer.

Planting time Spring–autumn.

Zone 4–11.

MISCANTHUS SINENSIS 'ZEBRINUS'

Zebra grass

This large, herbaceous perennial grass grows to a height of 6 ft (1.8 m) and spread of 19 in (50 cm). It suits perennial borders, water gardens, naturalized areas, screens and specimen planting.

Cultivation

Frost hardy, it requires a sunny situation and well-drained moist soil. Divide every 3–5 years to keep the plants growing vigorously, and cut back hard each winter. Propagate by division in spring.

Planting time Autumn, spring. *Zone 8.*

PACHYSANDRA TERMINALIS

This creeping evergreen perennial, a native of Japan, has leathery, ovate leaves with saw-tooth tips, clustered at

Rosmarinus officinalis

the ends of short stems. Tiny white flowers, sometimes pink or purple tinted, appear in terminal clusters in early summer. It makes a good ground cover, growing to 4 in (10 cm) high.

Cultivation

It is frost hardy, and will grow in most soils in sun or part-shade. Propagate by removing self-rooted layers or from cuttings. *Planting time* Autumn. *Zone 4–10.*

PENNISETUM SETACEUM

syn. *P. ruppellii*

African fountain grass

Native to tropical Africa, this herbaceous perennial grass has arching, coppery spikes with bearded bristles. Half-hardy, it grows to 3 ft (1 m) with a spread of 19 in (50 cm).

Cultivation

Plant in moist soil in full sun. It is not suitable as a lawn grass, but makes an attractive tall ground cover or a feature plant in a flower border. *Planting time* Autumn, spring. *Zone 8.*

ROSMARINUS OFFICINALIS

Rosemary

'Prostratus', the ground-hugging cultivar of this popular herb, is often planted to

Miscanthus sinensis 'Zebrinus'

Pennisetum setaceum

Pachysandra terminalis

spread over outcrops in the rock garden or as an alternative to grass. Its procumbent stems lend themselves to draping over a slope or beside steps.

Cultivation

Like many of the herbs originating in the Mediterranean region, rosemary likes well-drained soil in a full sun position. *Planting time* Autumn, spring. *Zone 8.*

VEGETABLES & HERBS

Nothing matches the flavor of home-grown vegetables or herbs. They can be picked at the moment of perfection and eaten or preserved within hours to the benefit of both the family's health and budget. Herbs were traditionally planted by themselves in small formal gardens, but you can also plant them as borders to flower or vegetable gardens. Most herbs are fairly low-growing, and their scent is a pleasure as you plant and weed. Set among the blooms in a cottage garden mix, their soft textures and varied greens stop a riot of colors.

Allium cepa

Allium porrum

ALLIUM

This is a very large genus which consists of more than 700 species of perennials and biennials. They range enormously in size, from 4 in–5 ft (10 cm–1.5 m), and grow in temperate climates around the world. Some species, such as the onions, garlic and chives, are edible. Common to all the plants in the genus is the oniony smell that is emitted when the leaves are bruised or pinched. The genus name derives from the Celtic word 'all', which means hot.

Cultivation

The onion species may need the protection of a cover if the soil is cold. Both the onion and ornamental species have the same pest and disease enemies such as onion fly, stem eelworm, rust and onion white rot.
Planting time Autumn, spring.
Annual.

Allium cepa
Onion, spring onion, scallion

Onions need a cool climate and a sunny, open position in a well-drained bed of soil. Sow the seeds or immature onions in mid-spring in holes ½ in (1 cm) deep and 12 in (30 cm) apart, and water moderately. Harvest in late summer when the leaves have begun to yellow. The onion was a popular vegetable among the Greeks and Romans but it was never eaten by the Egyptians because they regarded it as a sacred plant. The spring onion is an immature onion which has not yet made a bulb. It likes the same conditions as other onions. In a warm climate seeds can be sown at any time of the year.

Allium porrum
Leek

Easier to grow than the onion and more suited to cold climates, the leek likes a sunny spot and a moist light soil. Sow seeds in spring or summer or plant seedlings 8 in (20 cm) apart with 12 in (30 cm) between rows, filling each hole gently with water. Keep clear of weeds and, once the base of the leek is at least 1 in (2½ cm) thick, harvest as needed.

Allium sativum

Allium sativum
Garlic
There are two main types of garlic. The mauve flowered variety known as 'Giant Russian' *(A. giganteum)* or 'Jumbo' is very much larger and milder than the more potent, small or common garlic *(A. sativum)*, which has dainty white flowers. Individual cloves are planted in autumn in warmer areas or in spring where there is frost-risk. Good drainage, a rich organic soil and a sunny position are its requirements. Garlic will take up to 5 or 6 months to mature. Tall flower stalks should be removed for better flavor. Harvest when the leaves have turned yellow and fallen over. Handle gently to avoid bruising and allow to dry off and harden thoroughly before storage. Garlic planted near roses enhances their perfume and helps to keep aphids away. For at least 5000 years garlic has been used for culinary, medicinal and strength-giving purposes as well as a plague preventative and charm against vampires and witchcraft.

Allium schoenoprasum

Allium schoenoprasum
Chives
One of the most widely used herbs, this plant is also among the easiest to grow. Low growing, it can be used as a decorative border or grown in clumps in either the herb or cottage garden. However, remember if spraying for pests on, for example, roses, either cover the chives while spraying or take heed of the withholding period of the spray. If a

Artemisia dracunculus

Asparagus officinalis

constant supply of the useful green leaves is required be sure to remove the pinkish-purple flowerheads as they appear. A perennial that likes the sun, *Allium schoenoprasum* is grown from seed, or clumps can be divided every second year or so and placed into a newly worked position in the herb garden. This easily contained herb makes an ideal potted plant, either by itself or in a mixed bowl.
Zones 3–9 (perennial).

ANETHUM GRAVEOLENS

Dill

Originally from southwestern Asia, this deliciously aromatic annual grows to about 3 ft (1 m) high. Dill has a long, wiry root from which develops an upright, hollow stem with ferny foliage very similar to that of fennel (*Foeniculum vulgare*). Umbels of tiny bright yellow flowers develop at the stem tip and are followed by the pungent seeds. Dill is a wonderful culinary herb that is widely used in pickling and in a wide variety of fish dishes. Both the foliage and the seeds are used. The foliage is best used before flowering. It also has medicinal uses, most commonly as an aid to digestion.

Cultivation

Only moderately frost hardy, dill is easily grown in any moist, well-drained, humus-rich soil in sun. The seed is best sown in spring where it is to grow in the garden, because seedlings can be quite difficult to transplant. Dill often self-sows.
Planting time Spring. *Grow as an annual.*

ARTEMISIA DRACUNCULUS

Tarragon

Essential in French cuisine, tarragon is grown for its narrow, aromatic leaves which have a delicate, peppery aniseed flavor. Half-hardy, it grows up to 3 ft (1 m) high in the warmer months then dies back to a perennial rootstock over the winter months.

Cultivation

Full sun and a fertile, well-drained soil are its requirements. As it does not produce seed, propagate by division in early spring. The tarragon seed sometimes offered is the flavorless *A. dracunculoides* known as Russian tarragon. Tarragon loses most of its flavor during drying. Before the plant dies down for a winter's rest, gather the leaves and make tarragon vinegar and butter.

Planting time Spring. *Annual Zone 8–9; Perennial Zone 8–11.*

ASPARAGUS OFFICINALIS

Asparagus

A frost-hardy perennial of the lily family this vegetable seems to have been cultivated and eaten all over the world. Its culinary history dates as far back as the ancient Egyptians. Sow seeds in spring or set young plants in winter in 1 in (25 cm) deep trenches in a sunny part of the garden. Give asparagus a good 12 in (30 cm) between each plant so that its fleshy roots can wander freely. Select wilt and rust resistant varieties.

Cultivation

The soil should be well-drained and rich with compost or manure. Do not harvest the young shoots (spears) until the third spring, and always stop in time to allow sufficient shoots to mature to keep the plants going. The red berries should be picked before they go to seed and the plants should be mulched every summer.

Planting time Winter. *Zone 3–9 (perennial).*

BETA VULGARIS

Beet

A relatively easy vegetable to grow, beet is fast growing and should be given space and an open position. It needs a deep, fertile soil that has been previously cultivated. Sow seeds in autumn in 1 in (2½ cm) holes, 8 in (20 cm) apart. When the first leaves appear, weed out the weaker seedlings. Keep the soil moist and pull out the beet by hand.

Cultivation

In warm climates it can be harvested almost all year round, but in cold climates bulbs will need to be gathered and then stored over winter. It is susceptible to boron deficiency and white fly. It was once valued by the Romans and Greeks for its leaves rather than for the root itself.

Planting time Autumn, spring.
Annual.

Beta vulgaris var. *cicla*

Beta vulgaris var. *cicla*

Silverbeet, Swiss chard

Silverbeet is similar to spinach, but grows much better in warm climates. It has the same requirements as beet. It is easy to grow and will tolerate either shade or sun. Sow in mid-spring and summer. Snails and slugs are the only real problem. Harvest the leaves, a few at a time, as needed.

Capsicum annuum var. *annuum* 'Red Missile'

Brassica oleracea hybrid

BRASSICA

There are 30 species of this annual or biennial vegetable, some grown for cooking, oilseed and mustard, others for animal fodder. It is native to the Mediterranean and parts of Asia.

Cultivation

Most of the *Brassica* species love a lime-rich, moist, well-drained soil. Seedlings should be raised in containers and then carefully replanted 6 to 8 weeks later in a sheltered spot in soil that has been prepared previously for an earlier crop. Brassicas are more prone to pests and diseases than other vegetables so ensure all soil is weed-free and not wet. Club root is a common disease in these vegetables and crop rotation should be practiced.
Planting time Spring–autumn.
Annual.

Brassica oleracea Capitata group

Kale

The common cabbage belongs to the Capitata group within this diverse and highly hybridized species. By successive raising and planting out, cabbages can be enjoyed for most months of the year in all climates as this is one of the many genera where plants have been bred for most climatic zones.

Brassia oleracea Cymosa group

***Brassica oleracea* Cymosa group**

Broccoli

Broccoli is grown for its densely massed flower buds and fleshy stalks. Broccoli is best picked and eaten when young because once the yellow flowers begin to open it becomes coarse in both texture and flavor. Do not allow the plant to flower, as it will stop growing. Grubs and waterlogging are major problems with this plant.

CAPSICUM

The capsicum is closely related to the tomato, and like it, native to Central America and a lover of hot, humid summers. The genus contains both ornamental species, grown for their brightly colored fruit and edible types, which divide into the sweet or bell peppers. They can be cooked as a vegetable and eaten raw in salads. The chile peppers are used fresh or dry to add a sharp, hot flavor to cooking.

Cultivation

In colder areas, grow seedlings in pots for planting out when the last frost is over or in warmer areas straight into the garden. They demand a humus enriched, well-drained soil, plenty of both sun and water and regular fertilizing to ensure a quick, healthy crop.
Planting time Spring. *Annual.*

Capsicum annuum

Sweet bell pepper, capsicum

Capsicums are very high in vitamin C. Sow the seeds in containers using soil rich with compost indoors 8 weeks before the last frost. This plant is quite frost-tender and, once planted outside, seedlings may need to be covered to keep warm. Keep plants well watered. Capsicums contain more vitamin C and vitamin A if they are left to turn a deep red color. *C. annuum* var. *annuum* 'Red Missile' is a compact bush with conical red fruits.

CICHORIUM

This genus of perennials from the Mediterranean and the Middle East is distantly related to the lettuce. The two species in gardens, however, have little in common except their family relation—they are grown and used in the kitchen quite differently.

Cultivation

Like lettuce, the endive needs a friable, humus-enriched, but well-drained soil which should not be allowed to dry out as this will check the growth of the plant and make it too bitter for salads.
Planting time Late summer. *Annual.*

Cichorium endivia

Endive, curly endive

This is a relative of chicory, grown for its leaves. As with most salad vegetables, it needs a humus-rich soil which is kept moist so that it won't run to seed. Sow the seeds 12–15 in (30–38 cm) apart in a shaded position in late summer. Use liquid fertilizer every now and then as the plants are growing. The leaves are usually eaten green as a bitter salad; they resemble lettuce but are more sharply flavored.

Cichorium endivia

Cynara scolymus

Coriandrum sativum

CORIANDRUM SATIVUM

Coriander, cilantro, Chinese parsely

This herb is grown mainly for its seed and aromatic leaves. It is a fast-growing annual, reaching to 30 in (75 cm) high with parsley-like leaves and umbels of

Cucurbita pepo hybrid

tiny, white flowers in summer. The flowers are followed by small, round, aromatic seeds. Fresh leaves will provide an exotic tang in Asian and Mexican dishes. The dried seeds are used in curry powders, chutneys, confectionery, cakes as well as sauces.

Cultivation

Fully hardy, it requires full sun and a light, well-drained soil. Propagate from seed in early spring.
Planting time Spring. *Annual.*

CUCURBITA

This is an ancient vegetable genus which contains squashes, pumpkins, marrow, zucchinis and many others. The genus has been grown and interbred in gardens for so long that its botany is rather confused; most types are usually given as forms of *C. pepo.*

Cultivation

Most species of this genus are easy to raise and have the same need of a warm, rich soil. In warm climates sow from early spring to late summer. In cold climates sow indoors in early summer. To prepare the garden for seedlings dig

holes 12 in (30 cm) square, 3 ft (1 m) apart for bush varieties and 4 ft (1.2 m) apart for the trailing varieties of pumpkin. Fill with a good fertilizer mix. Water seedlings well before planting. Watch for slugs and keep well irrigated as they are water hungry. Harvest in summer and autumn.
Planting time Spring. *Annual.*

CYNARA SCOLYMUS

Artichoke

Native to the Mediterranean and a distant cousin of the thistle, the artichoke is one of many vegetables once considered to be an aphrodisiac. It has delicate, gray-green leaves and is easy to grow in most soils and positions. Make sure it has enough space (one or two plants will be enough in a small garden).

Cultivation

A rich soil will mean better production. Plant suckers rather than seeds 3 ft (1 m) apart in early spring. Remove yellowing leaves and stems in autumn. Cut the plump flower buds from the plants in spring and summer before the flowers begin to open. Watch for septoria leaf spot.
Planting time Spring. *Zone 8–9.*

DAUCUS CAROTA

Carrot

This famous root vegetable is native to Afghanistan and was introduced to Europe 600 years ago.

Cultivation

Sow in deep, warm, aerated soil that is loamy, in rows 10 in (25 cm) apart, making sure the earth is firmly compacted around the seeds. Keep the earth moist around the seedlings and thin the rows out when they are 1 in (2½ cm) high. The carrot gives a high yield even in a small garden and can be stored easily in bins or boxes between layers of sand. Once they are big enough to pick, avoid leaving them in the ground during wet weather as the root will split. The carrot is vulnerable to carrot-fly, greenfly and aphids.
Planting time Winter–spring. *Annual.*

Daucus carota

LACTUCA SATIVA

Lettuce

From the Latin, *lac*, meaning milk, referring to its milky white sap, this biennial originated in the Middle East and the Mediterranean. Praised through history for its healthy or sleep-inducing properties, lettuce is a salad plant with a very delicate root system. Popular types include the common Iceberg with globular heads like pale green cabbages, Cos lettuce with more open darker heads, and Mignonette with ruffled pink-tinted leaves. The cultivar 'Salad Bowl' has large frilly leaves.

Cultivation

Sow lettuce seeds in spring or summer in the open ground or sow in containers for later transplanting. Ensure that the seed is right for the climate as there are

many kinds of lettuce for different climates. The soil must be humus-rich and evenly moist. Thin the seedlings gradually until they are 12 in (30 cm) apart. Sudden changes in temperature can leave the lettuce open to disease. Ensure they do not flower. Water regularly over summer, avoiding excessive water on leaves. Watch for slugs and gray mold.
Planting time Spring–summer. *Annual.*

LYCOPERSICON LYCOPERSICUM

Tomato

This native of South America was regarded with suspicion for centuries because of its infamous relative, the deadly nightshade.

Cultivation

Its basic needs are sunshine, moist, well-drained soil and a frost-free area. In cold climates use a cover to keep the soil warm. In open ground plant the seedlings in rows 3 ft (1 m) apart and keep 12–24 in (30–60 cm) between each plant. Seedlings can be grown in windowsill pots and then gently planted out when 4 in (10 cm) high. It is essential that tomatoes be supported by stakes as they grow and sheltered from strong winds. Prune secondary shoots and keep soil moist, mulching if necessary. Pick tomatoes when they are ripe. Beware of slugs and birds eating the ripe fruit.
Planting time Spring. *Annual.*

Lycopersicon lycopersicum

Lactuca sativa 'Salad Bowl'

MENTHA

Mint

This is a large genus of herbs, some evergreen and some deciduous, from just about all the continents. They vary in size from tiny creeping ground covers to bushy plants about 15 in (40 cm) high, and in flavor from refreshing to so strong they must be used with circumspection.

Cultivation

As a rule, they are frost-hardy, like sunshine and rich soil and need lots of moisture (poor drainage does not matter) and are invasive growers, spreading rapidly by runners. To keep them from taking over, try growing them in large pots, watering regularly and repotting them annually.
Planting time Spring. *Zone 3–10.*

Mentha spicata

Spearmint

This fast-growing perennial, reaching 24 in (60 cm), is the most popular mint used in cooking. Spearmint has crinkly, dark green leaves and, as it has a tendency to put down roots all over the garden, is often best grown in a container or a separate bed. Fully hardy, it thrives in a sunny or partially shaded position in a moist, but well-drained soil. Plants should be cut back regularly to encourage fresh growth. Propagate by root division. This is the mint used in mint sauce, mint jelly and to flavor new potatoes, green peas and some salad dishes. Fresh sprigs are commonly used as a garnish in fruit drinks or desserts.

OCIMUM BASILICUM

Basil

A great favorite with cooks all over the world, basil is one of the most widely used herbs in Mediterranean cooking. It is a tender annual plant growing to 12 in (30 cm) with light green, oval leaves that have a delicious, warm, spicy fragrance. Small white flowers are carried in whorls towards the ends of the stems in late summer.

Cultivation

Full sun and a moderately rich, moist, but well-drained soil are its requirements. Grow this herb in a warm protected position. There are a number of varieties of basil including a compact small-leaf type; a crinkled, lettuce leaf variety and the beautiful 'Dark Opal' with rich purple stems and leaves. There are perennial varieties also, but their flavor is inferior. Regularly pinch back all basil plants to encourage bushy growth and to prevent them from going to seed too quickly. Propagate from seed sown when there is no frost. Keep a lookout for chewing insects or snails. Fresh leaves are best; freeze it for the winter; it loses its flavor when dried.
Planting time Spring. *Annual.*

ORIGANUM

Native to the Mediterranean region and parts of Europe and India, these frost-tender perennials are often grown as annuals in cooler climates.

Cultivation

They like sun and rich, well-drained soil. Trim regularly and propagate from seed in spring or by root division.
Planting time Spring. *Zone 3–9.*

Mentha spicata

Ocimum basilicum

Origanum vulgare 'Aureum'

Petroselinum crispum

Origanum vulgare
Oregano, wild marjoram
A close relative of marjoram, oregano has a sharper, more pungent flavor. It has a sprawling habit and grows to 12 in (30 cm) high with dark green, oval leaves and white or pink flowers in summer. 'Aureum' has yellow leaves and is also at home in the perennial garden.

PETROSELINUM CRISPUM
Parsley
Cultivated for thousands of years for its flavor and health-giving properties, parsley is still one of the most popular herbs grown. It is a biennial plant which grows to 12 in (30 cm high). The curly-leafed form and the stronger, flat-leafed Italian variety are the ones most commonly grown in gardens.

Cultivation
Parsley does best in full sun or light shade in warm climates. It likes a moist, well-drained position and regular feeding. For best flavor, harvest the leaves before the plant flowers. Propagate from seed. Soaking the seeds in warm water overnight before planting speeds up germination.
Planting time Spring–early autumn.
Biennial, grow as an annual.

PHASEOLUS VULGARIS
French bean, kidney bean, string bean, haricot bean
The major bean species both for green and dried beans, *Phaseolus vulgaris* displays great variation in both pod and seed characters, as well as plant growth habit. An annual, it was originally a climber but many cultivated strains are 'dwarf beans' that are better adapted to mechanical harvesting. The beans can also be divided into those grown as pulses, including the borlotti, pinto, haricot and navy beans, and those grown as green beans (a few are dual-purpose); these go by many names, including French beans, snap beans, string beans and stringless beans. The pods vary in length, whether they are round or flat, and in color from cream to yellow, green, blue-green, red or purple; seed color may vary almost as much. Popular green bean cultivars include 'Tendercrop', a dwarf with straight, plump green stringless pods; 'Blue Lake', a climber with very plump, long, tender pods; 'Kentucky Wonder Wax', a climber with large golden-yellow pods; and 'Royal Burgundy', a dwarf with curved, deep purple pods and purplish foliage.

Phaseolus vulgaris

Cultivation

Beans thrive with a long, warm growing season, plenty of sunlight and ample moisture. They prefer a humus-rich yet light and well-drained soil. Some are also suitable for planting in tubs or flower beds. Propagate from seed in autumn or spring. Watch for attack by slugs. *Planting time* Autumn, spring. *Grow as an annual.*

PISUM SATIVUM

Pea

There is an enormous range of peas, from the bush type which is good for humid climates, tall climbing plants which need trellising, to the newer snap pea edible when immature or fully developed.

Cultivation

Peas need a sunny, well-drained, rich, previously manured soil bed that contains some lime and dolomite for a good yield. Plant seedlings 2 in (5 cm) apart in rows 4 in (10 cm) apart. When the seedlings are 3 in (8 cm) high, stake them with short twigs. The tall varieties will need wire or plastic netting to support them as they grow. Keep weeds down and water when dry. Pick the pods from the lower stems. Watch for mildew, mites and also blight. *Planting time* Spring. *Annual.*

Pisum sativum

Rosmarinus officinalis

ROSMARINUS OFFICINALIS

Rosemary

Rosemary has been cultivated for centuries for flavoring food and for medicine. It will grow to 3 ft (1 m) high, has resinous, narrow, needle-like leaves and small flowers in shades of mauve-blue, off and on all year. Rosemary leaves can be used fresh or dried to flavor meat dishes, chicken, fish and vegetables. Dried branches can be used in wreath-making and the leaves in potpourri.

Cultivation

Half-hardy, rosemary can be grown outdoors in warm climates, but should be taken in for winter where temperatures fall below zero. It prefers a light, well-drained soil in a sheltered, sunny position. Propagate from cuttings or by layering.
Planting time Spring. *Zone 7–10.*

RUTA GRAVEOLENS

Rue

One of the bitter herbs used for warding off insects and disease, rue is also one of the most decorative herbs with its very pretty, gray-green, lacy leaves. It is a hardy perennial growing 24 in (60 cm) high with clusters of small yellow-green flowers in summer.

Salvia officinalis 'Purpurascens'

Ruta graveolens

Cultivation

Grow in a slightly alkaline, well-drained soil in full sun. Protect from strong winds and severe frost in cold climates. Trim after flowering. Propagate by division in spring or from stem cuttings in late summer. The leaves and flowers are used in small posies. Rue has been used in the past for medicinal purposes, but can be dangerous if taken in large doses and during pregnancy.
Planting time Spring. *Zone 4–8.*

SALVIA

This genus is mainly from the northern hemisphere and includes an enormous number of species. Most are aromatic and many are grown just for their brightly colored flowers.

Cultivation

Like all gray-leafed plants, this species of *Salvia* enjoys a well drained, full sun position in the herb garden or pot. It can be grown as a perennial, being cut back towards the end of summer, and is best replaced every second year or so to ensure a good supply of its sweet-smelling leaves.
Planting time Spring. *Zone 4–9.*

Salvia officinalis

Sage

Sage is a decorative, frost-hardy perennial plant which grows to 24 in (60 cm) high, with downy, gray-green, oval leaves and mauve-blue flowers on tall spikes during summer. There are several forms of sage: those with plum-red leaves, greenish-purple variegated leaves, tricolored leaves and golden variegated leaves. All are attractive and edible. The cultivar 'Purpurascens' is a decorative, purple-leaved sage. Grow in an open, sunny, well-drained position. In hot areas, plant in light shade. Propagate from cuttings. Trim frequently.

THYMUS

Thyme

There are many species and varieties of thyme, all of which are perennials with tiny, aromatic leaves and small flower spikes that appear during summer.

Cultivation

Thyme likes a light, well-drained soil and full sun if possible. It is generally hardy once established but may need winter protection in very cold areas. Keep well trimmed for compact growth. Propagate by division or layer stems. *Planting time* Spring. *Zone 5–9.*

Thymus vulgaris

Common thyme

This culinary thyme grows to 12 in (30 cm) high. The tiny, mid-green leaves are used in vinegars, butters and to flavor meat and vegetable dishes. Thyme tea aids digestion, sore throats and coughs.

ZEA MAYS

Sweet corn

With its origins in ancient Mexico, sweet corn has had an uphill battle to win a place on the dinner table in Europe, where it has been seen more as fodder than human fare, but Americans love their sweet corn.

Cultivation

It likes a nitrogen and lime-rich soil and needs hot weather to grow well. Sow in early summer in short rows 24 in (60 cm) apart. Weed gently and water thoroughly in really dry weather. Tie the stems to stakes as they grow taller and be sure to keep the soil firm around the plant base. *Planting time* Spring–summer. *Annual.*

Thymus vulgaris

Zea mays

FRUIT TREES, NUT TREES & OTHER FRUITS

Fruit trees are comely in habit and often beautiful in flower. Few are large, so they take up little space in your garden. Nut trees are really just fruit trees, but we eat their seeds rather than the fleshy coverings. Although not as popular as fruit trees, they are well worth growing and the crop keeps without having to be preserved. Fruit also grows on vines, such as grapes; and shrubs, such as blueberries. As their fruits tend to be soft and easily damaged on the way to market, if you grow your own, you can have the best.

Actinidia chinensis

Castanea sativa

ACTINIDIA CHINENSIS

syn. *A. deliciosa*

Kiwifruit, Chinese gooseberry

This deciduous vine is native to the Yangtze Valley in China and is now grown in warm areas around the world.

Cultivation

Plant on a sturdy trellis or pergola in deep soil which is high in nitrogen, in a sheltered spot away from wind, early frosts and hot sun. Prune regularly in summer and winter to ensure good quality fruit. Water well in summer. The first fruit will appear after 4 to 5 years. You must have a male and a female to produce fruit; grafted plants carrying both sexes are often available.
Planting time Autumn or late winter.
Zone 8–9.

CASTANEA SATIVA

Spanish chestnut, sweet chestnut

This fully hardy, deciduous Mediterranean native is valued for its timber, shade and edible fruit which is delicious roasted. It grows slowly to 50 ft (15 m), with dark green foliage and an open crown. The leaves, which turn brown in autumn, are oval and heavily serrated, with a hairy underside. Creamy golden, malodorous flowers bloom in early to mid-spring. In late summer to early spring, glossy brown chestnuts develop inside spiny pods.

Cultivation

This species enjoys warm summers and a rich, well-drained, acid soil, otherwise it can be prone to root rot. Propagate mainly from seed in autumn. It is prone to chestnut blight and has a tendency to sucker.
Planting time Autumn or early spring.
Zone 7–8.

CITRUS

Native to Southeast Asia, it is thought that citrus fruit trees were introduced to the Middle East and Europe in the time of the Romans.

Cultivation

They are half-hardy to frost-tender and do best in a warm, humid climate with mild winters. The attractive white flowers in spring and fruit in winter make them a valued tree. A nitrogen-rich, well-drained soil and a sunny position are their requirements. Water and fertilize well. They are attacked by a number of pests including scale insects and aphids. Although citrus are more reliable when grown from seed than most fruit trees, they are almost always budded to ensure the perpetuation of the desired variety. Understocks vary with type, but *Poncirus trifoliata*

gives greater resistance to cold and to certain viruses.
Planting time Spring or autumn. *Zone 9.*

Citrus limon

Lemon

Native to Pakistan and India, this just half-hardy tree or shrub is an attractive evergreen that grows to 14 ft (4 m) high and 10 ft (3 m) wide. The cultivar 'Meyer' is smaller than most lemons with a less acidic flavor, and is rather hardier than other lemons. Plant in well-drained soil and fertilize regularly with nitrogen. Propagate by budding. The lemon is less prone to disease than other citrus trees, but be careful of the fungus melanose (dark brown spots), which should be pruned off once it appears on the wood.

Citrus sinensis

Orange

An attractive tree to 14 ft (4 m) with a rounded head, glossy foliage and scented white flowers, oranges can be grown in most non-tropical climates. They will tolerate light frosts.

CYDONIA OBLONGA

Quince

Native to the Middle East, this is a moderately frost-hardy, deciduous tree growing 10–14 ft (3–4 m) high. Its soft green leaves turn an attractive golden yellow before falling.

Cultivation

Not fussy about soil, it is ideal for potting or for borders. Its aromatic fruit can be left on the tree for a few weeks after it ripens. Pick with care as it bruises easily. Prune minor branches or shoots which have produced fruit. Propagate from cuttings. It is vulnerable to fruit-fly and quince fleck.
Planting time Autumn or late winter.
Zone 8–9.

Cydonia oblonga

Citrus limon 'Meyer'

Citrus sinensis

DIOSPYROS VIRGINIANA

American persimmon, possum wood

This spreading tree can reach over 100 ft (30 m) in its native eastern USA, in alluvial river valley forests, but in cultivation it usually reaches 20–30 ft (6–9 m). It has cream flowers and sweet edible fruit, ripening to orange or purple-red. The timber (white ebony) is valued for its durability.

Cultivation

Fully frost hardy to frost tender, these trees prefer well-drained, moist soil, with ample water in the growing season and, being brittle, need shelter from strong wind. Propagate from seed. *Planting time* Autumn or late winter. *Zone 5–9.*

Ficus carica

Diospyros virginiana

FICUS CARICA

Fig

This small deciduous tree, indigenous to the countries surrounding the Mediterranean, produces edible fruit in autumn.

Cultivation

It needs a sunny position in a warm climate where dry summers are the norm, as rain can split the ripening fruit. Deep, fairly heavy soils hold the moisture necessary throughout the growing season, otherwise mulching will ensure the shallow roots are kept moist. *Planting time* Autumn or late winter. *Zone 8–9.*

FRAGARIA × ANANASSA

Garden strawberry

The name ananassa means 'pineapple-flavored', a curious description for the modern, large-fruited garden strawberry that arose from crossing American species. It has ovate leaflets that are glaucous above and white beneath. A wide range of strawberry cultivars have been developed to suit differing climatic conditions.

Cultivation

Grow these frost-hardy plants in beds or containers lined with straw, in free-draining, acidic soil. The plants need full

Juglans regia

sun or light shade and protection from wind; in cold climates grow them in slits in sheets of plastic. Propagate from seed in spring or autumn or by runners and replant with fresh stock every few years. Protect from snails, strawberry aphids and birds. Botrytis can be a problem in high rainfall areas.
Planting time Spring. *Zone 4–10.*

JUGLANS REGIA

Walnut

A forest tree, this species grows 50 ft (15 m) high and 30 ft (9 m) wide. It can take several years before the tree starts to bear any nuts so patience is required. 'Wilson's Wonder' fruits young, although its nuts are not thought to be of the very highest quality. A silver-gray trunk ends in a canopy of arching branches, making this a good source of shade in a spacious garden. Prune early to form a central leader and a well-spaced system of boughs.

Fragaria × ananassa

Cultivation

It is cold- and wind-hardy, although young trees may be damaged by harsh frost. Ensure that the soil is deep, loamy and well drained. Water well to increase nut production and pick the nuts from the ground after they have fallen. Large birds can be a problem as well as the erinose mite and nut-boring beetles.
Planting time Autumn or early spring. *Zone 7–8.*

MALUS

A member of the Rosaceae family, this genus contains the crab apple and the garden apple *(M. domestica)*; there are many species and varieties of both.

Malus × *domestica* 'Red Delicious'

Morus nigra

Cultivation

Species tolerate subtropical to subarctic conditions, although they do best in temperate climates with cold winters. Well-drained soil is essential for growth. They prefer deep, humus-rich, sandy loams in full light, although shade is tolerated. Plant in early spring in colder climates and autumn in warmer areas. Pruning consists basically of thinning out the branches of the tree to allow plenty of air and light around the fruit. Once established, it is rarely necessary to do more than shorten (in summer) the current season's over-long shoots. Thrips, mites, aphids, moth larvae and fruit-fly are just some among quite a few unwelcome guests which visit these trees. Apple trees are not fertile to their own pollen, so it is necessary to grow two or more varieties to produce a crop. The size of the tree depends on the understock, and in most gardens trees grafted on a 'dwarfing' stock will be best.
Planting time Autumn or early spring.
Zone 7–8.

Malus × *domestica* 'Red Delicious'

'Red Delicious' is an excellent dessert apple. Unfortunately, the apples do not keep well after being picked.

MORUS NIGRA

Black mulberry

From the same family as the fig tree, the deciduous mulberry has a 15–30 ft (4.5–9 m) tall trunk and wide-spreading branches. This slow-growing species has ornamental, heart-shaped leaves and black fruit. This tree commands a lot of space but can be grown in tubs or trained espalier as long as it has been pruned and shaped from early growth.

Cultivation

It loves a temperate climate and the fruit will ripen in early summer, becoming easy prey for passing birds. Propagate from seedlings. The white mulberry *(M. alba)* is more suitable for warm-winter climates, however, its fruit is not quite as good. Its leaves are fed to silkworms. Do not plant either *M. nigra* or *M. alba* where the fruit can fall on paving, as the fruit will stain it.
Planting time Autumn or late winter.
Zone 8–9.

PRUNUS

This large genus, mostly from the northern hemisphere, includes the edible stone fruits—cherries, plums, apricots, peaches, nectarines and almonds—and ornamental species and cultivars with beautiful flowers. While the genus includes several shrubby species, most are trees growing on average to 15 ft (4.5 m), although some can reach as much as 100 ft (30 m). Most of the familiar species are deciduous and bloom in spring (or late winter in mild climates) with scented, 5-petalled, pink or white flowers.

Cultivation

Plant in moist, well-drained soil in full sun but with some protection from strong wind for the spring blossom. Keep the ground around base of trees free of weeds and long grass and feed young trees with a high-nitrogen fertilizer. Many of the fruiting varieties respond well to espaliering. Propagate by grafting or from seed—named cultivars must be grafted or budded onto seedling stocks.

Planting time Autumn. *Zone 3–10.*

Prunus avium

Gean, mazzard, sweet cherry, wild cherry

Native to Europe and western Asia, this species is the major parent of the cultivated sweet cherries. It can reach 60 ft (18 m) in height. The pointed, dark green leaves are up to 6 in (15 cm) long and turn red, crimson and yellow before dropping. Profuse white flowers appear in late spring before the leaves and are followed by black-red fruit. Cultivated cherries are rarely self-fertile, so trees of 2 or more different clones are usually necessary for fruit production. Cherry wood is prone to fungus, so do not prune in winter or in wet weather.

Prunus avium

Prunus persica

Prunus persica

Peach, flowering peach, nectarine

Believed to have originated in China but introduced to the Mediterranean region over 1,000 years ago, the peach grows to 12 ft (3.5 m) or more, and bears abundant pinkish red flowers in early spring (late winter in mild climates). Its delicious midsummer fruit, varying in color from cream and pale pink to yellow or scarlet, is covered with a velvety down and contains a stone that is deeply pitted and grooved. *Prunus persica* var. *nectarina*, the nectarine, is almost identical to the peach in habit and flowers but its fruit are smooth skinned, mostly smaller and with a subtly different flavor.

PYRUS

Pear

Thousands of years of cultivation have produced many different shapes, sizes and fruit of pear trees, some more suitable for the domestic garden than others. Usually a large tree, it flourishes in a moist, mild climate.

Cultivation

Plant in a warm, protected spot where it will receive maximum sunlight. In a small garden, train it to grow on a lattice or wire frame. Alternatively, pear trees grafted onto quince stock are good for home gardens. It can stand a reasonable amount of water and responds well to loamy soil with the occasional boost of nitrogen-rich fertilizers. Cross-pollination is needed for productive fruiting. *Planting time* Autumn or early spring. *Zone 7–9.*

Rubus idaeus

Pyrus communis 'Beurre Bosc'

Pyrus communis 'Beurre Bosc'

This is popular worldwide for its large, sweet pears that are ideal for baking. It is prone to the pear scab fungus.

Pyrus ussuriensis

Manchurian pear

Also known as the Ussuri pear, this splendid tree is the largest growing of the pears and can reach 60 ft (18 m) or more, with a broad pyramidal shape. The tree is covered with a profusion of small, scented white flowers in spring which are followed by small, yellow-brown fruit. Its dark, shiny green leaves are almost heart shaped. They turn brilliant red and coral in autumn. *P. ussuriensis* makes a neat, attractive street tree.

RUBUS

This genus includes a large number of the berry fruits, including raspberries and blackberries. The plants produce long, trailing shoots known as canes, which bear fruit in their second season and then die. They need supporting frames to keep the fruit away from the ground, and to keep the plants under control—any shoot that lies on the ground will take root. In a small garden the plants can be trained against a wall or trellis.

Cultivation

Cool climates and an acidic, well-drained soil that holds water well are best. Make sure that the ground is well

clear of weeds before planting. Propagate from pieces of root or root suckers.
Planting time Early winter. *Zone 7–8.*

Rubus idaeus

Raspberry

Rubus idaeus from Europe is the main parent of the garden raspberries, though most modern cultivars have various American species in their background. All make tall lax bushes with delicious red fruit, much used for jam but also eaten fresh. There are both summer and autumn fruiting varieties; be sure to buy certified virus-free stocks and control aphids, which spread virus diseases.

VACCINIUM CORYMBOSUM

Blueberry

A fast-growing, deciduous shrub with handsome autumn colors. It looks best when planted as a thick hedge so that the flowers and berries form a mass of white or blue, depending on the season. 'Blue Ray' has delicious, sweet fruit.

Cultivation

It does well in cold climates and prefers a well-drained but constantly moist, loamy, acidic soil. It is self-fertile. Clear away weak branches in winter and shape so that light and air can reach the inner bush. The cooler the climate, the tastier the fruit will be. Propagate from cuttings. The blueberry is harder to reproduce than other berry fruit.
Planting time Early winter. *Zone 7–8.*

VITIS LABRUSCA

Fox grape

The parent of most of the non-Vitis vinifera grapes cultivated in the USA, this native of the eastern seaboard produces long, felty young shoots that require trellising for support. The large, shallowly 3-lobed leaves are deep green above and felty white beneath. 'Concord', 'Catawba' and 'Niagara' are popular cultivars in areas where summers are cool and short.

Cultivation

Grow in humus-rich, moisture-retentive but well-drained soil in full sun or part-shade. Fully to marginally frost hardy, they need cool winters and low summer humidity or mildew will be a major problem. Prune in mid-winter to control growth and encourage heavy fruiting. Propagate from cuttings in late winter.
Planting time Late winter. *Zone 4–9.*

Pyrus ussuriensis

Vaccinium corymbosum 'Blue Ray'

INDOOR PLANTS

The Victorians grew fuchsias on their window sills and ferns in miniature greenhouses, but the idea of plants as major features in interior design is a recent one. It was made possible by modern architecture, which increased the size of our windows, and electric light, which superseded gas and its plant-killing fumes. Indoor plants need adequate light for photosynthesis, and suitable humidity. Most of them drown rather than die of thirst, so you also need to water them with care. Some of the flowering types, such as cyclamens, gloxinias and poinsettias, are difficult to grow indoors. They will be spectacular, though temporary, delights.

Begonia × tuberhybrida

AECHMEA FASCIATA
Silver vase

Reminiscent of a formal flower arrangement, this Brazilian species of the diverse bromeliad genera has a 'vase' of silvery gray leaves irregularly barred green, from which emerges in summer a short, broad cluster of mauve-blue flowers among crowded, spiky bracts of a delicate clear pink. The rosettes, up to about 18 in (45 cm) high, do not clump up much.

Cultivation

In the tropics and subtropics they grow happily outdoors, most preferring filtered sun, a slightly raised bed and soil which is high in humus. Some tolerate surprisingly cool conditions. Usually, however, they are grown as indoor or hot house plants, potted in a coarse medium. Propagate by division (separating 'pups' with a sharp knife), or from seed.
Light Medium.

AGLAONEMA COMMUTATUM

Native to the Philippines and eastern Indonesia, this perennial subshrub has fleshy stems, branching from the base, which grow to about 18 in (45 cm) high,

Begonia fuchsioides

and bear slender-stalked leaves up to about 12 in (30 cm) long. The flowering stems have a narrow pale green spathe enclosing a small white spadix, and may appear through much of the year. In the original wild forms the leaves are dark green with subtle whitish feathering along the lateral veins, but cultivars have larger cream and yellow splashes.

Cultivation

In the tropics, aglaonemas are easily grown in any moist shady area beneath trees but in temperate regions they are grown indoors in containers. Propagation is normally by cuttings or offsets, which are easily rooted.
Light Medium.

BEGONIA
Begonia

Begonias are native to all tropical regions except Australia. The species all have waxy leaves and a succulent form. They do well in indoor potting mix with either peat moss, leafmold or well-rotted manure added to increase acidity.

Cultivation

Begonias need above average humidity and temperatures of 62–90° (16–30°C). Humidity can be maintained by standing the pot on a tray of pebbles and water. Keep soil moist but not soggy. Fertilize

in the spring growing season. Most begonias can be propagated from stem and leaf cuttings in spring, by division of rhizomes or from seed.
Light Medium–bright.

Begonia fuchsioides
A small-leafed species growing to around 30 in (75 cm), this dainty plant can be brought indoors when in flower or positioned on a covered terrace. Small pink flowers complement the waxy green leaves.

Begonia × tuberhybrida
The vibrant colors of the tuberous begonias make them bright house guests in the cooler months.

CALATHEA

Prayer plant

Native to South America and the West Indies, the plants in this large genus have decorative foliage. The long-stalked, mostly upright leaves are usually large. *C. zebrina* has velvety leaves marked by parallel stripes or bars of pale chartreuse.

Cultivation
Caltheas require high humidity achieved by misting frequently or standing the pot on a tray of pebbles and water. Do not allow to dry out totally and feed with half-strength fertilizer every 4 to 5 weeks when conditions are warm. Repot annually as they exhaust the soil and do not like to be overcrowded. Propagate by division in early spring.
Light Medium–bright.

CALCEOLARIA × HERBEOHYBRIDA

These low-growing annuals, which are ideally suited to greenhouse culture, have interesting flowers. The plants can be brought indoors when they bloom.

Calathea zebrina

Calcoolaria × horboohybrida

Cultivation
They need a lightly shaded position in well-drained soil. Protect them from the wind.
Light Medium–bright.

CYCLAMEN PERSICUM

Florist's cyclamen

From the woodlands of the Middle East, this is the most common species grown indoors. From the heart-shaped leaves, rise waxy flowers in shades of white and pink. It needs high humidity, so stand the plant on a tray of pebbles.

Cultivation
Water thoroughly, but avoid getting water in among the bases of the leaves,

then let the surface become just dry. Do not water in summer. Repot in autumn in potting mix with a sprinkling of lime and blood and bone; resume watering. *Light* Medium–bright.

DIEFFENBACHIA

Dumb cane

These decorative foliage plants from tropical America reach ceiling height when mature. The large, variegated leaves are oval-shaped. Popular indoor plants, they are easy to keep as long as humidity is maintained.

Cultivation

Bright to moderate light suits them. Allow the surface soil to become dry in between thorough waterings as root rot may occur if overwatered. Propagate in spring or summer from cuttings or stems laid horizontally in compost, but be careful to wash your hands. The poisonous sap causes the mouth and tongue to swell, rendering speech impossible. *Light* Medium–bright.

***Dieffenbachia seguine* 'Rudolph Roehrs'**

syn. *D. seguine* 'Roehrsii'

Growing to 3 ft (1 m) or more, this plant has sword-like, chartreuse leaves with mid-rib and edges in green.

DRACAENA MARGINATA

syn. *Pleomele*

A slow-growing tree or shrub from Madagascar, this species reaches 15–20 ft (4.5–6 m) in warm climates. Its narrow, sword-like leaves have red margins. The cultivar 'Tricolor' with a cream stripe and red edge is commonly grown as a houseplant. This species tolerates some shade and quite low winter temperatures but not frost. Dracaenas are often termed 'false palms' because of their

Cyclamen persicum

Dieffenbachia sp.

Dracaena marginata

cane-like stems and attractive crowns of sword-like leaves.

Cultivation
Very suitable for container growing, dracaenas need warmth to do their best. Plant in well-drained soil. Propagate from seed or by air-layering in spring or from stem cuttings in summer. Watch out for mealybugs.
Light Bright.

EPIPREMNUM AUREUM

syn. *Scindapsus aureus*

Pothos, devil's ivy

This evergreen climber is a fast-growing plant which can be kept in water for months or planted in rich, moisture-retentive soil. The apple-green, leaves are marbled with creamy white or gold.

Cultivation
It needs a humid and draft-free location. Water regularly during spring and summer, less in winter. Pinch off shoot tips to encourage branching. Propagate in late spring from leaf-bud or stem cuttings, which are kept in barely moist soil in a dark position until they have rooted.
Light Medium–bright.

EUPHORBIA PULCHERRIMA

Poinsettia, Mexican flame tree

Potted poinsettias are a familiar Christmas decoration, but this native of Mexico is only a garden plant in frost-free climates. It makes a rather open shrub up to 12 ft (3.5 m) tall, usually dropping its leaves as flowering commences. The broad bracts, which give each flower cluster the appearance of a single, huge flower, last many weeks. There are many named cultivars, which extend the color range from the original blood red to pink and cream. It thrives best in subtropical regions and likes fertile soil and sunshine. Most cultivars now sold for indoor use are semi-dwarf: 'Annette Hegg' is red, while 'Rosea' (pink) and 'Lemon Drop' (pale yellow) are similar except for color.

Cultivation
Plant in sun or part-shade in moist, well-drained soil. Propagate from cuttings in spring or summer, by division in early spring or autumn or from seed in autumn or spring.
Light Bright.

Epipremnum aureum

Euphorbia pulcherrima

Ficus lyatra

Ficus benjamina

FICUS

A genus of great variety, the species are grown for their foliage and tropical effect. Their leathery leaves allow them to tolerate a dry atmosphere.

Cultivation

Water moderately, keeping moist in the warmer months, and very little when the temperature is low. Overwatering may lead to leaf drop. Sponge leaves with a damp cloth. Propagate from stem or leaf-bud cuttings and repot when roots fill the pot.
Light Medium–bright.

Ficus benjamina
Weeping fig, weeping Chinese banyan
A tropical Asian evergreen tree, the weeping fig can reach 50 ft (15 m) in height and a much greater spread, and is sometimes supported by aerial roots. It has shiny, pointed, oval leaves, insignificant fruit and an invasive root system. This species and its cultivars are used extensively as potted houseplants; they need adequate water in summer, less in cooler months. 'Exotica' has twisted leaf tips; 'Variegata' has rich green leaves splashed with white.

Ficus lyrata
Fiddle-leaf fig
This handsome plant has huge, lustrous, dark green leaves shaped like a fiddle. It may grow to about 10 ft (3 m) indoors and will tolerate low light.

HOYA

These twining climbers with waxy foliage, native to Malaysia, China, India and tropical Australia, all bear clusters of scented, star-shaped flowers in summer. If the plant is supported on a frame and also slightly pot-bound it is more likely to flower.

Cultivation

Plant in any potting soil that drains well and allow the soil surface to become quite dry between waterings. As the new flowers come from the same spurs as the old ones it is best not to prune or pick. Propagate from semi-ripe cuttings in summer. Sticky honeydew drips from the flowers.
Light Bright–very bright.

Impatiens New Guinea hybrid

Hoya carnosa
Wax plant
Native to Australia, this twining plant can be grown against a small framework. From summer to autumn, its dark green, glossy, oval leaves are complemented by scented, star-shaped flowers.

IMPATIENS NEW GUINEA HYBRIDS

The decorative leaves vie for attention with the interesting flat, spurred flowers. These fast-growing perennials are suited to indoors in cooler areas or on enclosed verandas in warmer climates.

Cultivation
They prefer a moist, yet open draining soil in a draft-free position. Tip prune to ensure bushiness and propagate from seed or by cuttings.
Light Medium–bright.

JUSTICA CARNEA

Radiator plant
A small evergreen with veined leaves and pink flowers held aloft the foliage in late summer or autumn. They make ideal indoor plants as pests can be quickly detected before they disfigure the leaves.

Cultivation
Give these plants a well-drained moderately fertile soil; water well and fertilize during their growing season to ensure maximum quality blooms. Prune after flowering to maintain bushiness.
Light Medium–bright.

Hoya carnosa cultivar

Justicia carnea

SAINTPAULIA

African violet
The several thousand varieties of African violets are popular because of their foliage, compact nature, long flowering periods and wide range of flower colors. As they demand certain soil, it is easiest to plant them in commercial African violet mix. Constant temperature, moderate humidity and maximum, bright, indirect light will ensure long flowering.

Cultivation
Use room temperature water, and allow the surface soil to dry out a little

between waterings. Avoid splashing the foliage. Feed once a month in the warm season with half-strength, soluble fertilizer. African violets prefer to be slightly pot-bound to bloom well, but repot when very leafy. Propagate from leaf cuttings stuck in a layer of pebbles on top of a moist sand and peat mixture. *Light* Medium–bright.

Saintpaulia ionantha

This species has clusters of tubular, 5-lobed, violet-blue flowers of semi-succulent texture, growing on the stems above the leaves. The flowers can be single or double, and come in shades from white through mauve and blue to purple, and pale and deep pink to crimson.

Schefflera actinophylla

Saintpaulia ionatha

SANSEVIERIA TRIFASCIATA

Mother-in-law's tongue

From the central rosette of this Nigerian species emerge stiff, lance-shaped leaves 2–4 ft (0.6–1.2 m) long and 2 in (5 cm) or more wide. The dark green leaves are banded with gray-green and yellow. The plant sometimes has racemes of tubular, green flowers but rarely when grown indoors. 'Golden Hahnii' has broad leaves with golden yellow vertical stripes; 'Laurentii' has narrow, upright leaves with broad yellow margins.

Cultivation

Do not overwater, as this may cause rotting at the leaf bases and the roots. They need a minimum temperature of 50–60°F (10–15°C). Propagate from cuttings or by division in spring or summer. *Light* Medium–bright.

SCHEFFLERA

syn. *Brassaia, Heptapleurum*

These attractive, subtropical and tropical trees can grow to 6–14 ft (2–4 m) indoors and much taller outdoors. The glossy foliage is split into leaflets. They are easy to grow (but rarely flower) indoors.

Sansevieria trifasciata 'Laurentii'

Cultivation

Plant in a standard indoor potting soil, away from direct sunlight, with average to warm temperatures. Keep humidity high by misting or placing on a tray of pebbles and water. Water freely when in full growth, less at other times. Feed every 6 to 8 weeks in warmer weather with soluble plant food. Propagate by taking 4 in (10 cm) long stem cuttings from just below the nodes in spring.
Light Medium–bright.

Schefflera actinophylla
Queensland umbrella tree

The most common indoor species, its glossy foliage resembles segments of an umbrella. Long green stalks are crested by light green leaves. Indoors, it usually grows to about 6 ft (1.8 m) tall.

SPATHIPHYLLUM

Most species of this genus come from tropical America, but some are native to Malaysia. They are lush, with dark green, oval leaves that stand erect or arch slightly, and beautiful white, cream or green flowers, resembling arum lilies.

Cultivation

Grow in loose and fibrous, porous potting soil in filtered light. Water regularly, keeping the soil moist but not soggy, and allow it to dry out a little in winter. Feed every 4 to 6 weeks with half-strength, soluble fertilizer in spring and summer. Propagate by division in spring or summer.
Light Low–medium.

Spathiphyllum 'Mauna Loa'
Peace lily

The leathery, lance-shaped, glossy, mid-green leaves reach lengths of 18–24 in (45–60 cm). Oval, white, papery spathes, which surround white spadices, are borne intermittently, and age to green.

TILLANDSIA CYANEA
Pink quill

Rosettes of grass-like, arching leaves are usually deep green and often reddish brown when new. In summer to autumn the flowerheads rise on tall stems from among the foliage. It needs maximum humidity and is best grown in a compost of tree fern fiber, peat and sand.

Cultivation

Plant in well-drained sphagnum moss or grow on slabs of bark or driftwood. Propagate from offsets or by division.
Light Medium–bright.

Spathiphyllum 'Mauna Loa'

Tillandsia cyanea

CACTI & SUCCULENTS

Cacti are not the only family of succulent plants, but they show the succulent habit at its most wonderful. They are superb examples of how life adapts to flourish in the most uncompromising of environments. Unlike the cacti, other succulents store their reserves of water in succulent leaves rather than stems, and these are often marvellously shaped, colored and marked. Their habit varies from shrubby to just a few leaves on ground-hugging stems, and their flowers vary from the brilliance of the aloes and mesembryanthemums to being almost insignificant.

Aeonium arboreum 'Schwarzkopf'

Agave americana

AEONIUM

Native to the Canary Islands, the Mediterranean and northern Africa, this genus contains 40 short-lived, perennial or evergreen succulents. The species develop either as one large (or several smaller), compact, stemless rosette, or as several long, leathery stalks with rosettes on top. The foliage is lush and oval. Attractive star-shaped, pink, red, white or yellow flowers appear from the center of the leaf whorls.

Cultivation

These succulents prefer full sun or partial shade, light, well-drained soil and warmer temperatures. Prune stems after the bloom although the flowering rosette will usually die and single-rosette species will die out completely. Propagate from seed or leaf stem cuttings in spring and summer.
Flowering time Spring. *Zone 9.*

Aeonium arboreum 'Schwarzkopf'

This shrubby plant from southern Europe grows up to 24 in (60 cm) in height and 3 ft (1 m) in width. Its striking, stemmed rosettes have lance-shaped, purple-black leaves. In spring, after 2 or 3 years, little, starry, golden yellow flowers develop from the center of each rosette.

AGAVE

This genus consists of over 300 species native to South and Central America. The small species flower after 5 to 10 years; the tall species may not flower until they are 20 to 40 years old.

Cultivation

They all like well-drained, gritty soil, but will grow in poor soil. Although they need a very sunny position, young plants should be sheltered if in a frost area. They are drought tolerant, but need regular watering. Propagate from offsets or from seed in spring or summer.
Flowering time Spring/summer. *Zone 9.*

Agave americana
Century plant

This large succulent makes a very good accent plant in the garden, with a 10 ft (3 m) high and wide rosette of thick, fleshy, strap-shaped, gray-green leaves edged with sharp spines and pointed tips; a form with variegated leaves is popular. It flowers when it is 10 or more years old with a stalk of yellow flowers. The plant dies after flowering, leaving offsets which can then be used for propagation.

ALOE

Aloe

This diverse genus of rosetted plants is native to Africa and the Middle East. They range widely in habit, from low and shrubby, to tall and tree-like, with several types of vines and creepers also included. The whorled, lush, grayish green foliage is usually lanceolate and marked with white lines or patches. The flowers are very attractive and cylindrical. In red, yellow or orange, they appear in long-stemmed racemes.

Cultivation

These plants prefer moderate temperatures and are almost all half-hardy. The larger types prefer full sun, while the dwarf species enjoy semi-shade. Plant in rich, extremely porous soil and only water when the roots appear dry. Propagate from seed or stem cuttings. *Flowering time* Spring. *Zone 8–11.*

Aloe arborescens

Candelabra aloe, torch plant

This popular South African species has a shrubby habit and reaches up to 6–10 ft (2–3 m) in height when in flower. Its short-stemmed rosettes are composed of lush, grayish blue leaves up to 24 in (60 cm) long, slightly inward-curving and thorny-edged. Thick clusters of scarlet-red or yellow, cylindrical flowers develop along an upright stem in late winter to early spring. It is salt and drought resistant.

Aloe arborescens

Aloe vera

Aloe vera

syn. *Aloe barbadensis*

Medicinal aloe, medicine plant, burn plant

Renowned for its medicinal qualities, this short-stemmed species, its likely origin Arabia or northern Africa, grows to 24 in (60 cm) high and has rosettes of narrow, thick, lance-shaped, grayish green leaves with small whitish teeth on the margins. In summer, small orange-yellow flowers appear in spikes up to 3 ft (1 m) high. Its syrupy leaf juice is used in skin care products and for treatment of burns.

CEPHALOCEREUS SENILIS

Old man cactus

This erect, South American cactus grows slowly to 40 ft (12 m) tall in the wild but only 19 in (50 cm) in pots. It has up to 30 ribs, fine, short, yellowy white spines and a profusion of gray-white fleecy hair, which resembles an old man's whiskers. Mature plants develop thorny crowns from where trumpet-shaped, reddish pink spring flowers appear, although this is not usual on cultivated specimens. It is sometimes sold as a novelty item.

Cultivation

This frost-tender cactus is suitable for the greenhouse and requires full sun or partial shade and sandy, slightly alkaline soil. Water sparingly and propagate from seed or cuttings.
Flowering time Spring. *Zone 9.*

Cephalocereus senilis

DROSANTHEMUM

This genus contains approximately 95 species of perennial succulents native to South Africa. They have a spreading habit and vary in height, some reaching 3 ft (1 m). The leaves are densely covered in bright papillae and flowers range in color from pink and yellow to deep purple. Frost-tender, they require bright sunlight for the flowers to open fully.

Cultivation

Potted specimens can be kept indoors in winter in a warm, sunny position. Plant in well-drained, compost-enriched soil. Water sparingly in summer and keep fairly dry in winter. Propagate from seed or cuttings and replace plants about every 3 years.
Flowering time Summer. *Zone 9.*

Drosanthemum floribundum

This small, cushion-forming plant reaches up to 6 in (15 cm) in height. Its creeping branches take root as they grow and are covered with pairs of pale, gray-green, cylindrical leaves. A profusion of pink, daisy-like flowers are borne in summer.

ECHEVERIA

Hen and chicks

Native to the Americas, this large genus contains over 150 species of ornamental, perennial succulents valued for their habit, foliage and flowers. The species form in perfectly symmetrical, basal rosettes or in multi-stemmed bushes up to 3 ft (1 m) tall. Bell-shaped to cylindrical flowers bloom through the year.

Cultivation

Half-hardy to frost-tender, the succulents require full sun or semi-shade, very porous soil and light watering. Propagate from seed, offsets or cuttings, or by

division in spring and summer.
Flowering time Spring–summer.
Zone 8–9.

Echeveria elegans
Pearl echeveria
This half-hardy succulent develops in a thickly foliaged, basal rosette up to 2 in (5 cm) tall and 19 in (50 cm) in diameter. Its lush leaves are frosted blue-green with red margins. The bell-shaped, pinkish red flowers have yellow petal tips. 'Kesselringii' has gray-blue leaves in a loose rosette.

ECHINOCACTUS GRUSONII
Golden barrel cactus
Originating in Mexico, this popular, slow-growing cactus reaches up to 6 ft (2 m) in height and breadth. It has a single, globe-shaped, pale green body that stretches upwards in maturity, becoming barrel-shaped. This stem is heavily ribbed with numerous areoles sprouting radial, yellow spines. In summer, larger cacti produce a circle of yellow flowers from a crown at the top of the plant.

Echinocactus grusonii

Cultivation
Drought-resistant and frost-tender, the species requires well-drained soil and warmer temperatures. Full sun maintains the luster of the spines and the longevity of the flowers. This cactus is propagated from seed in spring. Young plants are prone to mealybug and spider mite.
Flowering time Summer. *Zone 9.*

Echeveria elegans

Drosanthemum floribundum

Echinopsis oxygona

ECHINOPSIS

This very popular genus contains over 35 species of cacti, native to South America, and growing up to 12 in (30 cm) tall. Ranging from single, basal, globe-shaped stems to readily colonizing, tubular and erect, these cacti are covered with spines and also have pronounced ribs. The species are highly valued for their brilliantly colored, funnel-shaped flowers which are up to 8 in (20 cm) long. The blooms only open at night and, unfortunately, are short-lived.

Cultivation

Half-hardy to frost-tender, these plants will survive in varying degrees of shade and require rich, well-drained soil and light water. Propagate in spring and summer from seed and offsets which are readily produced.
Flowering time Spring–summer. *Zone 9.*

Epiphyllum hybrids

Echinopsis oxygona
Easter lily cactus, barrel cactus
Originating in Brazil, this spherical, multi-branched cactus grows to 6 in (15 cm) in maturity and forms dense thickets up to 3 ft (1 m) in diameter. Long, slender, tapering, ribbed branches are covered with brown, black-tipped spines. These asparagus-like stems are inwardly curving and sprout fragrant, pinkish blue flowers from the tips.

EPIPHYLLUM OXYPETALUM

Belle de nuit
Ranging from Mexico to Brazil, this popular species has an upright growth habit to 6 ft (1.8 m) in height. Its multiple stems are up to 4 in (10 cm) wide, tapering to their bases and arching in maturity. The nocturnal, 6 in (15 cm) wide, white flowers have long, slightly curved tubes. They are intensely fragrant.

Cultivation

Frost-tender, species of *Epiphyllum* require a dry, cool spell during winter, and a light, sandy soil and strong light for optimum flowering. These cacti are ideal hanging basket plants, their trailing stems seeming to grow better if the roots are restricted. Propagate from seed in spring and cuttings in summer.
Flowering time Spring–summer. *Zone 10–12.*

HAWORTHIA

This genus of 150 dense, dwarf-like, perennial succulents originated in South Africa. The species are predominantly thicket-forming, developing in basal or short-stemmed rosettes. The decorative foliage is lanceolate to triangular.

Cultivation

Ranging from frost-hardy to frost-tender, these succulents require semi-shade to maintain healthy leaves. Keep slightly moist during the hotter months and dry in winter. Propagate by division or from offsets during spring to autumn. *Flowering time* Spring–summer. *Zone 8–9.*

Haworthia fasciata

The leaves of this succulent stand upright in neat rosettes. The tiny white flowers are carried in early summer on 15 in (40 cm) tall, bare stems. Half hardy, it is propagated by removing offsets.

KALANCHOE

This genus comprises approximately 200 species of perennial succulents native mostly to southern Asia and tropical and subtropical Africa. The species range in habit from erect and bushy to spreading and prostrate. The succulent pairs of opposing leaves vary from slender to rounded. The tubular or bell-shaped flowers have four petals and appear in branched terminal clusters.

Cultivation

These succulents require only light watering in the colder months and range from frost-hardy to frost-tender. Propagate from stem or leaf cuttings in late spring to summer, seed at the end of spring, or pot up plantlets that may form along leaf margins. *Flowering time* Late winter–summer. *Zone 11–12.*

Haworthia fasciata

Kalanchoe tomentosa

Kalanchoe tomentosa

Panda plant

This erect, shrubby Madagascan species grows gradually to 3 ft (1 m) tall with a spread of 8 in (20 cm). It has spoon-shaped, light gray-green leaves, covered with white felt, and yellowish green flowers tinged with purple on the lobes.

OPUNTIA

Prickly pear

This large, diverse genus is native to the USA, South America and the West Indies. Varying from prostrate to erect, and typically compact and branching, these cacti either develop flat, pad-like, jointed stems or branches with little tubular or three-angled leaves. Most species are covered with sharp spines and soft, hooked bristles, called 'glochids'. Open-petaled, mostly yellow flowers appear on larger plants in spring and summer.

Cultivation

Fully hardy to frost-tender, they require total sun and porous soil. Propagate from seed or cuttings in spring and summer. Several species have become serious pests in warmer countries, the worst being *O. stricta* in Australia and South Africa.
Flowering time Spring–summer. *Zone 9.*

Opuntia ficus-indica
syn. *O. engelmannii, O. megacantha*
Indian fig

With an upright, open habit, becoming compact and multi-stemmed in maturity, this species reaches 16 ft (5 m) in height and breadth. It has jointed stems composed of gray, oval pads up to 18 in (45 cm) long and usually covered with spines. Funnel-like, vivid yellow flowers appear from the stem tips in summer, followed by reddish yellow-purple, bristly but delicious fruit.

Schlumberga hybrids

Opuntia ficus-indica

SCHLUMBERGERA HYBRIDS

Christmas cactus

Christmas cacti are familiar flower shop potted plants. The genus consists of 6 species of bushy cacti from southeastern Brazil with flattened, spineless and rather weeping branches with indented notches at the margins. The bright flowers appear at the stem tips; they come in shades from palest pink to orange, magenta, scarlet and white. They are often grown in hanging baskets but do not cascade vigorously enough to cover the basket, looking their best in tall pots.

Cultivation

Species of *Schlumbergera* prefer mild, frost-free climates; in cooler areas they make excellent indoor plants. Plant in part-shade in rich, well-drained soil. Once they set their flower buds they do not like being moved to another position and could drop their buds. Propagate from stem cuttings in spring or early summer.
Flowering time Autumn–winter.
Zone 9–12.

SEDUM

Stonecrop

This very large genus contains over 500 species of predominantly evergreen succulents native to the northern hemisphere. These quick-growing plants vary widely in habit from carpet-forming to upright (up to 3 ft (1 m) tall). Their lush leaves may be tubular, lanceolate, oval or elliptical and the 5-petal ed flowers appear in terminal sprays.

Cultivation

Species range from fully hardy to frost-tender. Fertile, porous soil is preferred; however, some types will grow in most soil types. Propagate from seed in spring, stem cuttings in summer, or by division in spring or summer.
Flowering time Late summer–autumn.
Zone 8–9.

Sedum morganianum

Donkey's tail, burro tail

Native to Mexico, this branching, evergreen succulent has a compact habit which becomes weeping as the stems lengthen. Growing 3 ft (1 m) long, the stems are composed of bluish green, interlocking leaves that have a plump, lanceolate form. In cultivation, clusters of long, pinkish red, starry flowers may bloom at the stem tips in summer.

Sedum spectabile

This fully hardy, herbaceous succulent has a mound-forming habit with plump, fleshy, green or frosted gray leaves. In summer, flat-headed clusters of star-shaped pink flowers appear on short stems, usually with scattered leaves clasped close to the upright stems.

Sedum morganianum

YUCCA FILAMENTOSA

Golden barrel cactus

This plant grows in rosette-like clumps and has sharp, acutely pointed gray-green leaves which are almost 3 ft (1 m) long. The stiff foliage is softened by the large elegant spikes of lily-of-the-valley type flowers.

Cultivation

It needs full sun to flower well and is drought and frost resistant. Propagate by division.
Flowering time Summer. *Zone 8–9.*

Sedum spectabile

Yucca filamentosa

ORCHIDS

Orchids have a reputation for being glamorous, expensive and difficult. They are certainly glamorous, but new methods of propagation have made them much more affordable, and few are really difficult to grow. The orchid family is enormous; they are second only to the grasses in the plant kingdom. Wild orchids grow nearly everywhere, except in the Arctic and Antarctic. The most admired and coveted may be those from the tropics and subtropics of the old and new worlds, but the more modest temperate climate orchids are delightful too, and not as well known as they should be.

Cattleya hybrid

Cymbidium miniature hybrid

CATTLEYA

This large genus of epiphytes from Central and South America is perhaps the most admired of all orchids. The big ruffled hybrids of the flower shop, usually orchid-pink or white, are the best known: but there are more than 60 species and countless hybrids, the flowers ranging from miniatures only 2 in (5 cm) or so across to giants of 6 in (15 cm) or more. Just about every color but blue is available, though the brighter yellow-to-red shades tend to have smaller flowers. The genus is divided into two types: the bifoliate cattleyas, which have two thick leaves atop the stem-like pseudo-bulbs, and the unifoliates, which have only one. They mostly grow about 15 in (38 cm) tall, though they can spread into clumps as much as 3 ft (1 m) wide, and the flower sprays arise from the tops of the pseudo-bulbs. They appear, according to variety, in spring or autumn. The genus hybridizes very easily with the related *Laelia, Rhyncolaelia* and *Sophronitis,* and the resultant hybrids are often sold simply as 'cattleyas'. They are cultivated in the same way. The genus is named after an English orchid fancier, William Cattley, whose name is a guide to the pronunciation of the genus name.

Cultivation

All species of *Cattleya* prefer good light but not strong sunlight, a coarse potting mix, and a winter rest. They are propagated by division just as growth begins, which may be either in spring or in early autumn. This can be a messy job, as the roots tend to stick to the pot.

Flowering time Spring. *Zone 9.*

***Cattleya bifoliate* hybrids**

Cluster cattleya

There are many of these hybrids to choose from, with mostly rather small flowers in clusters, and almost all cool-growing; they can be grown out-of-doors in any frost-free, humid summer climate. They can be spring or autumn growing, and colors range from white through pink to magenta, with some in the yellow to coral range which carry genes from the dainty orange *C. aurantiaca*.

CYMBIDIUM MINIATURE HYBRIDS

The diminutive growing habits of these hybrids are gaining in favor with gardeners who have limited garden space. They have grass-like foliage, up to 19 in (50 cm), with many blooms on the miniature flower spikes which may need to be staked. Many have the rounded shape of the larger *Cymbidium* hybrids while others have blooms which are more spidery. Color ranges from green and yellows through to shades of pink and red.

Cultivation

Although these can be grown outdoors in temperate areas, they make ideal potted plants which can be brought indoors when flowering. Provide potted plants with a coarse, soil-free compost and place in a partial shade position away from pests. They can be divided after flowering and should be allowed to almost dry out during the colder winter months.

Flowering time Late winter. *Zone 9.*

DENDROBIUM

This is one of the largest of all the genera of orchids, with some 1500 species ranging from India, to China and Japan, Indonesia, New Guinea, Australia and New Zealand. It is also one of the most diverse. They can be evergreen or deciduous: most are epiphytic, but they vary in habit from clump-formers, which make fat pseudo-bulbs rather like those of a cattleya, to those whose bulbs have grown long and stem-like and which often carry their flowers in sprays in the axils of the fallen leaves. These last are divided into 'hard' and 'soft-caned' types: but though the hard types tend to be more upright in habit, the soft more floppy, even pendulous, the distinctions are not very consistent. The species and hybrids range from cool- to warm-growing: but in these days of high fuel costs, the warm-growing types are more often seen in bunches of imported 'Singapore orchids' than in what the orchid trade patronizingly calls 'amateur' greenhouses.

Cultivation

The largest and most diverse genus of the orchid family, they come from various habitats. All are epiphytic and like a free-draining mix in a temperate to warm, shady position.

Flowering time Winter, spring. *Zone 9.*

Dendrobium densiflorum

Dendrobium densiflorum

This attractive species has oval leaves to 6 in (15 cm) long and pendant flowering stems. These hold dense, elongated clusters of scented yellow and orange blooms.

Dendrobium Yamamoto hybrids
The name describes a group of Hawaiian bred hybrids developed from earlier crosses. They are strong plants with much to interest the enthusiast, such as a wide color range.

EPIDENDRUM IBAGUENSE

syn. *Epidendrum radicans*

Crucifix orchid
This common species from Mexico to Colombia has long, slender, cylindrical stems to over 3 ft (1 m) long with short leathery leaves along most of their length. The orange, red or mauve flowers, which can appear at any time of year, are only about 1 in (25 mm) wide, but each flower stem will have up to 20 open at any one time. In cooler climates, it should be grown in a greenhouse and given strong light. The common name is inspired by the shape of the labellum, which looks like a tiny golden cross standing in the center of each flower.

Dendrobium Yamamoto hybrid

Cultivation
Epidendrums thrive outdoors in a warm, frost-free climate in sun or light shade; in colder climates they need the protection of a sunny room or greenhouse. Water and fertilize plants from spring to autumn. Propagate by division or by removing rooted offsets.
Flowering time Winter–autumn.
Zone 9–12.

MILTONIOPSIS

syn. *Miltonia*

Pansy orchid
The several species of *Miltonia* are worth growing, but the popular pansy orchids are now reclassified in a genus of their own. There are about 5 species, but much more commonly grown are the many hybrids. These make round pseudo-bulbs with strap-shaped, rather pale green leaves; and the flowers are carried in small clusters, mostly in mid-

Epidendrum ibaguense

summer, a time when there are not many orchids in flower—though they can appear at any time from spring to autumn. Usually about 4 in (10 cm) wide, they are quite flat, like pansies; though the colors, white through clear pinks to red with flashes of gold on the labella, are not really pansy-like.

Cultivation

They like an open compost, light shade, and to be kept growing all year—a winter rest is not desirable. Propagate by division after flowering.
Flowering time Spring–autumn. *Zone 9.*

ODONTOGLOSSUM 'SAMARES'

Thousands of colorful hybrids have been developed suitable for greenhouse culture using *Odontoglossum*. Many other genera have also been utilized in the production of hybrids including those with *Cochlioda* (× *Odontioda*), *Oncidium* (× *Odontocidium*) and *Miltonia* (× *Odontonia*). Extravagant 'Samares' is a fine example. Its pure white petals are wavy and frilly-edged and each is decorated with a blood-red spot

Cultivation

Most odontoglossums are cool growing, and need only the usual orchid cultivation of coarse compost, plenty of water in summer and light shade. They do not need as definite a winter rest as cattleyas, but do not overwater then. They can be divided after flowering.
Flowering time Spring–autumn.
Zone 10–12.

ONCIDIUM VARICOSUM

This species from Brazil is typical of a large group that bears small flowers in large, branched sprays. The most prominent feature of each flower is the

Oncidium varicosum hybrid

Miltoniopsis hybrid

Odontoglossum Hybrid 'Samares'

Paphiopedilum insigne

Vanda hybrid

brilliant yellow labellum, the other parts being small and brownish. The flowers are popular with florists.

Cultivation

This plant likes light shade and only a short winter rest, an open, coarse potting mix and high humidity; it dislikes being overwatered. In the wild, many climb up their host tree, and are best potted with a slab of tree fern trunk to which it can cling. They can be propagated by division in spring.
Flowering time Spring–autumn.
Zone 10–11.

PAPHIOPEDILUM

Slipper orchid

The tropical slipper orchids used to be classed with the temperate ones in the genus *Cyprepedium,* but now they have been given a genus of their own. There are about 60 species from Indo-China and Indonesia, and though all are distinctive enough to be worth cultivating, the most important is the cool-growing *C. insigne*. This has been the parent of many hybrids and selected forms, but there are other hybrids available, developed from other species and many of these are intermediate- or even warm-growing. As a general rule, types with spotted leaves need warmer conditions than those with plain green leaves, but none is difficult to grow. All are clump-forming perennials, mostly terrestrial in habit, with no pseudobulbs; the leaves hug the ground and the flowers are borne above them.

Cultivation

They all like a rich compost and shade and should not be allowed to dry out, even in winter. They are propagated by division; mericlonal propagation does not suit them, so selected clones and hybrids remain expensive.
Flowering time Winter, early spring.
Zone 9.

Paphiopedilum insigne

This cool-growing species comes from Bangladesh and the nearby Himalayas, and is rather variable; there are many different named forms in cultivation. They are normally about 12 in (30 cm) tall in flower, and the waxy flowers combine shades of green, russet, cream and white in various patterns and markings; all-green forms are much admired. They look best when allowed to form generous clumps, and the flowers last for several weeks.

PHALAENOPSIS HYBRIDS

Thousands of hybrids have been produced from the species of this genus. Most are white or pink, and are very popular for the cut flower industry, much-used in floral arrangements and bouquets. Some notable examples are Alice Gloria 'Cecil Park', which is pure white; Bill Smoothey, pink with white edgings; and 'Carmela's Stripe', a striking hybrid with light pink petals with deep red veining and red lips.

Cultivation

Phalaenopsis require tropical and subtropical climates—or elsewhere a warmed but well-ventilated greenhouse—and filtered light, constant moisture and a rich but open and perfectly drained compost. They are apt to send roots out over the top of the pot: these should be left undisturbed if possible. Propagate by division in spring.
Flowering time Spring–autumn.
Zone 11–12.

VANDA

The most celebrated species of this epiphytic genus from Southeast Asia to northern Australia is *V. caerulea,* the blue orchid from the mountains of Thailand and Burma, where it used to be quite common. Sadly, it is now endangered. It is typical of its genus in its 3 ft (1 m) tall, stem-like, pseudo-bulbs with leathery leaves, from which the sprays of as many as 12, 4 in (10 cm) wide flowers appear in early autumn. Some of the 70 or so species are spring or summer flowering, and the color range is from white through cream and pink to orange—the blue is rare.

Cultivation

They are all warm-growing epiphytes, liking a very coarse compost and strong light, though preferably not full sunshine; they are outdoor plants only in the tropics. Keep them warm and watered all year, as they rarely take a winter rest, and propagate by removing rooted offsets. Most will need staking.
Flowering time Intermittently through the year. *Zone 10.*

Vanda Rothschildiana

Vanda hybrids

Most hybrids of this popular genus are derived from the infrequently cultivated *V. sandersanda.* Many of the clones have flowers up to 4 in (10 cm) wide in shades of pink or coral.

Vanda Rothschildiana
Blue orchid

This hybrid between *V. caerulea* and *V. sanderana* is easier to grow than *V. caerulea* itself. It bears sprays of 5 in (12 cm) or larger flowers in winter; they range in the different clones from light to deep violet-blue, the flowers being distinctly veined with a deeper shade; a well-grown plant can carry several sprays of flowers.

FERNS, PALMS & CYCADS

These three plants are grouped together as a coincidence of horticulture rather than botany. Indeed, it would be hard to select three more unrelated groups. Ferns have been around for hundreds of millions of years, while palms are among the most recent and highly evolved flowering plants. Cycads are a kind of bridge between the ferns and the conifers, the most primitive flowers. Despite their botanical differences, ferns, palms and cycads play similar roles in gardens. All are admired mainly for their leaves; they are valuable plants for shade; their most glamorous varieties are lovers of warm climates; and they often feature among indoor plants.

Adiantum aethiopicum

Asplenium bulbiferum

ADIANTUM

Maidenhair fern

Common throughout the tropics and subtropics, these half-hardy or tender ferns look delicate but grow vigorously in the right conditions. There are over 200 species worldwide, mostly ground-dwellers with an even greater number of cultivars.

Cultivation

They grow well in gardens with filtered sunlight and make perfect ground cover where there is any decaying organic matter such as leaf litter to keep the surface moist. Their fronds vary in length from 2 in (5 cm) to 3 ft (1 m) and turn from red to green as they grow. They have creeping rhizomes and polished, black-brown leaf stalks. Most species need repeated watering during summer.
Light Low–medium. *Zone 8–10.*

Adiantum aethiopicum

Common maidenhair

Originally from Africa and Australasia, this fern is one of the most popular and hardy of the genus. It flourishes in containers and hanging baskets (with frequent repotting) and in gardens, where it spreads via underground runners and forms large showy clumps of feathery fronds. It is half-hardy and grows to a height of nearly 3 ft (1 m).

ASPLENIUM BULBIFERUM

Hen and chicken fern, mother fern

This Australian and New Zealand native is one of the more widely cultivated species, easily grown in pots or hanging baskets. Typically fern-like in appearance, it has a tuft of arching, deep green, finely divided fronds up to 3 ft (1 m) long and 12 in (30 cm) wide. Small plantlets form on the fronds, mainly on the midrib.

Cultivation

Hardiness varies greatly with the species, as does the preferred growing environment. Most prefer woodland conditions with cool, moist, humus-rich soil and dappled shade. A few species, however, need sunnier locations and are reasonably tolerant of dry conditions. Propagate by spores, by division of established clumps, removing rooted pieces of rhizomes, or by growing on the frond-borne plantlets.
Light Medium. *Zone 9–11.*

CHAMAEROPS HUMILIS

European fan palm

Europe's most widespread native palm (native to southern Europe and the Mediterranean), this single-species genus is varied in its habit: it can have many trunks or one solitary trunk and be small or large, depending on its position. It is very resilient and perfect for temperate regions, being frost-hardy. It has been found covered in snow at high altitudes.

Cultivation

It prefers a sunny position and well-drained soil. A big clump makes a good lawn specimen and it can also be grown in a tub for long periods of time. Carpet fibers known as 'African hair' are made from the leaf sheaths, and leaf fibers have also been used as a substitute for flax.

Light Bright–very bright. *Zone 8–9.*

Cyathea australis

Chamaerops humilis

CYATHEA

syn. *Alsophila, Sphaeropteris*

Tree fern

These evergreen tree ferns, from tropical to subtropical areas of the world, can reach a height of 50 ft (15 m) although they are usually not as tall as that in gardens. Their palm-like trunks, from the summits of which the fronds spring, are composed of knitted-together aerial roots; below ground they have normal roots. Established plants need care in transplanting—ensure that the normal, subterranean roots are not damaged. The genus is characterized by its arching rosette of weeping or erect, bipinnate or tripinnate fronds.

Cultivation

Tree ferns prefer a warm climate but need plentiful water in warm weather and protection from the hot sun. They do well in tubs but eventually need replanting. Propagate from spores.

Light Low–medium. *Zone 9–11.*

Cyathea australis

syn. *Alsophila australis*

Rough tree fern

A native of eastern Australia, this majestic fern grows to 20 ft (6 m) or more high, with a slender blackish trunk and fronds up to almost 10 ft (3 m) long; foliage is deep green in shady situations, more yellowish in full sun. The frond bases are covered in narrow dark brown scales and are quite prickly to the touch. It adapts better than most tree ferns to low humidity but still demands plentiful summer water to grow well.

CYCAS REVOLUTA

Sago palm, Japanese sago cycad, Japanese fern palm

Native to the islands of southern Japan, this half-hardy evergreen suits temperate and subtropical regions. The trunk grows slowly to 10 ft (3 m), with a wide, flat crown of numerous glossy green leaves. Male cones are narrow cylinders up to 15 in (40 cm) long; female cones, brown and hairy, are half as long. Hairy vermilion seeds appear in autumn.

Cultivation

Water well in dry weather and fertilize lightly. Propagate from seed, basal suckers or trunk offsets.
Light Bright–very bright. *Zone 9–10.*

Cycas revoluta

CYRTOMIUM FALCATUM

syn. *Phanerophlebia falcata*

Holly fern

A native of East Asia, this species is easily recognized by the holly-like form and texture of its tough, glossy frond segments. It forms a dense clump about 2–3 ft in (60–90 cm) high. The spores are easily carried by the wind, so it has naturalized in countries with mild climates. It tolerates light frosts though the upper fronds can burn. It will grow in quite deep shade, although one of the most sun-tolerant of the ferns.

Cultivation

Most species are frost tender to moderately frost hardy and easy to grow. They grow well indoors in a well-lit position or in a conservatory or greenhouse. Propagate from spores, which germinate readily on moist bricks or mossy stones, or by division of clumps.
Light Low-medium. *Zone 9–11.*

DICKSONIA

This genus contains 30 large species of evergreen to semi-evergreen tree ferns native to the region stretching from Malaysia to Australia. These attractive ferns develop trunks in maturity and have arching, lance-shaped, multipinnate fronds with downy bases.

Cyrtomium falcatum

Dicksonia antarctica

Cultivation

The plants range from frost-hardy to frost-tender. Plant in peaty, damp soil with full or partial shade, and protect from the wind. Withered fronds should be frequently pruned. Propagate from spores in summer.
Light Low–medium. *Zone 8–10.*

Dicksonia antarctica

Soft tree fern, Tasmanian tree fern, New Zealand tree fern

Native to southeastern Australia and the giant of its genus, this tree fern can grow to 50 ft (15 m) with a trunk diameter of 6 ft (2 m). This fast and hardy grower favors a moist, sheltered position in the garden. Its lance-shaped fronds are up to 15 ft (4.5 m) long and its huge trunk is made of fibrous roots. Sections of trunk are used to make hanging baskets.

DRYOPTERIS ERYTHROSORA

Autumn fern, Japanese shield fern

Native to eastern Asia, this fern produces new fronds that range from copper to very bright red. As the fronds age they become glossy green. Bright red spore masses dot the undersides of the pinnules. A mature fern reaches 18 in (45 cm), spreading to 12 in (30 cm).

Cultivation

They require part-shade and moist, humus-rich soil. Remove fading fronds regularly. Protect from wind damage and do not overwater established plants. Propagate from spores in summer or by division in autumn or in winter.
Light Medium. *Zone 5–9.*

NEPHROLEPIS CORDIFOLIA

Fishbone fern, southern sword fern

Naturally found among rocks at the edges of rainforests, this fast-growing fern can survive in fairly dry and dark positions as well as in full sun. It is one of the toughest species in cultivation and a very easily grown plant—so much so that it can become a pest. Fronds grow to 3 ft (1 m). The cultivar 'Plumosa' is a slow-growing cultivar with lobed pinnae.

Cultivation

For ferns, they are extremely tolerant of dry conditions and are fast growing, provided they are given enough room to spread out and have well-composted, moist soil. Since they are sensitive to cold, these ferns are ideal for indoors, but be sure to provide lots of water in warm conditions. Propagate from spores or tissue culture, or by division.
Light Medium–bright. *Zone 10–12.*

Nephrolepis cordifolia

Dryotperis erythrosora

Phoenix canariensis

Pellaea rotundifolia

PELLAEA ROTUNDIFOLIA

Button fern, round-leafed fern, tarawera

Native to New Zealand, this species is a small, dark green, ground-dwelling fern found in damp open forests or drier rocky places. It has pinnate fronds with deep green, glossy round leaflets and long-creeping rhizomes.

Cultivation

Suitable for a garden or fernery with filtered sunlight, protected from drafts, it also thrives in rock gardens.
Light Low–medium. *Zone 8–9.*

PHOENIX

Date palm

This genus originates from tropical Africa, southern China, Asia and the Philippines. They feature a dense crown of long, pinnate leaves with stiff, sharp spines and a very rough trunk where the leaf base has broken away and left scarring. The flowers grow in clusters of thousands on some species. The bright red or golden fruit is usually edible. They are sun-lovers, and among the hardiest palms in cultivation. Species of *Phoenix* are valued as ornamental palms, and as a source of palm sugar, which is used widely in Asian cooking.

Cultivation

They tolerate hot winds and poor soil and the various species hybridize freely when grown together. Propagate from seeds.
Light Bright–very bright. *Zone 8–9.*

Phoenix canariensis

Canary Island date palm

Native to the Canary Islands, this shorter, heavier species has large, dark green fronds.

POLYSTICHUM SETIFERUM

Native to the damp woodlands and valleys of Europe, this large fern has bright green, soft, bipinnate fronds up to 4 ft (1.2 m) long. The central bud head and frond stems have a dense covering of large brown scales. Easily grown, it is popular in ferneries and gardens. 'Divisilobium Densum Erectum' is a form in which each leaflet is itself bipinnate, creating a dense feather duster of a frond. 'Plumosum Bevis' has elongated, sometimes crested-tipped fronds with widely spaced leaflets creating an airy, open effect.

Cultivation

They prefer part- to full shade and fertile, humus-rich, well-drained soil. The frond tips usually bear an abundance of small buds that become

Sabal palmetto

plantlets in their own right when conditions are favorable. Otherwise, propagate by sowing spores in summer or by division of the rhizomes in spring.
Light Low–medium. *Zone 7–9.*

SABAL PALMETTO

Palmetto, cabbage palm

Native to southeastern USA, this tall, thick palm grows up to 80 ft (25 m) tall and 12–18 in (30–45 cm) in diameter. The trunk is covered with continuous interlaced leaf bases and the fan-shaped leaves have an idiosyncratic twist. It flowers and bears fruit while it is still young.

Cultivation

This is a sun-lover, and should be planted in sandy soil in subtropical and tropical areas. Propagate from seed.
Light Bright–very bright. *Zone 10–11.*

WASHINGTONIA

Native to the rocky, dry areas of the southwestern USA and Mexico, the two species in this genus are large, single-standing fan palms. The trunk is fatter at the base and, in older trees, may be covered with a thick thatch of old leaves which extends almost to the ground. The crown is dense with no crown shaft and the stalks of the finely bladed leaves are broad and toothed.

Washingtonia filifera

Polystichum setiferum

Cultivation

It is suited to a sunny spot in warm areas or dry tropical climates. Propagate from seed.
Light Bright–very bright. *Zone 9–10.*

Washingtonia filifera

Washington palm, American cotton palm, desert fan palm, petticoat palm

This frost-hardy species has long, gray-green leaves and bears small white flowers in summer. It grows up to 50 ft (15 m) high. This palm lends its name to the city of Palm Springs, California.

Washingtonia robusta

Washington palm, thread palm, skyduster

At 80 ft (24 m) high, this is the taller species. Its flowers are creamy white.

CLIMBERS & CREEPERS

There's nothing as welcoming as a vine-covered arch over a front gate or a delicate rambler twining its way in and around window shutters to display its perfumed flowers to perfection. In these and other subtle ways, climbers play an important role in the overall garden landscape. Climbers set out to reach the high spots where there is less competition for light. Some provide a focal point in a small garden or in a tight spot, while other more adventurous types will sprawl over a garden shed, camouflaging it in no time.

Akebia quinata

Ampelopsis brevipedunculata 'Elegans'

AKEBIA QUINATA

Five-leaf akebia, chocolate vine

This woody, twining vine reaches up to 30 ft (9 m) or more. It has attractive bluish green leaves with 5 leaflets and remains evergreen in warmer climates. Fragrant, small, purple flowers bloom in spring and clusters of ornamental fruits develop in autumn. This native of China, Japan and Korea can be used as a ground cover.

Cultivation

Plant in full sun or shade in a well-drained, moist or dry soil. Prune back to the ground in winter or early spring to control the size of older, established plants, and re-train new shoots up the support structure. Propagate from softwood cuttings in summer or autumn. *Planting time* Early spring. *Zone 4–9.*

AMPELOPSIS BREVIPEDUNCULATA

syn. *Ampelopsis heterophylla, Vitis heterophylla*

Turquoise-berry vine, porcelain vine

This vigorous, deciduous climber will twine, with the aid of tendrils, 15 ft (4.5 m) or more. It has grape-like, lobed leaves, small greenish flowers in summer, and in autumn bunches of berries like miniature grapes that ripen from pale green to turquoise, bright blue and violet. The leaves of *Ampelopsis brevipedunculata* var. *maximowiczii* are larger than the species.

Cultivation

Grow in a sunny or partially shaded position in a moisture-retentive, but well-drained soil. They are fully hardy, grow rapidly and need strong support with plenty of room to spread. Cut back hard to the main branches when berries have finished. Propagate from cuttings in summer or by layering in fall. *Planting time* Summer, autumn. *Zone 4–9.*

CAMPSIS GRANDIFLORA

syn. *C. chinensis, Bignonia grandiflora*

Chinese trumpet creeper

This vigorous climber from China will reach up to 30 ft (9 m) with the aid of aerial rootlets clinging to a support. Deciduous and fast-growing, it produces trumpet-shaped scarlet to orange flowers in late summer and autumn.

Cultivation

Only just frost-hardy, it requires full sun in a well-drained, humus-rich soil. Prune in spring and propagate from semi-ripe cuttings taken in summer, or from layers or suckers.

Planting time Autumn, spring. *Zone 7–9.*

CLEMATIS

Virgin's bower, traveler's joy

These generally woody climbers are from moist temperate regions of the world, but nearly all the popular, larger-flowered garden plants have come from Japan and

China. They climb by twisting their tendrils around a support. Showy, bell-shaped or flattish flowers with 4 to 6 petals are followed by masses of fluffy seed heads.

Cultivation

They need well-drained, humus-rich, permanently cool soil with good moisture retention. The plants like to climb up to the sun with their roots in the shade. Prune old, twiggy growth in spring and propagate from cuttings or by layering in summer.

Planting time Autumn, spring. *Zone 5–9.*

Clematis montana

This vigorous, deciduous species from the Himalayas bears prolific, sweetly perfumed, white flowers with yellow anthers in clusters in late spring. Fast growing and fully hardy, it is ideal for covering a small shed or wall.

***Clematis* 'Nelly Moser'**

A woody climber which flowers in spring on last season's side shoots and again in autumn on the current season's growth. The individual flowers have 8 crinkly-edged petals of palest lilac-pink with a distinctive carmine midstripe.

DOLICHOS LABLAB

syn. *Lablab purpureus*

Hyacinth bean

A fast-growing vine with lovely dark green foliage with a purple cast and

Clematis montana

Dolichos lablab

Campsis grandiflora

Clematis 'Nelly Moser'

clusters of lilac to lavender and white pea-like flowers that bloom by mid-summer. After flowering, striking long, dark purple, leathery seed pods develop all over the plant. These are edible. It grows up to 10–15 ft (3–4.5 m) or more.

Cultivation

Seeds can be started indoors or where they are able to grow outdoors in a well-drained, loamy soil. Soak seeds in lukewarm water to speed germination. Plant in full sun to very light shade.
Planting time Spring. *Zone 9–12.*

GELSEMIUM SEMPERVIRENS

Carolina jasmine

An evergreen twiner with fragrant, yellow trumpet flowers, which appear in spring and in autumn.

Cultivation

Half-hardy, it likes a sunny, warm, sheltered position and a fertile, well-drained soil. It grows quickly to 10 ft (3 m) and can be trained on fences, walls, or a pergola near the house. All parts of the plant are poisonous and should be kept away from children. Thin out older growth after flowering. Propagate from semi-hardwood cuttings in summer.
Planting time Early Spring–autumn.
Zone 7–9.

HEDERA

Ivy

Useful for enhancing many a situation, ivies have long been well-loved, hardy evergreen creepers. They can be used for ground cover, clothing walls and fences, covering tree stumps and arches, growing up pillars and posts, edging borders and masonry work, trailing from containers and as indoor specimens.

Cultivation

In sun or shade they are adaptable to a wide variety of conditions, soils and climates. Regular pruning is recommended. Propagate from cuttings or rooted stems.
Planting time Spring, summer, autumn.
Zone 8.

Hedera helix

English ivy, common ivy

This fully hardy species will produce a dense, dark green cover. It is often used as a ground cover in shade where grass does not thrive, and is also excellent for climbing up walls and hiding fences. 'Variegata' has leaves marked with yellow and white and 'Goldheart' has leaves marked with yellow.

HIBBERTIA SCANDENS

Guinea flower, Guinea gold vine

A native of Australia, this soft twining climber or trailing plant can grow up to

Hedera helix 'Goldheart'

Gelsemium sempervirens

Hibbertia scandens

14 ft (4 m) high or be trained along the ground as an effective ground cover. It has broad, dark green leaves and large, showy, buttercup-yellow flowers from spring through the warmer months.

Cultivation

Any moderately fertile, well-drained soil is suitable. It will grow in full sun or semi-shade and is suitable for sandy, coastal gardens, as it tolerates salt spray. Half-hardy, it is ideal for warm climates. Lightly prune to shape in spring and propagate from semi-ripe tip cuttings in late summer. *Planting time* Autumn, spring. *Zone 8.*

HYDRANGEA PETIOLARIS

syn. *H. anomala* subsp. *petiolaris*

Climbing hydrangea

This deciduous, self-clinging climber grows up to 60–75 ft (18–23 m) and bears beautiful, flattened heads of small white flowers in summer. It has oval, finely toothed leaves, and is fully hardy.

Cultivation

Plant in humus-rich, well-drained, moist soil in full sun, with some protection from hot afternoon sun, and water regularly in summer. Propagate from semi-hardwood cuttings in summer. Prune after flowering, trimming close to the support. *Planting time* Spring, autumn. *Zone 4–8.*

Hydrangea petiolaris

Ipomoea × *multifida*

IPOMOEA

Morning glory

This fast-growing, twining climber has light green, heart-shaped leaves and can grow up to 15–20 ft (4.5–6 m). The old fashioned blue, white, purple, pink, red and bicolored flowers bloom all summer.

Cultivation

Soak seeds overnight before planting outdoors where they are to grow after the last frost. They can be sown indoors 4–6 weeks before planting out. Use peat

Lathyrus odoratus

pots that can be planted into the soil as plants resent transplanting. Plant in full sun or light shade in a moist, well-drained soil. Keep pruned so it does not grow into other plants.
Planting time Spring. *Zone 8–12.*

LATHYRUS ODORATUS

Sweet pea

The sweet pea is a fragrant spring flowering, cool weather annual, grown from seed. There are many varieties in the pink-blue shades. Some are tall growers needing support while others are self supporting, low-growing and shrub-like. Many have two-toned blooms.

Cultivation

Fully hardy, it is easily grown in a humus-rich, well-drained soil. Tall growers need the support of a sunny fence, trellis or tripod. Fertilize and water well as blooms begin to develop and pick flowers to encourage blooming.
Planting time Early spring. *Zone 8.*

LONICERA

Honeysuckle, woodbine

Honeysuckle are grown for their masses of perfumed flowers. They are perfect

Lonicera periclymenum

for covering arches, arbors and bowers, where they will provide a sweet summer evening fragrance.

Cultivation

Grow in a well-drained, moisture-retentive soil in sun or semi-shade. Propagate from cuttings in summer or late autumn.
Planting time Autumn, spring. *Zone 8.*

Lonicera pericylmenum

Woodbine

This plant has grayish green leaves and produces fragrant yellow-white flowers from summer to frost, followed by bright red berries. It grows to about 9 ft (2.6 m) high, making it suitable for smaller gardens. 'Graham Thomas' is an extremely fragrant, larger growing cultivar reaching up to 40 ft (12 m) in height.

MANDEVILLA

Native to tropical America, these woody-stemmed climbers are grown for their trumpet-shaped flowers, which are sometimes fragrant. Grow in warm, frost-free climates.

Cultivation

Soil should be deep, rich and well-drained. Provide ample water on hot days. Propagate from semi-ripe cuttings in summer. Set out container-grown plants after all frost danger has passed in northern areas.
Planting time Autumn, spring. *Zone 9.*

Mandevilla × amabilis 'Alice du Pont'

Polygonum aubertii

Passiflora caerulea

***Mandevilla × amabilis* 'Alice du Pont'**
syn. *Dipladenia × amabilis* 'Alice du Pont'
A twining climber growing up to 14 ft (4 m) with oval, glossy leaves and clusters of large, deep pink, scentless flowers through summer. It is frost-tender.

PASSIFLORA

Passion flower
Native chiefly to tropical South America, these tendril climbers have ornamental blossoms and fruit, notably the passion-fruit. Half-hardy to frost-tender, they are suited to warm areas.

Cultivation
Plant in a humus-rich, well-drained soil with a sunny aspect. Prune congested or overgrown plants in spring. Propagate from seed or semi-ripe cuttings or by layering in summer.
Planting time Spring. *Zone 9.*

Passiflora caerulea
Blue passion flower
In summer this half-hardy, fast-growing evergreen or semi-evergreen climber produces beautiful flowers with pale pink petals, banded with blue or purple.

POLYGONUM AUBERTII

syn. *Fallopia aubertii*
Silver lace vine
This extremely fast-growing, twining plant bears clusters of creamy pinkish white fragrant flower panicles that bloom from mid-summer into early autumn. When in bloom, the fluffy flowers give the plant a light, lacy appearance. Plants can reach up to 25–35 ft (8–10 m) high. This hardy plant is especially good for covering unattractive fences.

Cultivation
Plant in full sun to part shade in well-drained soil. Cut back hard in winter or early spring. Allow it to grow on sturdy supports or larger structures. If planting more than one vine along a structure, space plants 25–30 ft (8–9 m) apart. Propagate from stem cuttings in summer or by division.
Planting time Early spring. *Zone 4–8.*

ROSA

Rose

Climbing roses vary greatly in their habit from short-stemmed, rambling or pillar roses to tall vigorous climbers capable of reaching up to 20 ft (6 m) high. Species growing to around 4 ft (1.2 m) can cover walls and fences; short-stemmed roses are suitable for pillars; miniature climbers can cascade down retaining walls.

Cultivation

Most roses are fully hardy and require humus-rich soil, full sun and ample water. Give climbers room to develop and tie back canes as they grow. Remove spent blooms to prolong flowering. *Planting time* Autumn, early spring. *Zone 3–9.*

Rosa banksiae 'Lutea'

Rosa 'Iceberg Climbing'

Rosa banksiae 'Lutea'

This extremely vigorous, thornless climber will reach up to 15–25 ft (4.5–8 m). Clusters of small, yellow double flowers are borne in spring. Half-hardy, it needs warmth and protection.

Rosa 'Iceberg Climbing'

The clustered flowering 'Iceberg Climbing' is a sport of the popular white flowering rose. The rich, glossy green leaves are complemented by the clear white, shallowly cupped blooms with central yellow stamens.

Rosa 'New Dawn'

This rose bears pale pink flowers which bloom profusely on a plant growing 15–18 ft (4.5–5.5 m) high. This is one of the best climbers for a trellis or arbor.

Solanum jasminoides 'Album'

Rosa 'New Dawn'

SOLANUM

This is a large genus of annuals, perennials, shrubs, trees and climbers. The climbers are valued for their ornamental flowers, foliage and fruit. They are fast-growing and require fastening to a support.

Cultivation

They do best in a warm, sunny position in fertile, well-drained soil. Cut back congested growth in spring. Propagate from seed.

Planting time Autumn, spring. *Zone 8–11.*

Solanum jasminoides

Potato vine

From South America, this fast-growing, semi-evergreen climber reaches 20 ft (6 m) and bears showy clusters of pale blue flowers in summer and autumn, followed by small, purple berries. It is half-hardy. 'Album' is a white form.

THUNBERGIA

Clock vine

This genus contains 200 species of annual twisting climbers and perennial evergreen clump-forming shrubs which are native to Africa, Asia and Malagasy. Their attractive leaves have up to 5 lobes. The cylindrical blooms are borne individually from the leaf axils or in trusses. The species range from half-hardy to frost-tender.

Cultivation

They will grow in any reasonably rich soil with adequate drainage. Full sun is preferred, except during the summer months when partial shade and liberal water should be provided. Support stems and prune densely packed foliage during early spring. Propagate from seed in spring and semi-ripe cuttings in summer.

Planting time Autumn. *Zone 9.*

Thunbergia alata

Black-eyed Susan

Native to the tropics of Africa, this vigorous annual or perennial twisting climber grows quickly to 10 ft (3 m). Its deep green, cordate leaves grow to 3 in (8 cm) long. It bears masses of orange flowers with black throats all summer. It is perennial in frost-free areas.

TRACHELOSPERMUM JASMINOIDES

Star jasmine

Valued for its perfumed, star-shaped flowers, this evergreen, twining climber from China grows up to 25 ft (8 m) high. It has lance-shaped leaves, and hanging clusters of white flowers.

Cultivation

Frost-hardy, this plant does best in a sunny position in well-drained, fertile soil. It will flourish once established

Trachelospermum jasminoides

Thunbergia alata

Wisteria floribunda

Wisteria sinensis

Vitis labrusca

and is excellent for training on pillars, pergolas and arches. Propagate from semi-ripe cuttings in summer or autumn. *Planting time* Autumn, spring. *Zone 8–10.*

VITIS

This genus consists of deciduous woody-stemmed, tendril climbers. They are grown for their foliage and fruits.

Cultivation

Grow in humus-rich, moisture-retentive, but well-drained soil in full sun or partial shade. Propagate from hardwood cuttings taken in late autumn or winter. *Planting time* Late winter. *Zone 8.*

Vitis labrusca

Fox grape

This grape has large, shallowly 3-lobed leaves and large, purple-black fruit, which have a musky or 'foxy' flavor.

WISTERIA

Wisteria

With its drooping sprays of perfumed flowers, the deciduous wisteria is a popular plant for pergolas. Providing summer shade, the light green, luxuriant foliage is also attractive.

Cultivation

Wisterias like a sunny position and a humus-rich, well-drained soil. They become large, vigorous plants and need strong support for healthy future growth. Prune after flowering and again in late winter. Propagate from cuttings or by layering in late summer. *Planting time* Early spring. *Zone 4–9.*

Wisteria floribunda

Japanese wisteria

This vigorous, woody-stemmed climber up to 30 ft (9 m) or more bears pendulous, purple-blue flowers. The flowers are fragrant and are often produced after the leaves in spring. It is fully hardy.

Wisteria sinensis

syn. *W. chinensis*

Chinese wisteria

Native to China, this vigorous, fully hardy, woody-stemmed climber will reach up to 30 ft (9 m) high. The sprays of slightly fragrant, lavender-blue flowers appear in spring on bare branches before the leaves.

INDEX